Unchaining Solidarity

Unchaining Solidarity

On Mutual Aid and Anarchism with Catherine Malabou

Edited by
Dan Swain, Petr Urban, Catherine Malabou,
and Petr Kouba

ROWMAN & LITTLEFIELD
Lanham • Boulder • New York • London

Published by Rowman & Littlefield
An imprint of The Rowman & Littlefield Publishing Group, Inc.
4501 Forbes Boulevard, Suite 200, Lanham, Maryland 20706
www.rowman.com
86-90 Paul Street, London EC2A 4NE

British Library Cataloguing in Publication Information Available

Library of Congress Cataloguing-in-Publication Data

Names: Swain, Dan, editor. | Urban, Petr, 1977– editor. | Malabou, Catherine, editor. | Kouba, Petr, 1973– editor.
Title: Unchaining solidarity : on mutual aid and anarchism with Catherine Malabou / edited by Dan Swain, Petr Urban, Catherine Malabou and Petr Kouba.
Description: Lanham : Rowman & Littlefield, [2022] | Includes bibliographical references and index.
Identifiers: LCCN 2021034080 (print) | LCCN 2021034081 (ebook) | ISBN 9781538157954 (cloth) | ISBN 9781538157978 (paperback) | ISBN 9781538157961 (epub)
Subjects: LCSH: Malabou, Catherine—Criticism and interpretation. | Anarchism. | Solidarity. | Mutualism. | Neuroplasticity. | Biopolitics. | Biology—Social aspects.
Classification: LCC HX833 .U54 2022 (print) | LCC HX833 (ebook) | DDC 335/.83—dc23
LC record available at https://lccn.loc.gov/2021034080
LC ebook record available at https://lccn.loc.gov/2021034081

Unchaining Solidarity

On Mutual Aid and Anarchism with Catherine Malabou

Edited by
Dan Swain, Petr Urban, Catherine Malabou,
and Petr Kouba

ROWMAN & LITTLEFIELD
Lanham • Boulder • New York • London

Published by Rowman & Littlefield
An imprint of The Rowman & Littlefield Publishing Group, Inc.
4501 Forbes Boulevard, Suite 200, Lanham, Maryland 20706
www.rowman.com
86-90 Paul Street, London EC2A 4NE

British Library Cataloguing in Publication Information Available

Library of Congress Cataloguing-in-Publication Data

Names: Swain, Dan, editor. | Urban, Petr, 1977– editor. | Malabou, Catherine, editor. | Kouba, Petr, 1973– editor.
Title: Unchaining solidarity : on mutual aid and anarchism with Catherine Malabou / edited by Dan Swain, Petr Urban, Catherine Malabou and Petr Kouba.
Description: Lanham : Rowman & Littlefield, [2022] | Includes bibliographical references and index.
Identifiers: LCCN 2021034080 (print) | LCCN 2021034081 (ebook) | ISBN 9781538157954 (cloth) | ISBN 9781538157978 (paperback) | ISBN 9781538157961 (epub)
Subjects: LCSH: Malabou, Catherine—Criticism and interpretation. | Anarchism. | Solidarity. | Mutualism. | Neuroplasticity. | Biopolitics. | Biology—Social aspects.
Classification: LCC HX833 .U54 2022 (print) | LCC HX833 (ebook) | DDC 335/.83—dc23
LC record available at https://lccn.loc.gov/2021034080
LC ebook record available at https://lccn.loc.gov/2021034081

Contents

Acknowledgements

The editors would like to thank all the contributors to the volume, participants in the 2018 Politics of Plasticity Conference in Prague, and everyone else who has helped with the production of the book. The book is an outcome of the project 'Towards a New Ontology of Social Cohesion', grant number GA19–20031S of the Czech Science Foundation (GAČR), realised at the Institute of Philosophy of the Czech Academy of Sciences.

Acknowledgments

Chapter 1

Unchaining Solidarity, Mutual Aid and Anarchism

Dan Swain, Petr Urban,
Catherine Malabou and Petr Kouba

To think about solidarity, mutual aid and anarchism is to think about how we can and do live together, and how we might do so differently. Mutual aid is, in Peter Kropotkin's famous formulation, a factor of evolution, but also a conscious political strategy undertaken by activists in times of crisis. While this combination of biology and politics has been a source of controversy, and even embarrassment, recent developments demand a rethink. The contributions in this volume aim to renew interest in the idea of mutual aid, and to consider how biological claims might be incorporated into political projects without appearing as essentialist constraints. They thus point to the necessity of solidarity and mutual aid for understanding our social life, while releasing them from the biological and symbolic chains in which they often appear.

THE UNITY OF ORDER AND ANARCHY

Taking language in reverse: this is, by definition, an anarchist gesture, one that precisely conferred to the 'anarchists' their name. Until 1840, 'anarchist' had only designated the poor, the destitute, or the rebel. In *What is Property?* Joseph Proudhon uses it for the first time in a positive sense. He fictionalises a short dialogue between a young interlocutor and himself:

> 'Well! you are a democrat?', the young man asks – 'No'. – 'What! you would have a monarchy'. – 'No'. – 'A constitutionalist?' – 'God forbid!' – 'You are

This chapter is an outcome of the project 'Towards a New Ontology of Social Cohesion', grant number GA19–20031S of the Czech Science Foundation (GAČR), realised at the Institute of Philosophy of the Czech Academy of Sciences.

> then an aristocrat?' – 'Not at all'. – 'You want a mixed government?' – 'Still less'. – 'What are you, then?' – 'I am an anarchist'. 'Oh! I understand you; you speak satirically. This is a hit at the government'. – 'By no means. I have just given you my serious and well-considered profession of faith. Although a firm friend of order, I am (in the full force of the term) an anarchist'. (Proudhon 1994, 205)

Such an answer operates a total semantic revolution, a subversion even, of the initial meaning of 'anarchy' as chaos. 'The highest perfection of society, Proudhon also writes, is to be found in the unity of order and anarchy' (*Ibid.*). From Proudhon on, anarchism began to designate not only something different from, but also opposed to, disorder.

Proudhon was no doubt aware of the fact that the concept of solidarity had also undergone a semantic metamorphosis. From the Latin *solidus*, the French name *solidaire* used to characterise the link that united a debtor and creditor of a sum of money. Diderot and d'Alembert, in their *Encyclopédie*, coined the term 'solidarité' to designate 'interdependence' in general. A few decades later, in the early nineteenth century, 'solidarité' started to define a communion of interests and responsibilities, mutual responsibility. The semantic genesis of political anarchism was on its way.

The present book intends to prolong these linguistic metamorphic gestures by exploring the ways in which the 'unity of order and anarchy' is still alive and opening new, unheard forms of autonomous, self-organized and responsible occurrences of the common. It also aims at radicalising the emancipation of solidarity from the idea of debt, obligation, duty or guilt. This explains the injunction of 'unchaining solidarity' in the title. The texts that compose the volume, each in their own way, tend to *break the chains* that still sometimes imprison solidarity in different forms of dependence (ontological moral, political, ideological).

'Mutual aid', bridging solidarity and anarchism in the title, is both synonymous with and different from them. Coined by Peter Kropotkin in his 1902 book *Mutual Aid: A Factor of Evolution*, 'mutual aid' first refers to formations of animal networks of solidarity when confronted with extreme natural conditions.

Kropotkin asks himself to what extent the tendency that led to such formations was still present in human beings, and if the concept of political mutual aid was viable. He answers both of these questions positively after a long and brilliant analysis of 'mutuality' defined as 'altruism'. The relationship of mutuality with anarchism and solidarity is obvious: horizontality, autonomy and absence of leadership. Mutual aid however, according to its Kropotkinian determination, involves a type of relationship that is not necessarily comprised in anarchism and solidarity: *non-reciprocity*. Reciprocity is

Chapter 1

Unchaining Solidarity, Mutual Aid and Anarchism

Dan Swain, Petr Urban, Catherine Malabou and Petr Kouba

To think about solidarity, mutual aid and anarchism is to think about how we can and do live together, and how we might do so differently. Mutual aid is, in Peter Kropotkin's famous formulation, a factor of evolution, but also a conscious political strategy undertaken by activists in times of crisis. While this combination of biology and politics has been a source of controversy, and even embarrassment, recent developments demand a rethink. The contributions in this volume aim to renew interest in the idea of mutual aid, and to consider how biological claims might be incorporated into political projects without appearing as essentialist constraints. They thus point to the necessity of solidarity and mutual aid for understanding our social life, while releasing them from the biological and symbolic chains in which they often appear.

THE UNITY OF ORDER AND ANARCHY

Taking language in reverse: this is, by definition, an anarchist gesture, one that precisely conferred to the 'anarchists' their name. Until 1840, 'anarchist' had only designated the poor, the destitute, or the rebel. In *What is Property?* Joseph Proudhon uses it for the first time in a positive sense. He fictionalises a short dialogue between a young interlocutor and himself:

> 'Well! you are a democrat?', the young man asks – 'No'. – 'What! you would have a monarchy'. – 'No'. – 'A constitutionalist?' – 'God forbid!' – 'You are

This chapter is an outcome of the project 'Towards a New Ontology of Social Cohesion', grant number GA19–20031S of the Czech Science Foundation (GAČR), realised at the Institute of Philosophy of the Czech Academy of Sciences.

> then an aristocrat?' – 'Not at all'. – 'You want a mixed government?' – 'Still less'. – 'What are you, then?' – 'I am an anarchist'. 'Oh! I understand you; you speak satirically. This is a hit at the government'. – 'By no means. I have just given you my serious and well-considered profession of faith. Although a firm friend of order, I am (in the full force of the term) an anarchist'. (Proudhon 1994, 205)

Such an answer operates a total semantic revolution, a subversion even, of the initial meaning of 'anarchy' as chaos. 'The highest perfection of society, Proudhon also writes, is to be found in the unity of order and anarchy' (*Ibid.*). From Proudhon on, anarchism began to designate not only something different from, but also opposed to, disorder.

Proudhon was no doubt aware of the fact that the concept of solidarity had also undergone a semantic metamorphosis. From the Latin *solidus*, the French name *solidaire* used to characterise the link that united a debtor and creditor of a sum of money. Diderot and d'Alembert, in their *Encyclopédie*, coined the term 'solidarité' to designate 'interdependence' in general. A few decades later, in the early nineteenth century, 'solidarité' started to define a communion of interests and responsibilities, mutual responsibility. The semantic genesis of political anarchism was on its way.

The present book intends to prolong these linguistic metamorphic gestures by exploring the ways in which the 'unity of order and anarchy' is still alive and opening new, unheard forms of autonomous, self-organized and responsible occurrences of the common. It also aims at radicalising the emancipation of solidarity from the idea of debt, obligation, duty or guilt. This explains the injunction of 'unchaining solidarity' in the title. The texts that compose the volume, each in their own way, tend to *break the chains* that still sometimes imprison solidarity in different forms of dependence (ontological moral, political, ideological).

'Mutual aid', bridging solidarity and anarchism in the title, is both synonymous with and different from them. Coined by Peter Kropotkin in his 1902 book *Mutual Aid: A Factor of Evolution*, 'mutual aid' first refers to formations of animal networks of solidarity when confronted with extreme natural conditions.

Kropotkin asks himself to what extent the tendency that led to such formations was still present in human beings, and if the concept of political mutual aid was viable. He answers both of these questions positively after a long and brilliant analysis of 'mutuality' defined as 'altruism'. The relationship of mutuality with anarchism and solidarity is obvious: horizontality, autonomy and absence of leadership. Mutual aid however, according to its Kropotkinian determination, involves a type of relationship that is not necessarily comprised in anarchism and solidarity: *non-reciprocity*. Reciprocity is another chain that has to be broken. In that sense, non-reciprocity is also what profoundly transforms the immediate meaning of 'mutuality'.

The issue of mutual aid has opened an immense debate among philosophers, biologists and economists. They have understood it mainly as a tendency towards altruistic behaviours that benefit others at some cost to oneself. A vast majority of biologists have concluded, against Kropotkin, that altruistic behaviours in reality proceeded from a hidden form of egoism, and were disguised forms of self-interest. This would be true from a biological evolutionary perspective, but also from a moral perspective. Therefore, the only possible kinds of natural altruistic conduct would always be reciprocal. Helping others would only be possible if sustained by the expectation that others will help in return. Kin altruism (the sacrifice of the individual to preserve its kinship, behaviours meant to improve the genetic prospects of my children surviving and reproducing) and group selection (preservation of the group at the cost of destruction of other groups), are the most well-known forms of altruistic behaviours. The formal pattern of altruism would just be 'tit for tat'.

Things have recently evolved, with the development of a philosophical moral and pragmatic movement named 'effective altruism' in particular, whose prominent representative is the Australian philosopher Peter Singer. 'Altruistic impulses once limited to one's kin and one's own group might be extended to a wider circle by reasoning creatures who can see that they and their kin are one group among others, and from an impartial point of view no more important than others', Singer argues. 'Biological theories of the evolution of altruism through kin selection, reciprocity and group selection can be made compatible with the existence of non-reciprocal altruism toward strangers if they can accept this kind of expansion of the circle of altruism' (Singer 2011, 134–135).

Kropotkin's vision of mutual aid, which has become a major tenet of 'effective altruism', must nevertheless be distinguished from it. It is not a matter, for Kropotkin, of giving to unknown people that the donors will never meet, as Singer and effective altruists affirm. Anonymity is not the only way to sustain non-reciprocity. Anarchism is the affirmation that non-reciprocity can be built and cultivated in full awareness and publicity. It opens the possibility of a new meaning of both mutuality and aid emancipated from the necessity of counter-giving without disappearing as a person and a political subject. Non-reciprocity induces a new way of precisely understanding political subjectivity and politics through a revolutionary vision of the relationships between biology and history. Reflecting on all these semantic and political turns, our book tends to explore the *chiasmatic relationship* that exists between independence and community, autonomy and association, absence of central authority and collective strength.

The political context that gave birth to this book is diverse: a crisis of State-forms, a dwindling of democracy everywhere, abandonment of the poor and the sick by governments, withering of left-wing parties, the failure of social democracy, state socialism and party forms and of course, the ordeal of the pandemic, which made sensible, in so many ways, a feeling of abandonment and political and social helplessness.

Although this book was planned beforehand, emerging out of a conference held in Prague in 2018, the pandemic gave it fresh urgency. In its initial phases, much philosophical analysis of the pandemic focused on the state response of quarantines and lockdowns, approached in particular through categories and concepts of biopolitics and a fear of extending police and emergency powers. But this was only one side of the story. In many cases people acted faster than states, in demanding states take action, in taking their own preventative measures (a kind of 'lockdown from below') and in establishing networks to meet the needs that the state was failing to meet (see Cox 2020; Sitrin and Sembrar 2020). Whether by accident or from deep historical and institutional memory, the term *mutual aid* became the popular description for such groups. Writing in the *New Yorker*, Jia Tollentino (2020) noted how '"mutual aid" has entered the lexicon of the coronavirus era alongside "social distancing" and "flatten the curve"'. Indeed, in place of the faintly oxymoronic 'social distancing', many such groups insisted on 'physical distancing, but social solidarity'. Of course, such groups faced many challenges, navigating the state and resisting the logic of charity (see Illner 2020, chapter 9; Spade 2020), and to what extent they lived up to the standards they set themselves is beyond the scope of this book (although we do feature an insider's account of one of them). A year on, the demands of administering and distributing the vaccine seem to have put the focus once again on states, which risks eclipsing the self-organised initiative of the early phases. Rebecca Solnit (2020, xv) observes how, '[l]ike a near-death experience or a great loss or potentially fatal illness for an individual, collective disasters wake us up to who we are, who we can trust, what matters, and what doesn't. The difficulty is in how to stay awake when the ordinary returns'. Perhaps, then, this book might make a small contribution to keeping the revival of mutual aid alive, whatever comes next.

STRUCTURE AND CONTENTS OF THIS BOOK

This book is divided into three parts. It opens with a chapter by Catherine Malabou, which forms the foundation of the volume and so stands separately before the three parts. The intersection between *biology* and *politics* has been an enduring theme for Malabou over the past two decades. Her sustained engagement with neuroscience in works such as *What Should We Do with Our Brain?* (2008) and *The New Wounded* (2012) has sought to reincorporate the biological character of the brain into philosophy and psychoanalysis. Central to this is the concept of plasticity, 'the threefold movement of reception, donation and annihilation of form' (Malabou 2012, xiv). Malabou observes that the brain itself is plastic, and that recognising this requires rejecting biological determinism, rather than accepting it. Her recent work has turned to the anarchist tradition as itself an example of such plasticity, and to mutual aid as its cornerstone. Malabou's chapter in this volume interrogates the classical dichotomy between essentialism and discursivity that is characteristic of debates in contemporary anarchism, libertarianism and post-Marxism. She argues that essentialism and discursivity conceive mutual aid as the formation of chains between individuals or subjects, and that it is necessary to build new ways of thinking mutual aid as a type of relationship that 'can hold people together without chaining them'. Such an 'unchaining' would involve genuine self-organisation, be open to the new and alternative pathways, and seek to reconstruct connections and bonds between individuals without a structure guaranteed in advance by either biology or politics. The chapter concludes: 'It is time to think that connections can be links without chains. Mutual aid today is the paradoxical solidarity of the unchained, the inexhaustible resource of hope and energy for a politics of plasticity'.

Part I of this volume focuses directly on Malabou's work, with a particular emphasis on her concept of *plasticity* and its value for grasping and articulating forms of solidarity and sociality and their relationship to individual subjectivity. There is a growing number of books discussing plasticity and other aspects of Malabou's philosophy (e.g., Martinon 2007; Bhandar 2015; Wormald and Dahms 2018; Lynch 2019). However, the present volume is not limited to merely furthering those ongoing debates. Rather, it brings a new perspective to Malabou studies both because it tracks the shift in Malabou's work, towards a critical reading of anarchist and post-anarchist theories of free society, but also because it connects Malabou's philosophy with current debates on solidarity, cooperation and mutual aid.

Thomas Telios begins with a study of how solidarity in the form of mutual aid provides the ontological framework for human behaviour and practices and, at the same time, brings forward the social juncture in which it developed. Telios begins by approximating the notion of solidarity via Kropotkin's concept of mutual aid, arguing that mutual aid is best understood as a critical social-ontological constant. He argues that Kropotkin prefigures Sally Scholz's concept of political solidarity – which detaches solidarity from the need to share the same worldview – as well as pioneers the work of thinkers in contemporary social ontology such as Raimo Tuomela and Brian Epstein.

Telios elaborates on Malabou's appropriation of Kropotkin's concept of mutual aid, which he interprets against the background of her critique of the discursivity of French structuralism and her turn to an anti-reductionist type of materialism. The notion of mutual aid, Telios argues, enhances Malabou's conceptual arsenal in an important way as it 'provides the missing, long awaited, vector that illustrates the concrete politics that an abstract concept like that of plasticity can set in motion'. Since mutual aid does not oppose solidarity to individuality, such a politics does not coerce the subject to assimilate in an undifferentiated collective. Instead, mutual aid 'binds the given (social and political) reality to its necessarily existing alternative forms' and, at the same time, 'makes clear that these alternative forms of reality are possible only through mutual aid'.

Petr Kouba's chapter approaches the question from the opposite direction. If mutual aid is possible, even necessary, then why does it frequently not happen? What are the conditions that limit mutual aid's realisation? Kouba focuses on Malabou's distinction between destructive and constructive plasticity, arguing that while constructive plasticity makes possible mutual aid in the anarchist sense, destructive plasticity prevents and constrains it. Both forms of plasticity appear as a response to trauma, but destructive plasticity involves a pathological reaction to traumatic events that breaks down both individual and collective identities and 'turns the collective subjectivity of a community into something new, something that does not recognize itself anymore'. Kouba's chapter develops this distinction in critical dialogue with his interpretation of Heidegger's ontology, contrasting it with Heidegger's distinction between authentic and inauthentic existence and the different temporal dimensions involved in it. Destructive plasticity 'tears individual and collective subjectivity apart, creating space for a fake past that can never cover and redeem what has happened'. But, it still holds out the possibility for a constructive plasticity that 'allows people to live together anew when it brings them back to the fact of their coexistence in the world'.

Rasmus Sandnes Haukedal's chapter picks up on the theme of the relationship between necessity and contingency, the social and the individual. Haukedal draws on Malabou's reformulation of Hegel's philosophy of nature and her conceptualisation of Absolute Knowing (Malabou 2005). Absolute Knowing is the knowing that dialectics is caught up in its own game and that its agents cannot be disentangled. Consequently, the individual perspective is always already bound up with other perspectives which entails an ever-present possibility of explosion that radically changes the identity of the individual. Haukedal links this view to Malabou's argument that the brain's constant interaction with the environment makes a categorical division between the neuronal and the social impossible. In particular, he interrogates how the concept of Absolute Knowing fits with Malabou's ecological sense of agency and whether the distributed sense of agency converges on what Lambros Malafouris calls 'metaplasticity'. After exploring some similarities between Malabou, Donna Haraway, and Scott Gilbert who emphasise the symbiotic interrelations between organisms and ecosystems, Haukedal asks the question of whether the Gaia hypothesis provides a way of expanding the scope of Absolute Knowing. He concludes the chapter by suggesting that the Gaia hypothesis may extend its impact by adding a dimension of constitutive multi-species interplay.

Malabou's elaboration of the notion of plasticity – which opens up ways of thinking individuality and sociality beyond the anti-essentialism of post-anarchism and the false choice it poses between essentialism and discursivity – inspires Tim Elmo Feiten's attempt to develop a new reading of Max Stirner. In his chapter, Feiten opposes the recent reception of Stirner by post-anarchists and proposes an alternative reading of Stirner's account of self-empowerment as an embodied activity that draws its strength from the links between different forms of plasticity along the dimensions of the brain, body and culture. Feiten interprets Stirner's notion of property as analogous to Jakob von Uexküll's concept of *Umwelt* and frames Stirner's insurrection against ideology in terms of phenomenological accounts of embodiment. In contrast to existing scholarship which links Stirner's thought to Michel Foucault's reflections on 'ethic of the care for the self', Feiten distinguishes between the plastic subject that shapes itself according to external norms and Stirner's genuinely self-empowering way of taking up one's own plasticity in thought and action.

Feiten's reading of Stirner foregrounds the materialism of Stirner's thought and relates it in a novel way to the notion of plasticity. Materialism and plasticity become the key topics also in Arianne Conty's chapter which closes Part 1 of this book. Conty aims to elucidate Malabou's epigenetic theory of plasticity by placing it into dialogue with Gilbert Simondon's ontogenetic theory of individuation. Though Simondon's theories considerably predate the coining of the term 'new materialism' he should be considered, Conty argues, a 'new materialist' alongside Malabou whose work he profoundly influences. Conty examines how both Simondon and Malabou refute biological determinism by revealing the psychic content of genetic development while at the same time elucidating the biological substrate of all mental content. With respect to the question of human identity and subject formation Conty concludes that in both thinkers the human being is shown 'to be constituted by its relation to a past that remains its founding principle of potentiality, a past that exceeds the boundaries of cognition and individuated identity'. As a result, both Simondon and Malabou develop a materialist philosophical theory 'that provides a new interpretation of human freedom and its ability to construct an open future'.

Several chapters in Part I already touch on the political implications of their ontology, and in Part II these themes become more explicit. In particular, these chapters are all concerned with the connections between *anarchist politics* and *evolutionary theory*. Kropotkin's work means that the idea of mutual aid and anarchism are intimately historically entwined, but this has often appeared as much a source of embarrassment rather than strength. For much of the twentieth century dominant trends in evolutionary biology emphasised reciprocity over altruism and competition over cooperation, leading views such as Kropotkin's to be rejected as straightforwardly false. Kropotkin has also come under criticism within anarchism, starting with his friend and contemporary Errico Malatesta who charged him with a naïve optimism, and continued by post-anarchists, for whom Kropotkin appears the foremost representative of a 'classical anarchism' that was too infatuated with nineteenth-century scientific utopianism and essentialist ideas of the human (see Kinna 2016 for a critical discussion of this). The chapters in this section challenge this framing in various ways, defending Kropotkin's assertion that mutuality is at least as significant a part of nature as competition, if not more, and working to free 'classical' anarchism from assumptions of essentialism and determinism. They also resist solidarity and mutual aid's reduction to concealed forms of reciprocity, breaking the chain of 'tit-for-tat' with which they are often captured.

Gearóid Brinn and Georgina Butterfield begin with a study of how contemporary anarchists have understood the idea of human nature. They seek to reject both essentialist and anti-essentialist readings of the anarchist tradition by outlining a tradition they describe as 'realist anarchism', which identifies an anarchist impulse as one possibility among many. This perspective, they argue, has been present throughout anarchism's history, and is visible in the works of Errico Malatesta, Murray Bookchin, Noam Chomsky and David Graeber. They thus challenge the historical narrative and depiction of classical anarchism by post-anarchists and provide a concept of human nature that is compatible with a naturalist, materialist worldview. This worldview is strikingly similar to that articulated by Rasmus Sandnes Haukedal in Part 1, emphasising not what makes humans unique, but their continuity with and embeddedness in the non-human world. Seen from this point of view, competitiveness is as much in need of explanation as cooperation (perhaps more), and the fact that we see it otherwise 'points towards a remarkable capacity in humans for plasticity, in this case, in a potentially catastrophic way'. This capacity that has brought us to the brink of ecological catastrophe, but it is the same capacity we must mobilise to prevent it, and to establish new, more sustainable relationships.

Eugene Kuchinov's chapter probes some of the more radical conclusions of asserting this continuity between human and non-human nature. Engaging

in a close reading of Kropotkin, Kuchinov asks us to confront him as a radical not only in the field of social and political theory, but also in the implications of his ontology. Kuchinov radicalises Kropotkin's idea of nature in three directions: first, towards the idea of unity in plurality, in which (like in Brinn and Butterfield's account), elements of nature cannot be artificially separated from one another but have to be grasped together; second, in the idea of free nature, understood in terms of a harmony to which nature strives, and which mutuality enables by increasing the ability of elements of nature to act; and third, in Kropotkin's attempts to push mutual aid 'all the way down'. In Kuchinov's reading, this pushes Kropotkin to a kind of panpsychism, in which mutual aid is identified in nature itself. Kuchinov takes Kropotkin's assertion that society is *anterior* to man as only one stage in a process of anteriorisation, 'pushing the principle of mutual aid down into the depths of the pre-human'. Kuchinov asks the question of whether mutual aid can 'cross the transformative thresholds of nature' and operate between different species, and even between organic and non-organic life. Radicalising Kropotkin yet further, he suggests we might think in terms of a mutual aid 'armature', and places this in the context of debates about the Gaia and Medea hypotheses.

Kropotkin's insistence that society is anterior to man, both methodologically and ontologically, is precisely what many of his critics in mainstream evolutionary theory reject. The remaining two chapters in the section challenge this rejection directly. Jonas Faria Costa's chapter focuses on evolutionary game theory, which takes from classical game theory an assumption of methodological individualism that ignores the potential for collective reasoning. Costa argues that this assumption of individualism was both unwarranted and heavily ideologically determined by the Cold War and the dominance of neoclassical economics. Abandoning this assumption, as contemporary game theory is beginning to do, opens up an understanding of solidarity as a form of collective reasoning, and in this context Kropotkin's ideas demonstrate the coherence and viability of an alternative in evolutionary theory. This in turn rebounds on interpretations of the idea of mutual aid. Crucial to Costa's argument is that cooperative activity need not be based on 'tit-for-tat' reciprocity, but on the ability to form collective understandings of a common good. He thus rejects any interpretation of mutual aid as grounded in reciprocal altruism, reminding us of the slogan 'solidarity is not charity'.

One of the major culprits for importing methodological individualism into evolutionary theory is Richard Dawkins, who forms the primary target of Ole Martin Sandberg's chapter. Dawkins famously insists on a central role for selfish behaviour in evolution. Yet he also insists on a unique human capacity for moral behaviour, in which we act 'against our nature'. Sandberg identifies the striking parallels between this dualism and the religious ways of thinking that Dawkins so stridently resists and traces this view back to the ideas of Thomas Huxley, who sharply distinguished the 'cosmic process' that drove evolution from the 'ethical process' on which co-operation is based. The obvious contradictions with this approach were already noted by Kropotkin, who insisted (with Darwin) on giving morality a naturalistic grounding. Sandberg challenges some of the post-anarchist interpretations of Kropotkin, before bringing him into dialogue with Friedrich Nietzsche, arguing that despite their many differences they share a rejection of 'life-denying' forms of morality. Repeating a theme common to several chapters, Sandberg emphasises how symbolic and discursive understandings of our nature shape that nature itself: 'To believe in a particular theory of the world changes the way we act in the world and thus impacts the world'. He ends by repeating Kropotkin's final words from his essay on ethics: 'Yours is the choice'.

Part III picks up this activist injunction, focusing on mutual aid and solidarity as they motivate and are realised in *contemporary social movements*. Its title, 'at the end of the day it's just us', is taken from the words of Scott Crow, one of the founders of the Common Ground Collective, founded days after Hurricane Katrina to respond to the disaster (Plan C. 2019). Here, then, our contributors reflect on mutual aid and solidarity as something that activists can and must commit to and exercise themselves, but also confront the challenges and difficulties of working together, of committing to and forming an 'us' that does not subsume or deny differences. At the same time, mutual aid and solidarity appear in these chapters as practices that *challenge* and *interrupt* the *status quo* while having the potential to *transform* it, whether by extending and deepening existing forms of cooperation, unsettling existing hierarchies and social categories, or creating new subjects and social relations.

Jade Crimson Rose Da Costa begins this section with their reflections on the experience of organising mutual aid during the COVID-19 crisis, asking not just how the pandemic affected activism but also how activism shaped the pandemic. Writing as both activist and academic, she recounts the founding of The People's Pantry, a grassroots meal programme led by Women, Queer, and Trans Black, Indigenous and People of Colour (WQTBIPOC) activists that provides home-cooked meals and groceries in the Greater Toronto Area. Da Costa recounts how this project, and the wider network of 'CareMongering' of which it was a part, drew on existing forms of WQTBIPOC organising. The pandemic provided 'a moment of destruction in which, ironically, the restorative ethics of WQTBIPOC activists could extend into and thus reconstruct the public realm'. Central to this account is a different notion of plasticity from Malabou's, 'not as the process of receiving and giving form, but as the fluidification of Blackness within and through the ontologizing violence of western humanist ideologies'. In this reading, 'whiteness gains form through the concerted plasticization (read: abjection, subhuman rendering) of Blackness especially and the non-white Other more generally'. The virus, however, troubled these boundaries by revealing the fragility of all lives. Da Costa illustrates this through the sudden openness to the Black Lives Matter movement and slogan among White people that had previously disdained it, which testifies to the '(albeit brief) plasticization of whiteness, a process which was destructive in logic and yet constructive in outcome'. The chapter ends on an ambivalent note, unsure how far this brief moment might be extended.

Broadening the focus from the COVID crisis, Ewa Majewska develops a materialist feminist account of solidarity that draws on the experiences of contemporary feminist organising and the history of the Polish Solidarność movement. Central to this is the concept of the counterpublic, drawn from the work of Alexander Kluge and Oskar Negt and (later) Nancy Fraser, which are 'formed in the outskirts and margins of the classical, traditional public sphere' and 'express the need to gather and collectively debate common matters among the working classes, women, ethnic and sexual minorities'. Solidarność is understood as one such counterpublic, rooted as it was in the self-organisation of workers and combining demands for political freedoms with demands for social justice. Such movements challenge the exclusion of labour from politics and suggest that solidarity might be forged in the experience of working together. Following this line of thought, Majewska suggests that solidarity itself might be understood as a kind of labour, analogous to translation, 'consisting in learning the language of other, without claiming sameness and ignoring differences, while directly challenging alienation'. She sees such forms of solidarity at work in the feminist organising around #Metoo and against the Polish government's recent restricting of abortion rights. Such protests form their own counterpublics, 'focused around reproduction, choice and equality, but spreading towards very general notions of how society should be governed', but they are also constituted by various forms of weak, common and ordinary acts of resistance that suggest an alternative to a traditional, heroic model of political agency.

Dan Swain's chapter interrogates the common representation among activists of mutual aid as *prefigurative* – as a way of instantiating elements of a desired future society in order to bring both it and the kind of subjectivity it contains into being. This idea is a central feature of much literature on mutual aid, but often sits uneasily alongside the idea that mutual aid is also a deeply human (or even natural) tendency. The confidence that mutual aid is a naturally human practice can easily slip into the consolation (or worse) offered by essentialism and determinism. Swain's chapter thus asks how these ideas might be combined by examining contemporary debates in the concept of prefigurative politics and pursuing this through Marxist feminist understandings of socially reproductive labour, the labour of life-making. Although such theories reject the naturalisation of this labour, they still look to emancipatory potential within it, inviting 'reflection on the prefigurative potential of our practices of life-making in ways that can hardly avoid the terrain of biology, if not nature'.

Swain thus brings the book full circle, returning to Malabou's notion of political resistance, and suggesting a dialogue between these positions that 'might help us understand how we can (at least sometimes) see prefigurative potentials within the production and reproduction of life itself'.

BIBLIOGRAPHY

Bhandar, Brenna (ed.). 2015. *Plastic Materialities: Politics, Legality, and Metamorphosis in the Work of Catherine Malabou.* Durham, NC: Duke University Press.

Cox, Lawrence. 2020. "Forms of Social Movement in the Crisis: A View from Ireland." *Interface: A Journal for and about Social Movements* 12(1), 22–33.

Illner, Peer. 2020. *Disasters and Social Reproduction: Crisis Response Between the State and Community.* London: Pluto Press.

Kinna, Ruth. 2016. *Kropotkin and the Classical Anarchist Tradition.* Edinburgh: Edinburgh University Press.

Kropotkin, Peter. 1902. *Mutual Aid: A Factor of Evolution.* New York: McClure Phillips & Co.

Lynch, Thomas. 2019. *Apocalyptic Political Theory: Hegel, Taubes and Malabou.* London: Bloomsbury Academic.

Malabou, Catherine. 2005. *The Future of Hegel: Plasticity, Temporality and Dialectic.* London and New York: Routledge.

Malabou, Catherine. 2008. *What Should We Do with Our Brain?* New York: Fordham University Press.

Malabou, Catherine. 2012. *The New Wounded: From Neurosis to Brain Damage.* New York: Fordham University Press.

Martinon, Jean-Paul. 2007. *On Futurity: Malabou, Nancy, Derrida.* Basingstoke: Palgrave Macmillan.

Plan C. 2019. "'At the End of the Day It's Just Us' – Mutual Aid, Direct Action and Disasters." 8th October 2019. Accessed 29th April, 2021. https://www.weareplanc.org/blog/at-the-end-of-the-day-its-just-us-mutual-aid-direct-action-and-disasters/.

Proudhon, Pierre Joseph. 1994. *What Is Property?* Edited and translated by Donald R. Kelley and Bonnie G. Smith. Cambridge: Cambridge University Press.

Singer, Peter. 2011. *The Expanding Circle: Ethics, Evolution and Moral Progress.* Princeton: Princeton University Press.

Sitrin, Marina and Colectiva Sembrar (eds.). 2020. *Pandemic Solidarity.* London: Pluto Press.

Solnit, Rebecca. 2020. "Foreword." In *Pandemic Solidarity*, edited by Marina Sitrin and Colectiva Sembrar, xi–xv. London: Pluto.

Spade, Dean. 2020. *Mutual Aid: Building Solidarity During This Crisis (and the Next)*. London: Verso.

Tolentino, Jia. 2020. "What Mutual Aid Can Do During a Pandemic." *New Yorker*. Accessed 26th April, 2021. https://www.newyorker.com/magazine/2020/05/18/what-mutual-aid-can-do-during-a-pandemic.

Wormald, Thomas, and Isabell Dahms (eds.). 2018. *Thinking Catherine Malabou: Passionate Detachments*. London: Rowman & Littlefield International.

Chapter 2

Politics of Plasticity

Cooperation without Chains

Catherine Malabou

Three main characteristics are implied in the definition of *mutual aid*. The first one is social: mutual aid is a mode of organisation based on voluntary and reciprocal exchange of resources and services. The second one is moral: as opposed to charity, mutual aid does not connote moral superiority of the giver over the receiver. It is based on horizontal relationships that are supposed to exclude any feeling of guilt or debt. It is not based on empathy either, that is on the capacity to project oneself into the other's interiority. The third characteristic is dynamic: mutual aid is a problem-solving process that produces a result: security, equality and trust. Besides this, mutual aid organisations should be distinguished from conventional for-profit enterprises, entrepreneurship and the informal economy by two core features. First, they have explicit political and often environmental objectives. Second, they involve varying forms of co-operative, associative and solidarity relations. They include, for example, cooperatives, mutual associations, NGOs engaged in income-generating activities, women's self-help groups, community forestry and other organisations, associations of informal sector workers and social enterprise and fair-trade organisations and networks. The question I raise here is whether mutual aid can structure the collective today, and at the same time determine a new form of horizontal politics that challenges state authority as well as social hierarchy. I also ask if mutual aid can generate a philosophical inquiry emancipated from the idea of *chaining*, that is from the bonds, fetters or shackles of domination. These two questions are aimed at sketching the profile of a reelaboration of anarchism today.

Such questions arise from the identification of a shift in the morphology of democracy. The obsolescence of the welfare state has produced a loss of autonomy in political subjects, a sense of abandonment, accompanied by a radical individualism, that manifest themselves as a general incapacity to deal with social problems at both micro- and macroscopic levels without external institutionalised help: and this goes from neighbourhood issues and urban policy up to social and economic inequalities or ecological crisis.

There is consequently a need to reelaborate the concept of community outside the strict domain of state policy. Every democracy is based on mutuality. There is no social contract without mutuality. But mutual aid goes far beyond the sole idea of the social contract. What I intend to examine here is what exactly 'aid' is adding to 'mutuality'.

HOW TO EPISTEMOLOGICALLY SITUATE MUTUAL AID?

The need to rethink the concept of community with mutual aid also necessarily implies reconceptualising mutual aid itself. Such a necessity arises from the identification of inadequacies in the previous theories of mutual aid. A basic issue has to be raised anew: Why should people act in solidarity? What is the moral and political motor of cooperation? As we know, the traditional anarchist answer has revolved around the idea of altruism, an altruism that would have biological bases, as made clear by Kropotkin in his book *On Mutual Aid: A Factor of Evolution* (1902). Kropotkin grounds his social and political vision of mutual aid on the spontaneous animal solidarity that exists among members of the same species. Social solidarity would originally be a natural trend, the sophisticated translation of an instinct. There would be no need then, according to Kropotkin, to inquire about the motivations for mutual aid. Mutual aid would have its reason in itself as the result of a biological evolutionary tendency. Such an idea, however interesting and promising, has been strongly challenged. It has led to suspicious sociobiological assumptions, according to which evolutionary mechanics hide behind all social behaviours. Edward Wilson for example in his famous book *Sociobiology: The New Synthesis* (1975) has affirmed the existence of a direct link of causality between the biological and the social, raising strong opposition. A long controversy took place throughout the twentieth century between the advocates of natural altruism and those of natural biological 'egoism', a position often assigned rightly or not to Richard Dawkins and his famous book *The Selfish Gene* (1976).

The second main inadequacy of the traditional concept of mutual aid pertains to the difficulty of rigorously and definitely differentiating revolutionary anarchism from right-wing libertarianism. The idea that self-management and self-organisation can constitute coherent social and political forms finds itself also at the core of right-wing anarchist theories of the 'minimal state'.

In his book *Anarchy, State, and Utopia* (1974), Robert Nozick developed a defence of the state that restricts its activities to the protection of individual rights of life, liberty, property and contract. State power should not be used to redistribute income, to make people moral or to protect people from harming themselves. 'The minimal state', he writes,

> treats us as inviolate individuals, who may not be used in certain ways by others as means or tools or instruments or resources; it treats us as persons having individual rights with the dignity this constitutes. Treating us with respect by respecting our rights, it allows us, individually or with whom we choose, to choose our life and to realize our ends and our conception of ourselves, insofar as we can, aided by the voluntary cooperation of other individuals possessing the same dignity. How *dare* any state or group of individuals do more. Or less. (Nozick 1974, 35)

I am concerned with the question of how we can theoretically preserve, extend and develop the idea of mutual aid without falling back into sociobiological ideology on the one hand and ultra-liberal philosophy on the other.

This brings me to develop another important difficulty.

One might consider that the deconstruction of the traditional concept of mutual aid has already happened. Contemporary 'post-anarchism'[1] has insisted on the necessity of avoiding the dangers of both biologism and radical individualism.

However, and such is the difficulty, post-anarchism suffers from a conceptual weakness, which bars the way to an authentic thinking of participatory democracy, power shared leadership and cooperative decision-making. The current debate revolves around a very limited opposition, the opposition between *essentialism* and *discursivity*. Traditional anarchism, as well as libertarianism, are said to be essentialist by post-anarchists, who share with post-structuralist thinkers the systematic gesture of partitioning philosophy and politics into two categories: essentialism, precisely, and what appears as its emancipated contrary, discursivity.

New radical left theories fight against groundedness, ontological fixity, biological determinism, naturalism and humanism by opposing them to the constructed, contingent, changeable character of social determinations and struggles. If there is to be a culture of solidarity, they argue, it should be conceived as a culture of fluidity, transiency, in the absence of any natural basis.

Clearly, the central problem for anarchist theory and the current issue of cooperation and solidarity, declares Andrew Koch, 'is to build a non

[1] The term 'post-anarchism' was coined by Saul Newman (see Newman 2010, 34).

representational basis for anarchism [and mutual aid]. The character of human beings as benevolent or rational cannot be sustained with any more certainty than the claims that human beings are selfish and irrational. Anarchism must find its grounding outside any fixed structure' (Koch 2011, 42). This is of course directed against Kropotkin. In the collection where Andrew Koch's text is published, *Post-Anarchism: A Reader* (Rouselle and Evren 2011), Kropotkin is almost unanimously viewed as the thinker 'of the prototype of the properly human' (Koch 2011, 39), who understood biological evolution as the development of an immanent social rationality.

Another central critique of essentialism, and a major reference for the radical left today, even if not 'anarchist', is Ernesto Laclau and Chantal Mouffe's book *Hegemony and Socialist Strategy* (1985). They show that most struggles against subordination currently occur 'without passing in any way through parties or states' (Laclau and Mouffe 1985, 137). This refusal of a central apparatus and unifying structure supposes control of decisions that are not imposed from the outside, and cooperative organisation that allows groups to regulate themselves using their own resources. At the same time, such regulation cannot pertain to the classical anarchist vision of a battle between two poles, society against the state, to the extent that political struggles have become multiple and irreducible to any unity or universalism. 'We are faced here with a true polysemia. Feminism or ecology, for example, exist in multiple forms' (*Ibid.*, 152), there is a 'very proliferation of widely differing points of rupture' (*Ibid.*, 155). Mutual aid, then, has to be fostered out of and not against such contingency and multiplicity.

'Unfixity' they argue, 'has become the condition of every social identity', 'the social itself has no essence' (*Ibid.*, 82). They insist upon the indeterminacy of the social, its 'fundamental ambiguity [. . .], the impossibility of establishing in a definitive manner the meaning of any struggle, whether considered in isolation or through its fixing in a relational system' (*Ibid.*, 82).

Fixity and essentialism are also responsible, as I mentioned earlier, for the 'anti-democratic offensive' of the neo-liberal 'new right' that opposes the State in the name of individual freedom. Laclau and Mouffe's critique of Hayek and Nozick also lays its foundations on anti-essentialism. Libertarianism is a type of humanism that presupposes a naturality of the individual that allows him to develop it in any direction that facilitates wealth, security and freedom. Hayek 'proposes to reaffirm the "true" nature of liberalism as the doctrine which seeks to reduce to the minimum the power of the State' (Hayek 2011, 156). Democracy for him is only a 'means, a utilitarian device for safeguarding internal piece and individual freedom' (Laclau and Mouffe 1985, 156). Laclau and Mouffe also evoke Friedman and Nozick: 'In *Capitalism and Freedom*', they write, 'Milton Friedman declares that [the framework of the capitalist free market] is the only type of social organization which respects the the principle of individual liberty, as it constitutes the only economic system capable of coordinating the activities of a great number of people without recourse to coercion' (Laclau and Mouffe 1985, 156). We understand, from all this, that mutual aid, in the neo-liberal new right, pertains to the capacity of individuals to coordinate their actions for the sake of economic freedom.

Once again, there is a common point between left and right anarchism that is essentialism. Against these determinations, Laclau and Mouffe advocate for an 'equality without essence', which comes close to the arguments of post-anarchists (Laclau and Mouffe 1985, 140). Saul Newman, for example, declares that there is no natural or social tendency towards revolution: 'what is important is the unpredictability and contingency of politics', he writes (Newman 2011, 61). Furthermore, 'the political subject is not founded on essentialist conceptions of human nature; rather, the subject emerges in an unpredictable fashion through a rupturing of fixed social roles and identities' (Newman 2011, 51).

What, then, does constitute the social fabric if not discursivity, a structure that obeys constructed, symbolic rules that govern the shaping of communities and cannot be referred to any preexisting order? Resolutely cut off from nature, essence, or biology, mutual aid has to be structured like a language in order to appear genuinely emancipatory.

Such a conclusion seems to me challengeable. In my view, essentialism and discursivity share a common point to the extent that they conceive the collective as a series of *chains* between subjects. A chain is a length of rings that are connected together. Essentialism and discursivity cannot think of freedom without chains, and such is the reason why they are in reality not opposed. I defend here, on the contrary, a concept of mutual aid without chain. An *unchained solidarity.*

In order to develop my position, I will confront three types of chains: ontological, biological and discursive. The first two correspond to the two main dimensions of essentialism, the last one to their supposed deconstruction.

THE THREE CHAINS

Let's start with ontological chaining and refer to Plato for that purpose. For Plato, being is a chain, or rather a chain of chains, as all the parts of the cosmos are connected together through points of articulation, or structural joints. There is therefore a mutual solidarity between all these parts, that constitutes the cosmos as a *taxis*, an ordered totality. Dialectic, as a science, appears as the art of discovering the joints under the unity of the whole, and reciprocally reestablishing the whole out of the consideration of the joints.

A body for example, as Socrates explains in *Phaedrus*, is a totality in which all the organs act in mutual solidarity to the extent that they are simultaneously different and the same (Plato 1972).

Following this metaphor, he affirms that philosophy is the art of exhibiting the chains of things, the mutuality between all parts of the cosmos. In *Phaedrus*, 265[e], Socrates says that the philosopher has to know where to cut, and to determine 'where the natural joints are, and [should not] break any part, after the manner of a bad carver' (Plato 1972, 131). He adds 'just as the body, which is one, is naturally divisible into two, right and left, [. . .], so our our discourse is also divisible' (Plato 1972, 132). The dialectician has to decide where to cut and reassemble rightly in order not to butcher the logos.

According to such an understanding of the chain, mutuality and solidarity are seen as following from a preexisting order. The philosopher does not construct them, he or she just follows the preexisting lines of articulation. This model also sustains Plato's political thinking, according to which the social is ontologically structured, that is ideally cut, constituted and delineated according to predetermined lines of fractures.

The second type of 'essential' chaining is biological and concerns the link between individuals throughout evolution of several species, and the link between the members of the same species.

Kropotkin declares that: 'The mutual-aid tendency in man has so remote an origin, and is so deeply interwoven with all the past evolution of the human race, that is has been maintained by mankind up to the present time, notwithstanding all vicissitudes of history' (Kropotkin 1902, 32). The persistence of mutual aid through time pertains to the fact it is a tendency, an evolutionary trend, immanent to life. A reader of Darwin, Kropotkin affirms that natural selection is not the only evolutionary law. Living beings not only compete, they also cooperate. Darwin himself, Kropotkin affirms, came to that conclusion in *The Descent of Man*.

Mutual aid has nothing to do with any moral impulse, nor with love or even empathy. It depends on natural laws only. Living beings tend to form chains of solidarity in order to get protection against enemies and secure survival. Mutual support, which occurs for the adaptive sake of the community, requires the building of chains of cooperation.

Kropotkin describes and analyses protective behaviours among birds like parrots or cranes. He provides beautiful readings of migrating birds flying together, or associations between wolves for hunting. Kropotkin's contention is that human mutual aid is 'evolution of animal reign that speaks through us' (Kropotkin 1902, 39). Evolution orients our actions towards help, solidarity, communality and sustains the vision of a future better society grounded in self- institutionalised and self-managed organisations. 'In the long run', he writes, 'the practice of solidarity proves much more advantageous to the species than the development of individuals endowed with predatory inclinations' (Kropotkin 1902, 51).

If the idea of a biological chain (and the chain lexicon is extremely conspicuous in biology, if one thinks of food chain, protein chain, DNA chain) can be characterised as 'essentialist', it is not because it would proceed out of a preordered harmonious arrangement or distribution, like in Plato's model, but because it links all living beings across time and space along the evolutionary line.

It is striking to see that when Dawkins opposes the idea of natural altruism and advocates for the existence of a natural selfishness, he does it on the exact same basis as the scientists who he contradicts: *chain formation*. 'We are born selfish, he writes. [. . .] We are survival machines – robot vehicles blindly programmed to preserve the selfish molecules known as genes. This is a truth which still fills me with astonishment' (Dawkins 1976, 2).

Altruism, Dawkins argues, is just a mask for egoism. A bird or a bee risks their lives and health to bring their offspring into the world, not to help others, but in order for their genes to go on and survive. The digital information in a gene is effectively immortal and must be the primary unit of selection. 'The argument', he writes,

> is that we, and all other animals, are machines created by our genes. Like successful Chicago gangsters, our genes have survived, in some cases for millions of years, in a highly competitive world. [. . .] I shall argue that a predominant quality to be expected in a successful gene is ruthless selfishness. This gene selfishness will usually give rise to selfishness in individual behaviour. However [. . .], there are special circumstances in which a gene can achieve its own selfish goal best by fostering a limited form of altruism at the level of individual animals. [. . .] Much as we might wish to believe otherwise, universal love and the welfare of the species as a whole are concepts that simply do not make evolutionary sense. (Dawkins 1976, 4)

What are genes anyway? Chains! We can also think here of Michael Bradie's 1994 book, eloquently called *The Secret Chain: Evolution and Ethics* that insists on the irreducible links that exist between evolutionary trends and the development of morality.

I now come to discursivity, a paradigm that has become central in post-structuralism and post-anarchism. It is a striking fact that the discursive paradigm maintains the metaphor of chaining while challenging essentialism. Discursivity is conceived according to the model of the linguistic chain, made of articulated basic elements.

The first description of the linguistic chain appears in Saussure's *Course in General Linguistics*: 'Chain of speech', Saussure declares, is 'a succession of phonic unities (or phonemes) combined together on the syntagmatic line to form sentences statements in a given language' (Saussure 1916, 88).[2] Also:

> One definition of articulated speech might confirm that conclusion. In Latin, *articulus* means a member, part, or subdivision of a sequence; applied to speech, articulation designates either the subdivision of a spoken chain into syllables or the subdivision of the chain of meanings into significant units; *gegliederte Sprache* is used in the second sense in German. Using the second definition, we can say that what is natural to mankind is not oral speech but the faculty of constructing a language, i.e. a system of distinct signs corresponding to distinct ideas. (Saussure 1916, 88)

The articulation of language is a multi-differentiated structure: it designates the combination of different signs together but also the combination of two elements in each particular sign: the signified and the signifier.

The end of Saussure's sentence is fundamental: 'we can say that what is natural to mankind is not oral speech but the faculty of constructing a language, i.e. a system of distinct signs corresponding to distinct ideas' (Saussure 1916, 10). Hence the conclusion that 'what is natural is the capacity to invent a non-natural order'. The arbitrary system of language is what Saussure also calls 'discourse'. *Discourse*, or *discursivity*, refers to the constructed character of the linguistic articulated chains that break with any natural or ontological normativity or pre-arrangement. There is no *being* of language. No sign has any meaning in itself, it becomes meaningful only in its difference and articulation with other signs. This point has become fundamental in human sciences, in psychoanalysis for example, but all throughout the whole edifice of critical theory throughout the twentieth century. The unity of the discursive chain is *symbolic*, not natural once again, and 'symbolic' has been used as a contrary term to 'essential'.

What is a symbolic chain? What kind of mutuality is the discursive mutuality, that is, the relationality between the elements of an ensemble? What keeps them united, and how are they different from the aforementioned model of ontological and biological types of chains?

Laclau and Mouffe push the notion of symbolic chain to its most radical political limit. They argue that is has become impossible nowadays to assign political resistance to one class only – the proletariat. As Luxembourg and Gramsci already noticed, classical Marxism has then to be re-elaborated in terms of plural, multiple forms of struggles that cannot find their unity in a class, a group or a party. The concept of class is still essentialist as it is

[2] All quotes from Saussare 1916 in this chapter are my own translation.

governed by a logic of universality rooted in the objective determination of economy, what Althusser calls after Marx and Engels 'determination in the last instance', which is a logic that plays the part of a prearranged order. However, if this universal does not exist, it does not mean either that the social is constituted of juxtaposed particularities. *It is made of chains.*

These chains are formed by the different actors involved in the same types of struggle. They are opposed to essentialist ones, to the extent that they are precisely symbolic: 'The symbolic, i.e. overdetermined, character of social relations therefore implies that they lack an ultimate literality which would reduce them to necessary moments of an immanent law' (Laclau and Mouffe 1985, 84). The reference point of each chain is never an 'underlying principle external to itself' (*Ibid.*, 92). A chain is not governed by a unique, transcendental signifier, but each of its links has a different meaning. The chain 'overflows' with meanings, the signifiers overwhelm the signifieds. For example, 'woman' in feminist struggles is a 'floating signifier', not a transcendental signified. 'If we accept [. . .] that a discursive totality never exists in the form of a simply given and delimited positivity, the relational logic will be incomplete and pierced by contingency [. . .]. As the identities are purely relational, this is but another way of saying that there is no identity which can be fully constituted.' (*Ibid.*, 102).

Political resistance is therefore always fragmented, made of a plurality of chains, sometimes competing with each other, a characteristic that is particularly manifest in our time: feminism, ecology, anti-global movements, queer movements, and so on are coexisting, and their coexistence is both peaceful and conflictual.

The surplus of meaning, the overflowing proliferation of signifiers is not only internal to each chain, it permeates the mutual relationships between the different chains and floating signifiers. We are faced with two phenomena, the authors write: 'the asymmetry existing between the social growing proliferation of differences – a surplus of meaning of the "social", and the difficulties encountered by any discourse attempting to fix those differences as moments of a stable articulatory structure' (*Ibid.*, 82).

The last part of the sentence already announces what Laclau and Mouffe characterise as 'hegemony', a term that they borrow from Gramsci. Each element of each chain, as well as each chain itself, is governed by such a tendency, seeks to impose one signifier over the other, to fix temporarily one signifier as the dominant one, for example democracy, for example 'me too', for example 'sustainability' and so on. A particular link always seeks to represent the totality of the chain. It is a particularity that guarantees the momentaneous universal meaning of the chain, but such hegemony is contingent, temporary and changeable. The dominant term is a result of an overflow, an overdetermination, a displacement of the literal towards the metaphoric, not an essence, not a nature. Laclau and Mouffe declare: 'The logic of hegemony is a logic of articulation and contingency' (*Ibid.*, 75). Some privileged signifiers fix for a certain time the stability of a signifying chain (hence their temporary 'hegemony').

Hence, for example, 'the equivalential articulation between anti-racism, anti-sexism and anti-capitalism, requires a hegemonic construction which, in certain circumstances, may be the condition for the consolidation of each one of these struggles' (*Ibid.*, 166).

Laclau and Mouffe insist on the fact that most political struggles are designed as autonomous mutual aid networks in the sense I am discussing them. Hegemony does not contradict autonomy. 'Clearly', they say,

> when we speak here of the political character of [the] struggles, we do not do so in the restricted sense of demands which are situated at the level of the parties or of the State. [. . .] Certain contemporary feminist practices, for example, tend to transform the relationship between feminity and masculinity without passing in any way through parties or the State. (*Ibid.*, 137)

The confrontation between discursivity and essentialism thus appears as a competition between different modalities of chaining. That mutual aid can hold people together without chaining them is alien to both of them. Be it ontological, biological or discursive, the concept of chain is always normative, securing an order of concatenation that prevents improvisation, invention and spontaneity.

In the end, the difference between essentialist and discursive concepts of chaining is not that obvious.

DECORRELATED SUBJECTS

How, then, is it possible to challenge the idea of the chain?

Biology. First, it is important to notice that sociobiology has been deconstructed by biologists themselves. In 1975, Stephen Jay Gould, Richard Lewontin and other scientists from the Boston area wrote a letter to the *New York Review of Books* entitled, 'Against "Sociobiology"'. This open letter criticised Wilson's notion of a 'deterministic view of human society and human action' (Allen et al. 1975). This marked the beginning of a new turn in biology.

Contemporary molecular and evolutionary biology has undergone a profound revolution since the 1990s, thus achieving this turn. The current development of epigenetics, the insistence upon the malleability of the genome, the central role of brain plasticity, have displaced and debased the vision of biology as a deterministic science, dealing with codes, programmes, immanent laws *and chains*. Biology has deconstructed itself so to speak. It has brought to light the inadequacy of the chain model. The prefix 'epi' in 'epi-genesis' means 'at the surface'. Epigenetic mechanisms work at the surface of the DNA; they translate it into the RNA through processes that involve both chemical and environmental operations. Epigenetics is a biological improvisation, the jazz music of genetics. At another level, the study of brain plasticity, in which I have been interested for so many years, led me to radically challenge the essentialist/discursive opposition, as the most recent research in neurology has demonstrated that the functioning of the brain renders the distinction between the biological and the discursive superfluous and inaccurate. The brain is an organ, but is a symbolic one. The brain is the empirical structure from which language emerges, it is the locus of an indissociable unity between matter and meaning. An important characteristic of our time is the explosion of the organic/symbolic divide. There is no way in which we can draw a rigid line between the naturalistic and the discursive paradigm any longer. Brain plasticity is the plastic explosive that destroys both the essence and the floating signifier. It breaks the chains.

It is true that neural connections are often called neural chains. But these chains are extremely interesting to observe. As paradoxical as it may seem, they render improbable and contingent the relationship between connecting and linking. All brains areas are connected together in the global neural workspace, and yet their linking is temporary and transient, the patterns formed by momentarily wirings disappear.

Ontology. Laclau and Mouffe affirm that their *position* is not anti-realist:

> The fact that every object is constituted as an object of discourse has *nothing* to do with whether there is a world external to thought, or with the realism/idealism opposition. [. . .] What is denied is not that such objects exist externally to thought, but the rather different assertion that they could constitute themselves as objects outside any discursive conditions of emergence. (Laclau and Mouffe 1985, 94)

Speculative realism, or Object Oriented Ontology, affirm precisely the contrary, namely that objects can and do exist outside discursive conditions of emergence. We then need a decorrelated political ontology that breaks with the order of discourse as well as with the order of being.

The problem of anti-correlationism or speculative realism nevertheless is that it never addresses the social and political problem, and does not engage with this issue: What is an unchained chain of solidarity? What becomes of subjects once delinked, decorrelated from the real? And at the same time delinked, decorrelated from the symbolic?

Our time has cut the chains, for good or for worse. But after all, isn't this the right condition, the right time for anarchy?

Mutual aid of course proceeds from a need, the need to be together, to make connections. It is time, though, to think that connections can be links without chains. Mutual aid today is the paradoxical solidarity of the unchained.

CONCLUSION

Through his conception of mutual aid, Kropotkin operated a radical transformation of the philosophical core of anarchism. He did so by promoting 'life' as a political concept that he constructed outside the strict boundaries (and chains) of European metaphysics. As a geographer, and as we just saw, he elaborated his theory on the basis of his observations made during field trips in Siberia and Manchuria where he discovered that many animals were able to survive extremely severe conditions of life, wandering through immense territories devoid of artificial borders.

Once again, what he specifically calls 'mutual aid' is not only cooperation but more fundamentally a type of relation that allows for the maintenance of small variations in individuals, thus anticipating in many ways the most recent research in epigenetics. Contrary to the widely shared opinion that anarchism relies on a belief in the fundamental character of the Good, of Human Nature or the sacredness of the Individual, its vision of mutual aid does not constitute the substance of life, but only a contingent dynamic relation between living beings, always anterior to individuals, that preserves individual variations. In short, preservation of anteriority leads to the creation of a set of new state of an increased diversity. In Kropotkin's theory, multiplicity is always made possible by the return of the ancient. This return does not teleologically determine the multiple as it is transformable in its occurrences.

In the second half of his 1902 book, Kropotkin analyses the social destiny of mutual aid, leaving animals behind in order to examine human behaviours. He describes the multiplicity of the social egalitarian forms in contemporary world: clans, guilds, village communities, agricultural cooperation and unionism. These forms are transient. If they resist and recreate themselves each time they are attacked, they nevertheless do not constitute prisons with immutable rules or dogmatic party discipline.

Kropotkin does not say that these plastic egalitarian forms are 'biologically determined', that they just are remnants of an animal past. They bear witness to a *historisation of the biological*, as they render manifest the point of contact between nature and the social, which partly erases the frontiers between evolution and history.

There can be no history without the awareness of the return of anteriority. Primitive forms of mutual aid are not instinctual and blind though, they act as *memories* of a certain kind, without which history would not be possible. There are of course ruptures with this past, as proven with the emergence of capitalism, or the dissolution of small communities in current gigantic impersonal industrial cities. But the memories of anterior states are never lost.

The actors of mutual aid in contemporary societies are the 'anonymous masses'. In *Modern Science and Anarchism*, Kropotkin writes:

> Every social safeguard, all forms of social life in the tribe, the commune, and the early medieval town-republics; all forms of inter-tribal, and later on inter-provincial, relations, out of which international law was subsequently evolved; all forms of mutual support and all institutions for the preservation of peace – including the jury – were developed by the creative genius *of the anonymous masses*. While all the laws of every age, down to our own, always consisted of the same two elements: one which fixed and crystallized certain forms of life that were universally recognized as useful; the other which was a superstructure – sometimes even nothing but a cunning clause adroitly smuggled in in order to establish and strengthen the growing power of the nobles, the king, and the priest – to give it sanction. (Kropotkin 1903, 19)

'Anonymous masses' organise resistance to political hegemonies not because they are driven by a stubborn, unconscious natural trend, but because they *remember the past without having necessarily memorised it*. Biological life is a specific form of remembrance of things past that is why biological life is always already historical.

The Covid-19 crisis is the object of many philosophical analyses that heavily rely on Foucault's concept of biopolitics. Many thinkers argue that crisis management – terms of confinement, selection of patients, lack of material, cynicism of global leaders – is the result of biopolitical techniques of governmentality through which the lives of individuals are globally controlled, exploited, normalised and captured. It would of course be difficult to say the contrary. These analyses only understand 'life' as something passive and purely exposed to control and 'states of exception'. The resisting potential of life to such captures is never envisaged. The diverse manifestations of mutual aid that we see currently emerging are precisely the expressions of such a potential. There exists a biological resistance to biopolitics, a resistance which is all at once empirical and political. Mutual aid is the biological monument secretely erected in our lives in memory of ancestral forms of equality. Life is not the passive, blind, obscure dimension of being, that would only be enlightened by culture, language and the cut from organic determinism. The biological and the symbolic, the historical and the epigenetic are inseparable.

Therefore, we need a new reformulation of human rights, where the remembrance of the ancestral biological past should find its expression and formulation. Tentatively: 'All human beings are epigenetically born free and equal in dignity and rights. They are endowed with reason, conscience and memory, and should act towards one another in a spirit of brotherhood'.

Mutual aid of course proceeds from a memory, the non-conscious remembrance of past connections that allow for future possible social networks. It is time to think that connections can be links without chains. Mutual aid today is the paradoxical solidarity of the unchained, the inexhaustible resource of hope and energy for a politics of plasticity.

BIBLIOGRAPHY

Allen, Elizabeth, Barbara Beckwith, Jon Beckwith, Steven Chorover, David Culver, Margaret Duncan, Steven J. Gould, Ruth Hubbard, Hiroshi Inouye, Anthony Leeds, Richard Lewontin, Chuck Madansky, Larry Miller, Reed Pyeritz, Peter Bent, Miriam Rosenthal, Herb Schreier. 1975. "Against 'Sociobiology'." *The New York Review of Books*, 13 November.

Bradie, Michael. 1994. *The Secret Chain: Evolution and Ethics*. New York: SUNY Press.

Dawkins, Richard. 1976. *The Selfish Gene*. New York: Oxford University Press.

Hayek, Friedrich. 1960. *The Constitution of Liberty*. Chicago: Chicago University Press.

Koch, Andrew M. 2011. "Post-Structuralism and the Epistemological Basis of Anarchism." In *Post-Anarchism: A Reader*, edited by Duane Rousselle and Süreyyya Evren, 23–45. London: Pluto Press.

Kropotkin, Peter. 1902. *Mutual Aid: A Factor of Evolution*. New York: McClure Phillips & Co.

Kropotkin, Peter. 1903. *Modern Science and Anarchism*. London: Anarchist Library.

Laclau, Ernesto, Chantal Mouffe. 1985. *Hegemony and Socialist Strategy: Towards a Radical Democratic Politics*. London: Verso.

Newman, Saul. 2010. *The Politics of Postanarchism*. Edinburgh: Edinburgh University Press.

Newman, Saul. 2011. "Post-Anarchism and Radical Politics Today." In *Post-Anarchism: A Reader*, edited by Duane Rousselle and Süreyyya Evren, 46–68. London: Pluto Press.

Nozick, Robert. 1974. *Anarchism, State and Utopia*. New York: Basic Books.

Plato. 1972. *Phaedrus*. Edited and translated by Reginal Hackforth. Cambridge: Cambridge University Press.

de Saussure, Ferdinand. 1916. *Cours de linguistique générale*. Paris: Payot.

Wilson, Edward O. 1975. *Sociobiology: The New Synthesis*. Cambridge: Harvard University Press.

Part I

'AN INTERNAL PRINCIPLE OF COOPERATION, ASSISTANCE AND REPAIR' – SOLIDARITY AND PLASTICITY

Chapter 3

Solidarity as Necessity

Subject, Structure, Practices

Thomas Telios

Intersectionality is not just a rapidly developing feminist theory. It also constitutes a promising research agenda, providing a theoretically demanding and elaborate conceptual framework intended to serve not only as a tool for analytical diagnoses of societal phenomena but also as a compass and blueprint for emancipatory political action. Born from the practical necessity of accounting for the discriminatory experiences of Black women who were un(der)represented within the mainstream of White, middle-class, heterosexual feminism, intersectionality's theoretical roots go back to the manifestos and pathbreaking writings of activist groups and scholars from a variety of fields. These include Black feminism (bell hooks 1984), critical race and women of colour feminism (Spelman 1988; Moraga and Anzaldúa 1984), Black lesbian socialist activism (the Combahee River Collective), French poststructuralist philosophy (primarily Jacques Derrida and Michel Foucault) and, finally, postcolonial and anti-Eurocentric feminism (Mohanty 1988). A quite recent sociological tradition, intersectionality surfaced in the United States at the end of the 1980s and the beginning of the 1990s in the writings of Kimberlé Crenshaw (1989), Patricia Hill Collins (1990) and Chela Sandoval (1991) and was consolidated into a global theory within the following decade. Michele Tracy Berger and Kathleen Guidroz attested, as early as 2009, to the relevance of intersectionality when they declared that 'to be an informed social theorist or methodologist in many fields of inquiry [. . .] one must grapple with the implications of intersectionality' (2009, 7). Seven years later, in her rendition of the intellectual history of the concept, Hancock (2016) contended that intersectionality had become – just thirty years after its introduction – something even more significant, namely a matter of 'social literacy' (Hancock 2016, 4).

Intersectionality consists, first and foremost, of the assertion that 'social identity categories such as race, gender, class, sexuality, and ability are interconnected and operate simultaneously to produce experiences of both privilege and marginalization' (Smooth 2013, 11). Accordingly, it provides the theoretical and methodological tools to analyse historically embedded modes of subjectivity production that generate or perpetuate different axes of discrimination and subordination. At the same time, intersectionality aims to offer forms of resistance and self-determination 'vis-à-vis [. . .] power-laden social relations and conditions' (Lykke 2011, 51). In this light, intersectionality is not a mere theoretical instrument that presumes that the subject is a product or intersection where different modes of subjectivity production encounter each other and are therefore always-already 'potentially at a crossroads' (Townsend-Bell 2013, 43). Intersectionality is also a political device the potentiality of which emerges due to the clash that is generated as the different modes of subjectivity production cross each other in the subject.

Nevertheless, and despite the vast and ever-growing literature on intersectionality, the status of the relation between the partial identities that originate from the different modes of subjectivity production is still fiercely debated within the intersectional discourse. Judith Butler is critical of what she has pejoratively called 'that embarrassed "etc." at the end of the list' (1990, 182), thus rejecting the possibility of an exhaustive list including all possible modes of subjectivity production. In a similar gesture, Wendy Brown argues that 'we are not fabricated as subjects in *discrete* units' (Brown 1997, 86; emphasis added), meaning that the different domains of discrimination and subjectivation that intersectionality highlights as parts of the subject's identity are incapable of compartmentalising and dividing the subject, which can only appear as an integral individual. In response to these concerns, intersectional theorists have emphasised that given the complexity of social structuration and stratification, intersectionality is meant to 'foreground a richer and more complex ontology than approaches that attempt to reduce people to one category at a time' (Phoenix and Pattynama 2006, 187). In this light, intersectional theorists attempt to expand the modes of subjectivity production, acknowledging 'the crucial importance of the separation of the different analytical levels in which social divisions need to be examined' (Yuval-Davis 2006, 202). They take as a starting point the need for 'theory formation and research which accounts for the diverse conditions which gave rise to the constitution of differences as well as their historical interconnectedness' (Knapp 1999, 130) and juxtapose this to monosemantic accounts of subjectivity that tend to address the subject as the product of only one mode of subjectivity production. Among the various theoretical propositions that have been suggested to solve this Gordian knot, I return to Yuval-Davis's older call for 'a richer and more complex ontology' (Yuval-Davis 2006, 195). She points out that, 'each social division has a different ontological basis, which is irreducible to other social divisions' (*Ibid.*). Drawing on Roy Bhaskar's dialectical critical realist philosophy, Lena Gunnarsson has recently argued that it is possible to think of those multiple and shifting identities as each depicting a social position 'that intra-acts with other social positions but which nevertheless has its own irreducible properties' (Gunnarsson 2017, 11).

In what follows, I make a similar claim and turn to the notion of solidarity as a heuristic model. Thereby I do not only intend to explain how the identities that house the subject's body relate to one another. More importantly, I aim also to illustrate what kind of political practices correspond to this kind of structuration of subjectivity. Having sketched the main tenets of intersectional thought in this section, I begin the next section by approximating the notion of solidarity via the concept of Peter Kropotkin's concept of mutual aid, arguing that mutual aid is best understood as a *social-ontological constant.* I then turn to Catherine Malabou's materialist interpretation of Kropotkin's concept of mutual aid to corroborate the political significance of mutual aid within this framework. Finally, I demonstrate how this reappropriation of mutual aid helps us to rethink not only how different identities relate to one another in the subject's body but also the kind of practices that correspond to such an understanding of subjectivity. As will be shown, the latter is rendered possible due to certain Spinozist elements that permeate the philosophies of both Kropotkin and Malabou and will be proven pivotal in this regard.

FOUNDING SOLIDARITY: PETER KROPOTKIN'S CONCEPT OF MUTUAL AID

When dealing with Kropotkin's concept of mutual aid (1902) as a theory of solidarity, the first thing to bear in mind is that we must avoid understanding solidarity as an intentional, one-sided practice (Bayertz 1999; Wilde 2013) where the person who acts in solidarity is expected to bear the costs of his/her actions (cf. Sangiovanni 2015) and the beneficiary of solidarity is often expected (cf. Wildt 1999) to act in a correspondingly solidary way when in the exact same position as the person(s) who already showed solidarity to him/her in the first place (see Costa this volume).

For Kropotkin, mutual aid is another name for what he passionately describes as the 'far wider, even though more vague feeling or instinct of human solidarity and sociability which moves me' (Kropotkin 1902, xiii). Love, sympathy and self-sacrifice are but mere expressions of this most fundamental feeling or instinct, 'upon which Society is based' (*Ibid.*). According to Kropotkin, mutual aid reveals itself, first, as an anthropological characteristic pertaining to the nature of human beings, not as a quality shaped or adopted through processes of socialisation. In maintaining this, he anticipates the neuroscientific work of Michael Tomasello. In his *Why We Cooperate*, Tomasello attempts, through a series of experiments with young great apes and young children, to provide an answer to modernity's fundamental dilemma: 'whether humans are born cooperative and helpful and society later corrupts them (e.g., Rousseau), or whether they are born selfish and unhelpful and society teaches them better (e.g., Hobbes)' (Tomasello 2009, 3). Kropotkin addresses the same question, but he brackets the dilemma and reorients the question. Mutual aid must be seen as a natural law that frames human behaviour to the extent that it constitutes an intrinsic structure of human practices. Therefore, it need not be evaluated as morally good (Rousseau) or morally bad (Hobbes). Mutual aid, for Kropotkin, is morally not assessable and as such a neutral tool that can both delimit and enhance human action and can thus prove equally detrimental and productive.

Second, mutual aid is characterised as a descriptive constant and not as a normative principle dictating (human) practices. The later becomes apparent through Kropotkin's depiction of the appearances and transformations that the concept of mutual aid has undergone throughout history. In this regard, it is important to point out that, for Kropotkin, mutual aid is not a teleological or progressivist vector of completion and perfection, driving the development of humankind to better and higher forms of existence. Against belligerent Hobbesians and vying (vulgar) Darwinists, Kropotkin aims to make us aware of the fact that there have been times throughout history where solidarity was practised effectively. This (perhaps even unconsciously practiced) solidarity is all the more significant to the extent that these solidary practices took place amid a mindset that privileges self-centeredness and solipsism, waging 'a war on the idea of interdependency' (Butler 2015, 67). Further, by demonstrating how mutual aid has permeated human history from antiquity, via the Middle Ages, to late- and post-capitalist societies, Kropotkin conceptualises mutual aid as a transhistorical constant in a twofold way: On the one hand, as a constant that is possible and feasible without being compulsory. As Nightingale puts it: in his analysis Kropotkin 'does not tell us what he thinks solidarity *could* or *ought* to be'[1] (Nightingale 2015, 79). On the other hand, Kropotkin discloses mutual aid as a historically conditioned constant, not as a principle. Every time mutual aid breaks through it takes on the particular and concrete traits of the historical context within which it is embedded. From this perspective, it helps to reconstruct ex post what took place without nevertheless

[1] If not otherwise indicated, the emphasis in the quotes is original.

subsuming historical events within a predominant and overarching narrative (cf. Kropotkin 1902, 6).[2]

Third, mutual aid does not just manifest an underlying and preexisting, intersubjective, relation between two members of a family, guild, town and so on. It also underscores that in addition to these intersubjective relations there is yet another bond at work that binds this time the subject to its surrounding group or community and renders the subject identifiable through the qualities of that surrounding group. Contra Max Stirner's individualist (if not egoistic) anarchism, Kropotkin opposes his collective (and not merely social) anarchism, where the group enriches and enhances, instead of constraining and delimiting, the subject and its development.

Fourth, and finally, the entanglement of the subject with its surrounding group raises a question concerning the relation between the immediate group that encompasses the subject and further concentric or even disjoint sets of social groups. Crucial in this regard is a debate that permeates the literature on Kropotkin and that delves into the question of whether his concept of mutual aid bears any similarity to Émile Durkheim's notion of mechanical solidarity, despite the undoubted absence of a documented, direct connection between them (cf. Gehlke 1915; Crowder 1991; Williams 2014). While the reasons why mutual aid does not resemble organic solidarity are obvious, since the latter is based on regimes of labour division, when it comes to mechanical solidarity the case seems more complicated. Nightingale points out that, though, 'Kropotkin's political prescriptions are not intended to encourage similarity or sameness' (Nightingale 2015, 98). This is especially important given that Durkheim introduced the concept of mechanical solidarity precisely in order to account for professional similarities and family relations that are not chosen but inherited, aimed at automatically reproducing the very concrete family or societal structures from which they arise. In this light, it is neither assimilation nor the forfeiting of individuality but a sense of what we would nowadays call communitarian (cf. Ritter 1980) inclusivity, belonging and attachment that he postulates when writing that 'without the whole the "ego" is nothing; that our "I" cannot even come to a self-definition without the "thou"' (Kropotkin 1922, 11).

Seen in this way, Kropotkin's concept of mutual aid bears similarities to preceding concepts of solidarity, just as it also anticipates a series of similar concepts. When arguing, for instance, that 'the ant, the bird, the marmot, the savage have read neither Kant nor the Fathers of the Church nor even Moses. And yet all have the same idea of good and evil' (Kropotkin 1970, 91), it is

2 See also Genter (2017, 17) according to whom, 'by stressing the unpredictable, open-ended nature of the evolutionary process [. . .] Kropotkin echoed Spinoza's contempt for metanarratives of human development'.

obvious that Kropotkin recognises in the iteration of practices of mutual aid the origin of ethical feelings that Adam Smith (2002) had also recognised in practices of sympathy. Further, by inviting us to 'arrange matters so that each man may see his interest bound up with the interests of others' (Kropotkin 1886, 16), Kropotkin prefigures Sally Scholz's concept of political solidarity since both Kropotkin and Scholz disconnect solidarity from the sharing of the same worldviews and recalibrate it as 'a response to a situation of injustice or oppression' (Scholz 2008, 34) that strives for 'a society without exploiters and without rulers' (Kropotkin 1886, 16).

Nevertheless, Kropotkin's concept of mutual aid is best understood as pioneering the work of thinkers such as Raimo Tuomela and Brian Epstein, which would subsequently render mutual aid a *social-ontological constant*. For Tuomela, 'social ontology is not only a study of the basic nature of social reality, but at least in part a study of what the best-explaining social scientific theories need to appeal to in their postulated ontologies' (2013, ix). Emphasising the praxeological (in contrast to the metaphysical) character of social ontology, Epstein argues that '[s]ocial ontology should not be thought of as the study of "ontological claims" such as "social groups exist" or "there are no social spirits". But instead, it is the study of *ontological building relations between different kinds of entities*' (2016, 149). Instead of the exhaustive listings of the properties of things that we know from classical ontology, social ontology operates on the following twofold basis: it provides us with the guidelines that help qualify certain entities as the objects and the things that the social order consists of while at the same time offering us the necessary toolkit to address those only allegedly ahistorical (ontological) entities as what they have always been, namely historical (social) procedures of becoming.[3] As we have seen, mutual aid indeed provides for the ontological framework for human behaviour and practices, just as it brings forward, through the forms it acquires, the social juncture in which it developed. As an explicit social-ontological constant, mutual aid is additionally capable of (i) bringing to the fore an intrinsic mode of the subject's way of be(com)ing, (ii) serving as a hermeneutical toolkit according to which we can analyse a given historical situation and (iii) acting as a compass and blueprint for practices

[3] I would even go as far and argue that mutual aid is for Kropotkin a *critical* social-ontological constant. As Reha Kadakal defines the task of a critical social ontology,

> '[s]ocial theory as critical ontology grasps social reality not simply in terms of a positivist notion of "facts", but rather in terms of its very processes of becoming, and it attempts to comprehend these processes through questions that are simultaneously theoretical and normative' (Reha 2015, 167).

Unfortunately, I cannot delve deeper in this debate here. For some primary reference, cf. though Testa 2015, Renault 2016, Thompson 2017 and Telios 2019.

that correspond to the subject's historical composition and derive from this theoretical analysis.

CATHERINE MALABOU AS A READER OF KROPOTKIN

Catherine Malabou took up Kropotkin's concept of mutual aid in a series of recent papers. The most significant of these are undoubtedly the paper given in Prague in February 2018 which was developed into Malabou's chapter in this volume and the paper delivered in April 2020 for the wandering and collectivist artistic project *Fall Semester* based in New York in 2020. While the first paper tackles the concept of mutual aid theoretically, the second highlights its practical-political implications. To a certain extent, my chapter is merely an attempt to explain and link these two papers with one another by demonstrating why Malabou's reappropriation of mutual aid in the first paper is capable of deploying the political implications that she sketches in the second.

Turning to Malabou's reappropriation of Kropotkin's concept of mutual aid, it is important to underline that this is best understood through the lens of her critique of the discursivity of French poststructuralism and her subsequent turn to materialism, which she launched with her *What Should We Do with Our Brain?* (2008). This work is essential not only because Malabou outs herself in it as an 'entirely materialist' (2008, 13) thinker. More importantly, this book is important because it lays the foundation for a materialism that does not regress to a mere reversion of idealism. On the contrary, the materialism that Malabou carves out is a new type of anti-reductionist materialism that – just like intersectionality – is inclusive, pluralistic and antihierarchical. As Malabou states with regard to the debate on whether the subject's practices trace back to a purely biologically determined brain or historically contingent consciousness, the 'reasonable materialism' that she advocates addresses the subject as the joint and collective product of both its underlying biological-neuronal and socialised information. This new form of materialism respects and factors into its analysis and critiques the different modes of subjectivity production and tries to expand and enhance its range with the ever-growing modes of subjectivity production. Seen this way, what should be apparent is not only the compatibility of this *collectivist* – as I would call it – materialism with the intersectional understanding of subjectivity sketched above. Furthermore, this should also clarify why Malabou joins her voice to a broad variety of thinkers from fields of contemporary metaphysics, speculative realism and/or object-oriented ontologies in their critique of the primacy of lingualism and discursivity. The materialism that Malabou posits does not tolerate the distinguished position that poststructuralists bestow on language.

Within this framework, Malabou identifies the following three characteristics as inherent to the concept of mutual aid. Mutual aid is (i) social; (ii) moral; and (iii) dynamic. As Malabou defines those notions, mutual aid is *social* because it 'is a mode of organization based on voluntary and reciprocal exchange of resources and services' (Malabou 2018, 1). It is *moral* because it promotes 'horizontal relationships' (*Ibid.*). It is *dynamic* because it is 'a problem-solving process that produces a result: security, equality and trust' (*Ibid.*). The similarities between the three dimensions of mutual aid and the characteristics of mutual aid (not only in its role as a *social-ontological constant*) as sketched above are clear. Yet there is a further reason why the concept of mutual aid helps Malabou to enhance her conceptual arsenal with another plastic concept. This reason is that mutual aid provides the missing, long-awaited, vector that illustrates the concrete politics that an abstract concept like that of plasticity can set in motion.[4] Malabou is categorical in affirming the political advantages that the concept of mutual aid offers. If we are to overcome the current, irrefutable 'shift in the morphology of democracy' (*Ibid.*), then we 'need to reelaborate the concept of community outside the strict domain of state policy' (*Ibid.*). The latter must take place and expand 'at both micro and macroscopic levels without external institutionalized help: and this goes from neighborhood issues, urban policy up to social and economic inequalities or ecological crisis' (*Ibid.*). Mutual aid comes in to provide for this 'chain' as Malabou calls it, or 'plastic chain' as I would like to address it by paying tribute to Malabou's key concept. As Malabou acknowledges right away, though, a plastic chain is a (performative) contradiction. But then again, it is precisely in the double character of plasticity – as both a plastic and an explosive operation (cf. Malabou 2004, 9) – that the promise of a chain with mutually bound parts lies. While a chain is the sum of parts that are indestructibly and inescapably tied together, a plastic chain is a collective articulation of joints and links that depend on one another and are defined by being attached to one another. Just as Malabou's materialism is collective in the sense that it is inclusive and postulates interdependence, the notion of the plastic chain is equally all-embracing while respecting the autonomy of the parts that are linked together to form its joints.

In this respect, mutual aid is called upon to prove that it can overcome the pitfall of essentialism as well as the all too hasty identification of anarchic forms of self-organisation with the minimisation or extinction of the state

[4] I do not assume here that Malabou's concept of plasticity is lacking in practical applications; quite the contrary. The past few years bear witness to a rising tide of what can be described as plasticity studies, where the concept of plasticity has been fervently implemented in a series of disciplines spanning from educational methodologies and the arts to areas including the philosophy of law, the critique of political economy, digitalisation, cybernetics, literature studies and feminist philosophy.

that characterises 'ultra-liberal philosophy' (Malabou 2018, 3). Malabou is certainly not wrong when she interprets some of Kropotkin's arguments as falling into a kind of essentialism in the form of biological determinism, since 'it links all living beings across time and space along the evolutionary line' (Malabou 2018, 7).[5] I think, however, that Malabou would agree that passages similar to the one just mentioned can be read differently. Instead of seeing in mutual aid another essentialist grand narrative capable of joining the scattered pieces of the history of humankind, mutual aid can be interpreted as proof that, against the narrative and legitimisation of solipsism and individualism brought forward by Western modernity, an alternative storyline is possible. Malabou would then again be right to counter-argue that this understanding of mutual aid as, for instance, a materialised and practicalised Derridean *dif-ferance* still relapses into what she calls a discursive form of essentialism. As she points out, this time quoting Saussure, articulation of speech

> designates either the subdivision of a spoken chain into syllables or the subdivision of the chain of meanings into significant units [. . .]. Using the second definition, we can say that what is natural to mankind is not oral speech but the faculty of constructing a language, i.e. a system of distinct signs corresponding to distinct ideas. (Saussure 1916, 88, cited in Malabou 2018, 8)

My last line of defence would then be to argue that mutual aid as a social-ontological constant does not function as a normative principle that, as soon as it has been restored as an *agens movens* of history, demands that we either act according to its dictates or await a messianic improvement of a certain political situation. On the contrary, addressing mutual aid as an ex post, merely hermeneutical tool helps us to create a link between what is given and what is contingent, that is, with the alternative forms that the given can assume. Mutual aid does not oppose solidarity to individuality. It does not coerce the subject to fuse with other subjects, since this would result in the loss of the individual's singularity and in the individual's assimilation in a collective that is itself an individualistic entity given that it is integral and undifferentiated. Rather, mutual aid binds the given (social and political) reality to its necessarily existing alternative forms. At the same time, it makes clear that these alternative forms of reality are possible only through mutual aid, since it is mutual aid that showcases their possibility. Does this coincide with a fallback to essentialist patterns, in which mutual aid is a transhistorical truth? Not at all. Essentialism is the preponderance, by means of exclusion and universalisation, of a single identity, or the postulation of that identity's

[5] Herein she follows the post-anarchist critique of Saul Newman (2001) and Andrew Koch (1993) instead of Brian Morris's (2014) line of argumentation, which I find more plausible.

impossibility. Mutual aid is opposed both to this unified identity and to its declaration as dead. Instead, mutual aid brings forward the existence of this intersectionally subjectivated being that by the logic of its social structuration cannot but communicate and include in its existence all possible identities. To that Malabou would agree. After all, as she concludes: 'Mutual aid of course proceeds from a need, the need to be together, to make connections. It is time, though, to think that connections can be links without chains. Mutual aid today is the paradoxical solidarity of the unchained' (Malabou 2018, 14).

The only thing that remains to be seen is on what grounds the necessity of mutual aid can be founded, and for that we will need to turn to Spinoza.

SPINOZA: NECESSITY AND METAMORPHOSIS

If what brings Malabou and intersectionality together is this novel understanding of materialism that is opposed to hierarchies and fosters inclusivity and pluralism, then what *genuinely* binds Malabou and Kropotkin are the Spinozist elements shared by both philosophers' views.[6]

Kropotkin's most relevant account of Spinoza is the one he offers in his *Ethics: Origin and Development* (1922), a magnificent and unfortunately mostly overlooked history of Western Ethics. For Kropotkin, Spinoza – just like Hobbes – immanentised morality by denying an 'extra-natural origin of morality' (Kropotkin 1922, 95). At the same time, and contrary to Hobbes, Spinoza did not 'conceive morality as something based on coercion exerted by the State' (*Ibid.*, 96). Spinoza rejected the view of moral concepts as 'revelations from above' (*Ibid.*, 167), whether political or divine, arguing instead that 'the moral conceptions of man are merely the further development of the moral habits of mutual aid, which are so generally inherent in social animals that they may be called a *law* of Nature' (*Ibid.*, 166). This naturalisation of mutual aid is what differentiates Kropotkin's reading of Spinoza from that of other anarchist thinkers, and the following two factors are essential to grasping the latter: first, the *origination* of mutual aid as a naturalist tendency or condition, and second, the clarification of the character of this natural characteristic as either *necessary or obligatory*.

[6] Within Malabou's philosophy, we find an alternative way to found the necessity of collectivity that is not Spinozist but Hegelian in origin. The argument would thus be to turn to Malabou's (2004) interpretation of the operation that the process of simplification (*Vereinfachung*) designates within Hegelian dialectics (cf. Malabou 2004, 146–152). From this perspective, collectivity would not be necessary from a naturalist perspective, as is the case with Spinoza. Rather, it would be necessary from a logical/conceptual perspective. Unfortunately, such a comparison regarding the different foundations of necessity, no matter how fruitful, is beyond the scope of this article.

Concerning the former, Kropotkin's argument, from Part III of Spinoza's *Ethics*, is in a nutshell the following: Body and mind are inseparable from one another. The mind is intelligible through the way it thinks, and the body through the space it acquires in the way it acts. Nevertheless, these are modes of approximation that correspond to the different qualities that mind and body possess and do not testify to a distinction in the way that the body and the mind exist. On the contrary, body and mind share one important qualification, namely the fact that they actively strive for what brings pleasure. In this light, Spinoza's philosophy acquires both a eudemonistic and an actionist character. The subject is not just in need of happiness but is actively and interventionistically seeking to achieve it (cf. Kropotkin 1922, 97). Reformulating Spinoza, Kropotkin asserts that 'we endeavour to bring into existence everything which we imagine conduces to joy' (Spinoza cited in Kropotkin 1922, 96). Herein lies the crux and the pivotal point of Kropotkin's fascination with Spinoza: What is conducive to joy, furthers the mind to its completion, and, last but not least, motivates the body to act, is their dependence on something, an *Other*, residing *outside* the subject. As Kropotkin declares, the cornerstone of Spinoza's philosophy of morality lies in the realisation that '[l]ove is just *pleasure with the accompanying idea of an external cause*' (Note III:13). Love – and along with it pleasure, mental development, actions and ways of thinking – is not an intentional expression of the subject directed wilfully at another subject. Rather, it is the realisation of a relation between the Other and the subject that binds them. The origin of pleasure is externalised and attached to a place outside the subject. The latter alludes to a process in which an externality is detected as conditioning the subject's way of becoming. Put succinctly, Spinoza's naturalisation of the mutuality defining the subject's way of be(com)ing lies in interdependency – the mutual dependency of the subject on its other and of the other's dependency on the subject.

This insight brings us to Kropotkin's second focal point in Spinoza's philosophy, concerning the dialectic of necessity and obligation. The latter has always been a pressing matter among the various tendencies of nineteenth-century anarchist philosophy (cf. Crowder 1991; Cohen 2006; Colson 2007) since – following the example of Pierre-Joseph Proudhon (1870)[7] – the anarchists saw in nature 'a matrix that made freedom possible and desirable but not necessary' (Cohen 2006, 79). Kropotkin deviates in this regard from the majority of his fellow anarchist thinkers and does not hesitate to assert that 'there is nothing in

[7] Proudhon deserves to be further mentioned for bringing forward one of the most original understandings of what shortly will be called the 'collective subject', or, according to Malabou, the subject eventuating as a collective event. In his 'Philosophy of Progress' (2012), Proudhon lays down the foundation for an ontological understanding of a subjectivity that, as he states, 'has as a synonym the group' (Proudhon 2012, 23). Unfortunately, I cannot delve deeper here. Nevertheless, I wholeheartedly refer the reader to the excellent work of Rothman (2016) on this issue.

nature, wrote Spinoza, that is *obligatory*: there is only the *necessary*' (Kropotkin 1922, 96). The nuance here is essential. Spinoza writes in his first scholium to proposition I: XXXIII that: 'A thing is called "necessary" either by reason of its essence or by reason of its cause. For a thing's existence follows necessarily either from its essence and definition or from a given efficient cause' (Spinoza 1901, 71). Mutual aid falls under the second part of the definition. It is necessary by reason of its cause because if the other (who is external to the subject) did not condition the subject, there would be no pleasure, and subsequently no development of the mind nor incentive for the body to act. Even when Kropotkin asserts that 'morality, for its realization and development, has no need of the conception of *obligation*, or, in general, of any *confirmation from without*' (Kropotkin 1922, 192), he does not turn against identifying the subject as dependent on an entity that lies outside of it. Rather, the mutuality that Spinoza detects between subjects is a structural modality that brings to the fore the historicity of the subject's becoming, as vectored through the Other.

With regard to Malabou's reading of Spinoza, it is important to realise that this too bears the marks of Malabou's collectivist materialism. For Malabou, this involves emancipating the accidental and putting it on a par with the (subject's) essence instead of addressing it as merely contingent, transient and therefore unworthy.[8] Spinoza does not appear among the chorus of thinkers (such as Hegel, Heidegger and Freud) that Malabou subjects to her plastic reading. Just as Kropotkin is an author who proposes *a vision of the link between biology, ethics and politics without elaborating a biologism* (Malabou 2020), Spinoza is 'the first philosopher to recognize the ontological, or essential, importance of the nervous system' (Malabou 2012b, 18f.). Yet there is a passage in Spinoza's Ethics that Malabou mentions in passing in her *The New Wounded* (2012a), before taking it up again in her *The Ontology of the Accident* (2012b), that is crucial to my argument. In this passage, Spinoza uses the motif of death as a metaphor for the radical transformation inflicted upon a subject from an unforeseeable external cause – one that leaves the subject so radically altered that it is unrecognisable. Even if, phenotypically, the subject seems unaltered, 'there is no reason', writes Spinoza in his first scholium to IV: XXXIX, 'which compels me to maintain that a body does not die, unless it becomes a corpse; nay, experience would seem to point to the opposite conclusion. It sometimes happens, that a man undergoes such changes, that I should hardly call him the same' (Spinoza 1901, 216). Malabou recognises in this metonymic potentiality that Spinoza attributes to death the 'annihilating metamorphic power' (Malabou 2007, 201) that she

[8] In her attempt to illustrate this materialism Malabou utilises also rhetorical means and the figure of the *asyndeton* is the most prominent of them (cf. Malabou 2012b, 62). Unfortunately, I cannot elaborate further on this matter here.

calls *destructive plasticity*. In the *Ontology*, Malabou revisits this Spinozan conceptualisation of death, which henceforth encompasses and connotes (i) 'a radical personality change' (2012b, 33); (ii) a partial alteration in the subject's body or affective state; and (iii) the dying out of a concrete and particular body organ, without its entailing the death of the entire body. If, for Kropotkin, Spinoza sketches processes of subjectivation in which the subject, seeking to find pleasure *from without*, must attach itself to this other, Malabou detects in Spinoza the depiction of a process in which – every time the subject encounters its other – an unprecedented and unforeseeable transformational process is initiated, in which the subject may not lose itself but is transformed to something different. In this light, Malabou and Kropotkin find in Spinoza an interlocutor who helps them to explain dependency without having to relinquish autonomy. In addition, Malabou finds in Spinoza the origins of a plastic process of fundamental transformation, since what should have been a contingent and unimportant accident results in the complete transformation of the subject and in the emergence of a new essence. Seen this way, the subject occurs as an event, a collective event, a συμβεβηκός. No subject originates solipsistically on its own but as the joint ensemble of the subject bound to the other outside of it.[9] Tying the subject to its other results in a process that, as Malabou writes in accordance with Spinoza, results in 'the *transformation of the body into another body in the same body*' (Malabou 2012b, 34; emphasis added). And this transformation, which is triggered in the subject every time it encounters the other, belongs for Spinoza and Malabou, just as for Kropotkin, to the nature of the subject.

CONCLUSION: SOLIDARITY AS MUTUAL AID – FROM STRUCTURAL MODALITY TO ORGANISED PRACTICES

Where do these insights leave us regarding mutual aid as a heuristic device[10] for tackling the intersectional conundrum?

[9] Malabou follows the Greek view of the event as συμβάν, from the verb συμβαίνειν, which means: 'at the same time to follow from, to ensure and to arrive, to happen' (Malabou 2004, 12). In doing so, she concentrates only on the one strand of meaning of the verb συμβαίνειν – to be precise, on the meaning that locates the scholastic accident in συμβάν. There is, however, another chain of connotations inherent in συμβάν that drives or causes both the eventfulness and the classification of a feature as an accident, and this lies in the collectivity implied by the prefix συν-. The word συμβάν denotes a collectively executed practice, a collectively executed occurrence, the concurrent rise and appearance of something (συν-βαίνω, συν: together + βαίνω: to go), and thus the realisation that the subject eventuates as a collective conditioned through the other that co-originates simultaneously. On this point, see Telios (2021).

[10] Malabou would most likely have used the term hermeneutic motor scheme (cf. Malabou 2009, 13).

Returning to where we began, namely the intersectional conundrum, how can mutual aid that functions as a *social-ontological, collectivist-materialist, naturalist and necessary constant* help us to reconsider the way in which identities relate to one another and to the body? To start with, mutuality in the form of a *social-ontological* human disposition debunks methodological individualism once and for all as an ideological illusion. It shows that, due to the constant of mutuality, a *prima philosophia* based on a single, unified and universalised identity instead of a pluralist one can only be indicative of political pathologies and authoritarian mechanisms of appropriation. Second, it makes the search for the other identities hyperbolic. Mutuality will always pulse through the subject. Seeking to broaden the horizon of relations of interdependence and enhance intersectionality's list with even more axes of subjectivity production is not embarrassing (contra Butler). Rather, the intersectional methodology constitutes a scientific imperative derived from the nature of the subject's be(com)ing. Additionally, only if we keep expanding the horizons of possible attachments that bring forward the subject and revolve around the microscopic spheres of the subject's life (spheres that are camouflaged under the alleged cloak of freedom and self-determination) will we ever be capable of carving out practices that account for the subject's singular construction at the crossroads of different modes of subjectivity production.[11]

Moving on to the *collectivist-materialist* elements of Malabou's rendition of the concept (inclusivity, pluralism, flat hierarchies), the first element is that such an antihierarchical concept of mutual aid is opposed to classifications of the different modes of identity production in primary and secondary. All identities, like all links in the mutual plastic chain, must be considered as contributing equally to the subject's development and structuration. Further, they ought to be regarded as irreducible and incommensurable to one another. Being bound together in the subject's body does not entail that the different identities forfeit their uniqueness or autonomy. Quite the contrary. After having penetrated the subject by bringing it forward according to the ideological content of the respective modes of subjectivity production, all identities continue to house the body of the subject. When the context appears, they spring forward, forcing the subject to act, thereby revealing the respective identities. Finally, mutual aid's inclusivity helps us to bring together different modes of production without having to straighten them or make them coherent, subsuming them in a cohesive narrative. Seen in this way, attesting that

[11] In this light, I would argue that Kropotkin's concept of mutual aid, if applied to the intersectionality debate on how the different identities relate to one another, answers the fundamental question concerning the existential right of intersectionality, especially against the abovementioned critiques from Butler and Brown.

the subject is more than a discursive act, the reproduction of class mechanisms, gender, the exchange of electrical or chemical signals and so on, is not enough. Rather, we must recognise that these identities, when found within the subject's body, mutually inform each other. This makes it essential to turn to the entanglement of those identities and to thematise the respective reconfiguration of these entanglements according to each and every case. Again, mutuality as an inclusive, pluralist, and antihierarchical modality makes us aware of the fact that there can be no structurally predominant identity that overshadows the others. Rather, all identities and their entanglements must be thematised alike and in respect to their historical situation.[12]

Finally, mutual aid discloses the subject as a collective amalgam of modes of subjectivity production and not as an inert entity waiting to be codified and signified by them. Seen in this way, such an understanding of mutual aid is opposed to a line of intersectionalist thought in which the subject is ascribed self-reflective competencies that render it capable of becoming aware of the axes of inequality and discrimination that cross through it. Rather, mutual aid finds in the other the cause of the subject, a cause located as coming '*from without*'. Diagnosed as a relation underlying the production of subjectivity, mutuality demonstrates the constitutive role of the other as a vector of subjectivity production. This does not mean, however, that there is no reflexive potentiality left for the subject. Spinoza's motif of death, as explicated by Malabou, seems to be essential to explicating how the subject can be collective and mutually informed (from one identity to the other, from one subject to the other) without forfeiting its singularity. The latter pertains to the fact that acknowledging the subject's socially constructed collective subjectivity does not entail that the subject must continuously act out all of its multiple identities. The subject may be a woman, a woman of colour, a worker, a lesbian, an activist, a mother, a citizen of a certain state, a graduate from a certain university, a member of an urban community, an atheist and so on. but it is not *only* a woman, *or only* a woman of colour, *or only* a worker, *or only* a lesbian, *or only* an activist, *or only* a mother, *or only* a citizen of a certain state, *or only* a graduate from a certain university, *or only* a member of an urban community, *or only* an atheist and so on. Rather, the subject *is*, at each and every point in time, the simultaneous and sedimented palimpsest of all these identities. Nevertheless, this does not entail that the subject must necessarily *perform* all of these identities in a simultaneous way. The subject can also behave and perform *exclusively* as a woman, *or/and* a woman of colour, *or/and* a worker, *or/and* a lesbian, *or/and* an activist, *or/and* a mother, *or/and* a citizen of a certain state, *or/and* a graduate from a certain university, *or/a*nd

[12] Seen this way, Malabou's reconceptualisation of mutual aid helps to answer the question concerning the modes of entanglement of the different identities within the subject's body.

a member of an urban community and so on. In this light, the subject consists of all those identities but not all of the identities that encounter each other in the subject's body have to be performed. Many lay dormant and suspended, springing forward only when they find themselves in a favourable context, one that fits their respective mode of subjectivity production. They are all constitutive components of the subject and help the subject to eventuate as their collective event,[13] a συμβεβηκός. However, neither the subject nor these particular identities are reducible to one another. Seen in this way, mutual aid helps us to explain these internal deferments and transformations as Spinozist 'transformation[s] of the body into another body in the same body' (Malabou 2012b, 34).[14]

From this perspective, the concept of mutual aid provides us with valuable insights into pressing matters that loom large over debates within the theory of intersectionality. At the same time, however, it helps us to revisit issues regarding what kind of political practices can be carved out from such an understanding of subjectivity. It is from this perspective that we can finally turn to Malabou's last paper on Kropotkin's mutual aid where – as mentioned above – Malabou occupies herself with its practical-political implications. The internal structuration of the intersectional subject alongside the social-ontological, collective-materialist, naturalist and contingent lines is not the only political application that can be derived from mutual aid. Mutual aid is also capable of serving as the compass and blueprint for political practices by defining the actors who – structured alongside those characteristics of mutuality – have been implanted the capability to also express and exert mutuality.[15] Malabou calls the latter the 'historization of the biological' (Malabou 2018, 13; 2020) and does not hesitate to proclaim the agent of this mutualist New International. As she declares: '[t]he actors of mutual aid in contemporary societies are the "anonymous masses"'(Malabou 2018, 14; 2020). In this light, mutual aid does not just manifest itself as a heuristic device that helps us to explain the necessary social-ontological structuration of subjectivity as a collective entity. As such it helps us also demonstrate how such a structuration of subjectivity necessitates

[13] Hints of a collective subject can also be found in a shorter piece by Malabou, which unfortunately has yet to receive the scholarly attention it deserves. In her 'The Crowd' (2015), Malabou draws attention to Elias Canetti's critique of Freud, who resisted viewing the masses in a positive way. What Freud, according to Canetti, overlooks is not only that there are 'crowds around me' (Canetti, cited in Malabou 2015, 27). More crucially, Freud overlooks that there are also 'crowds *within* me' (*Ibid*., emphasis added).

[14] From this perspective, the Spinozist elements that permeate both Kropotkin's and Malabou's concepts of mutual aid help us to rethink the relation of each identity to the overarching and collective event that is the subject.

[15] The following three quotes appeared originally in Malabou's recent paper presented in New York (2020) that in contrast to her 2018 paper presented in Prague – which dealt with the analytics of mutual aid – tackles the *politics* of mutual aid. While reworking her paper for this volume though, Catherine Malabou decided to fuse the main ideas from the two papers.

collective practices as its solely appropriate form of action. Collective forms of practice are not to be engaged in only when individual actions have failed. Rather, collective forms of practice must be regarded as the primary mode of emancipatory, self-determining action. Anonymous masses can 'organize resistance to political hegemonies', (*Ibid.*; Malabou 2020, 16) as Malabou points out, precisely because they correspond to, translate and materialize the collective structuration of the subject into practice. Seen in this way, mutual aid, like intersectionality, stops being a mere heuristic device for expressing the subject's way of becoming. Mutual aid becomes a political necessity.

BIBLIOGRAPHY

Andersen, Tawny. 2020. "Ontological Violence: Catherine Malabou on Plasticity, Performativity, and Writing the Feminine." *Culture, Theory and Critique* 61(1): 4–21.

Berger, Michele Tracy, and Kathleen Guidroz. 2009. *The Intersectional Approach: Transforming the Academy through Race, Class, and Gender.* Chapel Hill: University of North Carolina Press.

Brown, Wendy. 1997. "The Impossibility of Women's Studies." *Differences: A Journal of Feminist Cultural Studies* 9(3): 79–101.

Butler, Judith. 1990. *Gender Trouble: Feminism and the Subversion of Identity.* New York: Routledge.

Butler, Judith. 2015. *Notes Toward a Performative Theory of Assembly.* Cambridge: Harvard University Press.

Call, Lewis. 1999. "Anarchy in the Matrix." *Anarchist Studies* 7(2): 95–117.

Call, Lewis. 2003. *Postmodern Anarchism.* Lanham, MD: Lexington Books.

Cohn, Jesse S. 2006. *Anarchism and the Crisis of Representation: Hermeneutics, Aesthetics, Politics.* Selinsgrove: Susquehanna University Press.

Collins, Patricia Hill. 1990. *Black Feminist Thought: Knowledge, Consciousness and the Politics of Empowerment.* New York: Routledge.

Colson, Daniel. 2007. "Anarchist Readings of Spinoza." *Journal of French Philosophy* 17(2): 90–129.

Crenshaw, Kimberlé Williams. 1989. "Demarginalizing the Intersection of Race and Sex: A Black Feminist Critique of Antidiscrimination Doctrine, Feminist Theory and Antiracist Politics." *University of Chicago Legal Forum* 140: 139–167.

Crowder, George. 1991. *Classical Anarchism: The Political Thought of Godwin, Proudhon, Bakunin, and Kropotkin.* Oxford: Clarendon Press.

Epstein, Brian. 2016. "Framework for Social Ontology." *Philosophy of the Social Sciences*, 46(2): 147–167.

Galloway, Alexander R. 2013. "The Poverty of Philosophy: Realism and Post-Fordism." *Critical Inquiry* 39(2): 347–366.

Gehlke, Charles Elmer. 1915. *Émile Durkheim's Contributions to Sociological Theory.* New York: Columbia University.

Genter, Robert B. 2017. "Barnett Newman and the Anarchist Sublime." *Anarchist Studies* 25(1): 8–31.

Gunnarsson, Lena. 2015. "Why We Keep Separating the 'Inseparable': Dialecticizing Intersectionality." *European Journal of Women's Studies* 24(2): 114–127.

Hancock, Ange-Marie. 2016. *Intersectionality: An Intellectual History*. Oxford: Oxford University Press.

hooks, bell. 1984. *Feminist Theory: From Margin to Center*. Cambridge, MA: South End Press.

James, Ian. 2012. *The New French Philosophy*. Cambridge: Polity Press.

Kadakal, Reha. 2015. "Toward a Critical Ontology of the Social: Hegel, Lukács, and the Challenge of Mediation." *Globalization, Critique and Social Theory: Diagnoses and Challenges* 33: 165–188.

Knapp, Gudrun-Axeli. 1999. "Fragile Foundations, Strong Traditions, Situated Questioning: Critical Theory in German-Speaking Feminism." In *Adorno, Culture and Feminism*, edited by Maggie O'Neill, 119–140. London: Sage.

Koch, Andrew. 1993. "Poststructuralism and the Epistemological Basis of Anarchism." *Philosophy of the Social Sciences* 23(3): 327–351.

Kropotkin, Peter. 1886. *The Place of Anarchism in Socialistic Evolution. An Address Delivered in Paris*. London: W. Reeves.

Kropotkin, Peter. 1902. *Mutual Aid: A Factor of Evolution*. New York: McClure Phillips & Co.

Kropotkin, Peter. 1922. *Ethics: Origin and Development*. London: The Anarchist Library.

Kropotkin, Peter. 1970. *Kropotkin's Revolutionary Pamphlets: A Collection of Writings by Peter Kropotkin*, edited by Roger N. Baldwin. New York: Dover Publications.

Lykke, Nina. 2011. *Feminist Studies: A Guide to Intersectional Theory, Methodology and Writing*. New York: Routledge.

Malabou, Catherine. 2004. *The Future of Hegel: Plasticity, Temporality and Dialectic*. London/New York: Routledge.

Malabou, Catherine. 2008. *What Should We Do with Our Brain?* New York: Fordham University Press.

Malabou, Catherine. 2009. *Plasticity at the Dusk of Writing: Dialectic, Destruction, Deconstruction*. New York: Columbia University Press.

Malabou, Catherine. 2012a. *The New Wounded: From Neurosis to Brain Damage*. New York: Fordham University Press.

Malabou, Catherine. 2012b. *The Ontology of the Accident: An Essay on Destructive Plasticity*. Cambridge: Polity Press.

Malabou, Catherine. 2015. "The Crowd." *The Oxford Literary Review* 37(1): 25–44.

Malabou, Catherine. 2018. "Mutual Aid Beyond Discursivity." Conference presentation, February 23rd, 2018, Prague.

Malabou, Catherine. 2020. "Rethinking Mutual Aid: Kropotkin and Singer in Debate." Retrieved on 25th April 2021 from: https://fallsemester.org/2020-1/2020/4/8/catherine-malabou-rethinking-mutual-aid-kropotkin-and-singer-in-debate.

Martinon, Jean-Paul. 2007. *On Futurity: Malabou, Nancy and Derrida*. Basingstoke: Palgrave Macmillan.

May, Todd. 1994. *The Political Philosophy of Poststructuralist Anarchism*. University Park: The Pennsylvania State University Press.

Mohanty, Chandra Talpade. 1988. "Under Western Eyes: Feminist Scholarship and Colonial Discourses." *Feminist Review* 30 (Autumn): 61–88.

Moraga, Cherríe, and Gloria Anzaldúa. 1984. *This Bridge Called My Back: Writings by Radical Women of Color*. New York: Kitchen Table Press.

Morland, David. 2004. "Anti-capitalism and Poststructuralist Anarchism." In *Changing Anarchism: Anarchist Theory and Practice in a Global Age*, edited by Jon Purkis and James Bowen, 23–38. Manchester: Manchester University Press.

Morris, Brian. 2014. *Anthropology, Ecology, and Anarchism: A Brian Morris Reader*. Dexter: PM Press.

Newman, Saul. 2001. *From Bakunin to Lacan*. Oxford: Lexington Books.

Newman, Saul. 2004. "Anarchism and the Politics of Ressentiment." In *I am Not a Man, I Am Dynamite: Friedrich Nietzsche and the Anarchist Tradition*, edited by John Moore, 107–126. Brooklyn: Autonomedia.

Nightingale, John. 2015. *The Concept of Solidarity in Anarchist Thought*. PhD thesis, Loughborough University.

Phoenix, Ann, and Pamela Pattynama. 2006. "Intersectionality." *European Journal of Women's Studies* 13(3): 187–192.

Proudhon, Pierre-Joseph. 1870. *De la Justice dans la Révolution et dans l'Église: Nouveaux Principes de Philosophie Pratique*, Vol. 3. Paris: Marpon et Flammarion.

Proudhon, Pierre-Joseph. 2012. "The Philosophy of Progress." Retrieved on 11th December 2020 from https://www.libertarian-labyrinth.org/working-translations/the-philosophy-of-progress-revised-translation/.

Renault, Emmanuel. 2016. "Critical Theory and Processual Social Ontology." *Journal of Social Ontology* 2(1): 17–32.

Ritter, Alan. 1980. *Anarchism: A Theoretical Analysis*. Cambridge: Cambridge University Press.

Rothman, Hayyim. 2016. *Reason's Rebellion, or Anarchism Out of the Sources of Spinozism*. PhD thesis, Boston College.

Sandoval, Chela. 1991. "U.S. Third World Feminism: The Theory and Method of Oppositional Consciousness in the Postmodern World." *Genders* 10: 1–24.

Sangiovanni, Andrea. 2015. "Solidarity as Joint Action." *Journal of Applied Philosophy* 32: 340–359.

Scholz, Sally J. 2008. *Political Solidarity*. University Park: The Pennsylvania State University Press:

Smith, Adam. 2002. *The Theory of Moral Sentiments*. Cambridge: Cambridge University Press.

Smooth, Wendy G. 2013. "Intersectionality: From Theoretical Framework to Policy Intervention." In *Situating Intersectionality: Politics, Policy, and Power*, edited by Angelia R. Wilson, 11–41. New York: Palgrave.

Spelman, Elizabeth V. 1988. *Inessential Woman: Problems of Exclusion in Feminist Thought*. Boston: Beacon.

Spinoza, Baruch. 1901. *Spinoza's Works. Vol. 2. The Ethics*. London: George Bell & Sons.

Telios, Thomas. 2019. "Why Still Reification? Towards a Critical Social Ontology." In *Georg Lukács and the Possibilities of Critical Social Ontology*, edited by Michael J. Thompson, 223–266. Leiden: Brill.

Telios, Thomas. 2021. *Das Subjekt als Gemeinwesen: Zur Konstitution kollektiver Handlungsfähigkeit*. Baden-Baden: Nomos Verlag.

Testa, Italo. 2015. "Ontology of the False State. On the Relation Between Critical Theory, Social Philosophy, and Social Ontology." *Journal of Social Ontology* 1(2): 271–300.

Thompson, Michael J. 2017. "Collective Intentionality, Social Domination, and Reification." *Journal of Social Ontology* 3(2): 207–229.

Tomasello, Michael. 2009. *Why We Cooperate*. Cambridge, MA: MIT Press.

Townsend-Bell, Erica E. 2013: "Intersectional Advances? Inclusionary and Intersectional State Action in Uruguay." In *Situating Intersectionality: Politics, Policy, and Power*, edited by Angelia R. Wilson, 43–61. New York: Palgrave.

Tuomela, Raimo. 2013. *Social Ontology: Collective Intentionality and Group Agents*. Oxford: OUP.

Wildt, Andreas. 1999. "Solidarity: Its History and Contemporary Definition." In *Solidarity*, edited by Kurt Bayertz, 209–222. Dordrecht: Kluwer.

Williams, Tyler. 2013. "Plasticity, in Retrospect: Changing the Future of the Humanities." *Diacritics* 41(1): 6–25.

Williams, Dana M. 2014. "A Society in Revolt or Under Analysis? Investigating the Dialogue Between 19th-Century Anarchists and Sociologists." *Critical Sociology* 40(3): 469–492.

Yuval-Davis, Nira. 2006. "Intersectionality and Feminist Politics." *European Journal of Women's Studies* 13(3): 193–209.

Chapter 4

What Prevents Mutual Aid? On Trauma and Destructive Plasticity

Petr Kouba

When summarising the basic features of the anarchist view of social reality, Cindy Milstein describes mutual aid as follows: As opposed to competition, which involves an idea of lack, where only a few can win out, mutual aid

> implies a lavish, boundless sense of generosity, in which people support each other and each other's projects. It expresses an openhanded spirit of abundance, in which kindness is never in short supply. It points to new relations of sharing and helping, mentoring and giving back, as the very basis for social organization. Mutual aid communalizes compassion, thereby translating into greater 'social security' for everyone – without need for top-down institutions. It is solidarity in action, writ large, whether on the local or global level. (Milstein 2010, 56)

As such, mutual aid creates social relations of equality that undermine all social hierarchies. It avoids the paternalism of charity gestures, where the donator is in a position of authority, while the receiver always remains inferior. Regardless of how generous it is, charity still involves an attitude of self-interest. Mutual aid, on the contrary, makes space for collective joy, spontaneity, freedom and self-organisation.

Seeing all the prospects of mutual aid outlined by anarchist theory, one could question their conditions of possibility. Relations of solidarity, free collaboration and spontaneous social cohesion can be explained in terms of

This chapter is an outcome of the project 'Towards a New Ontology of Social Cohesion', grant number GA19–20031S of the Czech Science Foundation (GAČR), realised at the Institute of Philosophy of the Czech Academy of Sciences.

the ontological, biological or discursive structures that make them possible. But their examination can also go beyond any image of ontological, biological or discursive chains, which would radicalise the emancipatory impulse contained in anarchist theory. In the study that opens this volume, Catherine Malabou seeks to describe a mutual aid that does not rely on any ontological, biological or ideological chains. She attempts to outline a social and political theory 'that breaks with the order of discourse as well as with the order of being' (Malabou, this volume).

Following Malabou's impulse, I would like to ask a slightly different question than the other studies presented in this volume. Rather than asking what makes possible relations of solidarity, spontaneous collaboration and voluntary association, one could ask the other way around: What makes mutual aid seem impossible? What prevents us from living in solidarity, free collaboration and voluntary association if they seem to be so beneficial? Why are we, again and again, trapped in selfishness and competitiveness, no matter whether they are individual or collective?

To answer those questions, it is necessary to draw a line between Malabou's most recent work on anarchy and her previous work on plasticity. If the concept of plasticity is introduced into social ontology, it opens a unique view on mutual aid. With the help of Malabou's analysis of traumatising events in social reality, it is possible to understand the atomisation, isolation and fragile integrity of groups that appear to be incapable of mutual aid. Such groups do not lack cooperation, solidarity and social cohesion. Rather, the way they perform collective cooperation, solidarity and cohesion is formed by destructive plasticity. Their collective structure is therefore rigid and intolerant to others. Such groups are based on the logic of competition and fight. They must constantly struggle for their place under the sun, and the same applies to their members.

Besides destructive plasticity, Malabou also recognises constructive plasticity, which could explain why competition and fight are not the only destinies of humankind. Constructive plasticity can enable formation of new alliances as well as invention of new forms of cooperation. With the help of constructive plasticity, we are able to overcome ethnic, class, ideological and cultural boundaries that separate us; we can discover meanings of solidarity and equality that issue from the very fact that we live together in the same world. Constructive plasticity can be both uniting and liberating. It is thanks to constructive plasticity that mutual aid can become possible. Not as a utopia, but as a very expression of our co-existence with others.

To arrive at such a view of mutual aid, it is necessary to read Malabou together with Heidegger. A systematic exploration of constructive and destructive plasticity requires an investigation into Heidegger's fundamental ontology, which offers a useful conceptual counterpart to Malabou's philosophy. However, it is not her own reading of Heidegger that is at stake here (Malabou 2011). Malabou's conception of constructive and destructive plasticity obviously goes beyond any distinction between authentic and inauthentic existence. Yet, the concepts of authenticity and inauthenticity still remain on the scene, for example when she relates the destructive plasticity to 'inauthenticity' with its fragile facticity and made up history (Malabou 2012c, 151). To deconstruct any dualism of authenticity and inauthenticity, I would like to suggest my interpretation of Heidegger's fundamental ontology, which opens also a possibility of the third mode of existence as well as a possibility of total breakdown of individual or collective existence (Kouba 2015). Such a confrontation with Heidegger's social ontology and its temporal conditions can open a path to critical examination of the factors that prevent or enable mutual aid in the anarchist sense of the term.

HEIDEGGERIAN SOCIAL ONTOLOGY

It is well known that Heidegger grasps our coexistence with others in terms of proximity and distance. In *Being and Time*, he argues that we are always already familiar with others, which is why we need to mind our distance to them. When analysing our coexistence, he focuses on the semantic structure of the world that brings us close to others (Heidegger 1962, 155) We essentially care for others because we have the same world. The world we share enables all social interactions including negligence, cooperation or competition. All social relations are forms of solicitude, which is a constitutive feature of our existence. When it comes to positive modes of solicitude, Heidegger distinguishes two extreme possibilities: there is a solicitude that manipulates, making the Other dependent and dominated, and a solicitude that liberates, as it respects and preserves the autonomy of the Other (Heidegger 1962, 158–59). It is obvious that a true being together always involves some distance. Eventually, all forms of togetherness are fundamentally broken by our finitude, which individualises our existence. In the end, we are all alone in relation to the utmost possibility of death. But at the same time it is the possibility of death that warrants the personal integrity of existence.

What is true for individual existence, however, applies also to collective existence. It is not only the integrity of individual existence, but also the cohesion of a community that is given by our openness to the ultimate possibility of end. Being-with-Others that expresses such collective cohesion is called 'destiny' (*Geschick*) (Heidegger 1996, 436). Heidegger's conceptualisation of collective integrity has been often reproached for its romantic tone and proximity to nationalism. But in fact it is supposed to serve as a merely formal tool for expressing a collective experience that is decisive and active.

It does not necessarily concern a nation; it can be a political party, church or any other community that is actively involved in its own historicality. What matters, however, is a collective attitude to the possibility of end, which is experienced 'only in communicating and struggling' [*in der Mitteilung und im Kampf*] (Heidegger 1962, 436). When it comes to social cohesion, it is the logic of fighting, facing death and taking over the same historical possibilities of communicating and struggling that seems to be decisive for Heidegger.

The importance of death is emphasised because the meaning of the authentic existence – in its individual or collective form – is determined by the temporal dimension of the future. While the authentic existence holds together as it opens itself for the certain uncertainty of the future, the inauthentic existence loses its dynamic consistency by taking its possibilities merely from the present. Contrary to the inconstancy of the inauthentic existence that is distracted and dispersed in whatever momentarily offers itself, the authentic existence maintains its existential constancy (*Ständigkeit*), for it is focused on the only possibility whose meaning remains in the future (Heidegger 1962, 442).

SOCIAL PLASTICITY

The fundamental ontology, with its depiction of Being-with-others, solicitude, individual and collective historicality, is obviously far from expressing the nature of mutual aid. It is also debatable how far Heidegger can elucidate what prevents mutual aid. It seems that the reason why he cannot come to terms with mutual aid remains in his view of finitude. The limitations of the Heideggerian ontology of finitude, in its common presentation, are undeniable. Death can be treated as the uniting principle of both individual and collective existence only because it is, in *Being and Time*, regarded with certain formalism – as an ultimate end of an individual or collective existence. Even though it is emotionally opened and experienced through anxiety, it is a death that is not yet. Suffering, experiencing misery and contingency of life can therefore never bring a radical discontinuity of meaning. For even if the semantic structure of the world collapses in anxiety, there is still some meaning to be found in one's own existence.

Such an ontology of finitude, however, can be revised in view of the phenomenology of trauma, which Malabou outlines in her *Ontology of the Accident*, where she explicitly describes her approach to trauma as phenomenological (Malabou 2012b, 6). In this work and above all in her chef d´oeuvre *The New Wounded* she draws a picture of traumatic events that radically change individual or collective existence (Malabou 2012b). Using her expertise in neuropathology, she demonstrates how traumatic experiences open a gap in existence; they introduce a discontinuity of meaning that cannot be simply surmounted. After traumatic experiences we cannot live as we used to live, since we cannot recognise ourselves anymore. The traumatic experiences create a post-traumatic subjectivity that is torn away from the previous existence. This is quite evident in the case of serious brain injury that Malabou uses as a model of traumatic event:

> [b]rain lesions are paradigmatic in the sense that they are the *very example* of violent, meaningless, unexpected and unforeseeable shock that transforms the identity of the subject, interrupts his relation to himself and permanently disorganizes the process of his auto-affection. (Malabou 2012c, 157)

But, following contemporary psychiatry and neurology, Malabou refers to the phenomenon of trauma in a much broader sense. With regard to the rising number of post-traumatic stress disorders in today's world she suggests that trauma is to be seen as a general phenomenon. Not only the victims of wars and terrorism, but also the long-term unemployed, oppressed or marginalised suffer from post-traumatic stress disorder:

> it is striking to note that today's victims of sociopolitical traumas present the same profile as victims of natural catastrophes (tsunamis, earthquakes, floods) or grave accidents (serious domestic accidents, explosions, fires). We have entered a new age of political violence in which politics is defined by the renunciation of any hope of endowing violence with a political sense. (Malabou 2012c, 155)

The rape culture denounced by the #MeToo movement and the history of violence exposed by Black Lives Matter activists testify that social and political theory can hardly overestimate the role of trauma in today's world. Trauma appears to be a common denominator for all those whose lives have been shattered and disrupted without the possibility to answer the question: Why is this happening to *me*?

An insight into the nature of trauma that shows the contingency, fragility and finitude of human existence can therefore explain what would otherwise remain unexplainable. It is the experience of the new wounded, as Malabou calls them, that is, the experience of those who have lost the track of their lives and cannot get back to what they used to be.

However, the experience of trauma does not necessarily mean that traumatised people inevitably get stuck in apathy, emotional detachment from reality, loss of motivation or show signs of violent, self-destructive behaviour. Milder forms of trauma in particular allow for various forms of adaptation that cope with discomfort, unhappiness and suffering. To explain various reactions to trauma, Malabou enriches the conceptualisation of plasticity by distinguishing constructive plasticity from destructive plasticity.

In biology, medicine and neuroscience, plasticity is commonly viewed positively, as a formative process, which maintains equilibrium between the receiving and giving of form. 'It is understood as a sort of natural sculpting that forms our identity, an identity modeled by experience and that makes us subjects of a history, a singular, recognizable, identifiable history, with all its events, gaps, and future' (Malabou 2012b, 3). Against such a positive view of plasticity Malabou places destructive plasticity, which annihilates the equilibrium of living forms, thwarts new connections and freezes life. Destructive plasticity represents a pathological reaction to a traumatic event that cannot be balanced, and therefore turns life into pieces. Destructive plasticity brings 'the deserting of subjectivity, the distancing of the individual who becomes a stranger to herself, who no longer recognizes herself, who no longer remembers her self' (Malabou 2012b, 6). The old way of existence is here replaced by a new, rigid form without any continuity, or mediation. It is a sudden transformation that is suffered, rather than being actively performed.

What matters in this regard is that the difference between constructive and destructive plasticity functions not only on the individual level of life, but appears also in collective processes. If individual existence can be broken by a traumatic event, the same can happen to the life of a community. Destructive plasticity then turns the collective subjectivity of a community into something new, something that does not recognise itself anymore. No matter if it is due to war, terrorism, sudden epidemics, economic crisis, massive unemployment or famine, traumatic events give rise to new collective subjects that cannot return to previous ways of life. The past of the traumatised community becomes another, strangely distant past, if it is not totally destroyed and sentenced to oblivion. For traumatised people, life can never be the same as it used to be.

As far as the collective sphere of life is concerned, destructive plasticity brings strange fruits. Unresolved collective trauma can lead to atomisation of society and distinctive individualism where everyone cares only for his or her own good. On the other hand, it can boost the 'collective egoism' that Buber mentions in his reading of Kropotkin and other 'utopian socialists' (Buber 1996, 41–42). Destructive plasticity would then explain why people tend to create self-enclosed communities that are hostile to their outside. For such communities all outsiders automatically represent the traumatic experience that can be repeated at any moment. The communities that arise out of traumatic events become more paranoid and fragile the more they need to fight for purity, safety and homogeneity of their own interiority. The social cohesion of those groups is firm, but their atmosphere is unbreathable. The main principle of their collective lives is a fight for survival. In the name of this fight, people believe that the life of the individual can be sacrificed for a higher cause: be it nation, party, state, army or church. Those big, collective entities, however, do not have to exist in advance. They often arise as the byproduct of the traumatic event itself. So it was in the case of assimilated European Jews during the Holocaust, or in the case of Bosnians who did not consider themselves Muslims until they were selected as a target of ethnic cleansing during the civil war in former Yugoslavia. The collective identity of those groups was nothing but a product of the violent identification they were subjected to.

Besides the tendency towards self-enclosure and mistrust of strangers, collectives formed by destructive plasticity have a firm bond with their leaders. As much as individuals are ready to sacrifice their lives for the sake of groups, social groups marked by traumatic experience need strong leaders. Even if authoritarian leaders cynically take advantage of the traumatised communities, those communities still long for strong, charismatic leaders who will unite them and crush their enemies to dust.

As opposed to destructive plasticity, constructive plasticity allows for a much more relaxed relation to one's own collective existence. Constructive plasticity makes possible new connections; it constantly opens new possibilities. Therefore, it allows communities to relate freely to their members and non-members. Instead of creating exclusive groups, it fosters open relations to the outside. Constructive plasticity does not force anyone to live in a permanent fear of enemies. Its spirit is not based on fight, competition or struggle for survival. Societies modelled by constructive plasticity are capable of collaboration and solidarity not only within themselves, but also in relation to other groups and individuals. Constructive plasticity also undermines all rigid, hierarchical structures and their paternalistic attitudes, replacing them with atmosphere of equality, tolerance and spontaneity. It provides a luxury of mutual trust. Communities formed by constructive plasticity enjoy the feeling of inexhaustible surplus and richness of life, as their members explore new possibilities and new connections.

To put it simply and to get to my point, I would like to hold the thesis that it is constructive plasticity that makes possible mutual aid in the anarchist sense of the term, while destructive plasticity in society prevents it. The reason why we are – first and foremost – not able to enjoy mutual aid with all its benefits for our social and personal life is destructive plasticity, which either dissolves society into atomised individuals, or imprisons it in collective selfishness.

TEMPORALITY OF PLASTICITY

Yet, if one views the social life in this way, does not it resemble the Heideggerian difference between the authentic and inauthentic existence with all its notoriously known problems? Does not it mean that the difference between authentic and inauthentic existence is here replaced by the dichotomy of constructive plasticity and destructive plasticity, where all pathological features of social life are explained in terms of destructive plasticity, while the beneficial factors are granted to constructive plasticity? Do we not find here again an opposition of inconsistency, social conformity and gregariousness on one side, and true consistency, freedom and resoluteness on the other? How can one avoid such suspicion if Malabou refers to inauthenticity when describing the nature of destructive plasticity?

> By virtue of its pathological force of deformation and its destructive plasticity, in fact, such an event introduces an *inauthenticity*, a *facticity* within psychic life. It creates another history, a past that does not exist and, in this sense, constitutes a 'neurotic imposture'. (Malabou 2012c, 151)

The Heideggerian language here is obvious. But one would definitely miss the target with the claim that *destructive plasticity* is just another term for *inauthenticity*, while *constructive plasticity* is a new term for *authenticity*. What clearly demonstrates that this is not Malabou's point is her reference to the temporal structure of destructive plasticity. For the traumatic event that throws the subject into 'a past that does not exist' has nothing to do with the temporal dimension of present which determines the inauthentic existence in *Being and Time*. To understand this, it is necessary to explain the temporal character of the traumatic event that profoundly disrupts subject's existence and transforms the very experience of one's own past.

According to Malabou, destructive plasticity can never be understood in itself, since it is always already related to some traumatic event. In her polemics with Slavoj Žižek and psychoanalytic approach to trauma in general, she does not accept a psychoanalytic perspective which claims that trauma has always already occurred because it is preceded by some previous trauma that has made it possible (Malabou 2012a, 226). She does not want to believe that every empirical shock must be embedded in some original *Urtrauma* which hides its meaning. Following contemporary neurobiological and socio-political views on trauma, she takes up a position that does not make it possible to ask in the old psychoanalytic way: Why am I suffering so much? Why is this happening to me?

What is decisive for Malabou's approach to trauma is a difference between two meanings of the word 'event': 'the event conceived of as an internal immanent determination (*Erlebnis*) and an encounter that occurs from outside (*Ereignis*)' (Malabou 2012a, 227). She refuses to read traumatic accidents as inner experiences of personal life and takes them as events in the strong sense of the term, that is, as something that comes by chance from the outside, testifying thus to the total contingency of life. A trauma so conceived represents a material, empirical and meaningless interruption of life. After such traumatising events, if they are strong enough, 'a new subject emerges with no reference to the past or to her previous identity' (Malabou 2012a, 227). Post-traumatic subjectivity cannot relate to its previous life; being torn away from its original past, it necessarily fabricates a new, fantastic past. This is the work of destructive plasticity. In Malabou's words, 'we need to think of a destructive plasticity, that is a capacity to explode, that cannot, by any means, be assimilated by the psyche, even in dreams' (Malabou 2012a, 233).

But how should one grasp this destructive plasticity in terms of temporality, if the traumatic event is to be a purely empirical, meaningless disruption of human existence?

What can help here is a meticulous reading of Heidegger's *Being and Time* (Kouba 2015, 84–86). Attention to the inherent logics of the temporality of existence, as depicted in *Being and Time*, makes it evident that there are not only two modes of existence. In fact, besides the authentic existence whose temporality is oriented towards future, and the inauthentic existence whose temporality gets stuck in the present, there is a third mode of existence whose temporality remains in having-been. Even though this third mode of temporality is never described, or even mentioned in *Being and Time*, it must be taken into account. With the help of this third mode of temporality one can then elucidate the temporal structure of 'always already' that psychoanalysis finds in all traumatic experiences. The third mode of existence expresses the experience of those who are trapped in their past, those whose having-been incarcerates and overwhelms their present and their future.

The oddity of destructive plasticity, however, reaches beyond the third mode of temporality that is fully determined by the dimension of the having-been. The traumatic event, as Malabou views it, forces us to accept the radical contingency and possible discontinuity of human existence. That the individual existence can be disrupted to the point that it cannot recognise itself anymore and has to start with a newly fabricated history testifies to the radical finitude of human life. An empirical and materialistic view of traumatic events leads to the idea that individual existence can be disrupted from outside only because it is open to ruptures from inside. This corresponds to the in-depth analysis of anxiety that Heidegger presents in *Being and Time* (Kouba 2015, 86–88). A careful reading of his analysis, which actually goes beyond his own strategy but closely follows the logic of his text, shows that anxiety does not simply bring existence to its individual self-consistency. The temporal characteristics of anxiety, as described in *Being and Time*, demonstrate that one of the temporal ecstasies is actually missing in anxiety. What is lacking in anxiety is the temporal dimension of the present, which opens a bottomless gap where only the having-been of the attunement and the future of understanding meet. If this profound abyss of experience is not covered up by the relation to present beings, human existence collapses and disintegrates. This temporal fragility of human existence, which lurks in its deepest bottom, then explains why subjectivity can be traumatised by sudden and unexpected events. Traumatic events do not grow from the third mode of existence that remains imprisoned in its having-been. They address the essential finitude of the existence that is tormented and destroyed by its own temporal dis-unity.

SOCIAL ONTOLOGY IN VIEW OF DESTRUCTIVE PLASTICITY

Presuming there is an analogy between the temporal structure of individual and collective existence in *Being and Time*, it is then possible to ask what it says about destructive and constructive plasticity on the social level of life. One could probably and quite elegantly assert that the traumatic experience in the past leads to the endless repetition of this past. It would be tempting to show how this confinement – which might appear on the individual or collective level of experience – prevents us from living fully in the present and opening ourselves for the future. The Bosnian filmmaker Emir Kusturica presents this temporal schema in his film *Underground*: the heroes of his film are still fighting the Second World War instead of living in the present and understanding the challenges of the future; they are trapped in their past acting as if this past has never ceased. Such a depiction, however, is still too poetic to express the disturbing nature of destructive plasticity. It is certainly not enough to assume that destructive plasticity can be adequately explained in terms of the third mode of existence that remains in the endless repetition of what has always already been.

Through the traumatic events the individual and collective subjectivity is not just tied to a past that can be neither solved nor forgotten. Destructive plasticity tears individual and collective subjectivity apart, creating space for a fake past that can never cover and redeem what has happened. No self-blaming, no heroic boasting can fulfil the gaping abyss that makes no sense. This is perhaps why post-traumatic subjectivity is so often haunted by depression or self-destruction. Alcohol, drugs, self-harm or finally suicide only testify how deep this abyss can be, how deep we can fall.

It is no coincidence that in our times, whose main symptom is, according to Malabou, a rising number of traumatic events, we see so much self-destruction: terrorist attacks, armed conflicts, economic crisis, environmental crisis, pandemics. Who can distinguish what is the cause and what is the consequence? Destructive plasticity does not simply bring us back to what has always already been. It introduces a collective suicide that is presented as a struggle for survival in a permanent need to compete with others. Step by step, one trauma after another, destructive plasticity forces us to find our place in *anti-society*, where all relations to others are impossible, and in *anti-world*, where we can find no meaning to live for.

Exaggerated as it may sound, it is no dark fantasy. It has already started; destructive plasticity has been at work for a long time. As Jean-Luc Nancy demonstrates it in his *Being Singular Plural*, anti-society and anti-world have been established through ethnic cleansings the model of which is for him the urbicide of Sarajevo (Nancy 2000, 145–158). Spaces of coexistence where meaning is produced and shared in the indefinite plurality of origins were systematically annihilated not only in the Balkans, but in all the Central and East European countries that lost their Jewish and German populations after the Second World War. Ethnic and cultural homogenisation of human populations, which strangely resembles the diminishing diversity of natural species, has continued successfully since then. A fantasy of community without strangers, a dream of perfectly homogenous society that remains faithful to its 'proper' ethnic and cultural roots thus comes to its realisation.

In this devastating process, destructive plasticity harnesses joint forces of our political authorities. The role of charismatic, authoritarian leaders in the functioning of destructive plasticity is decisive. It is their task to unite people and lead them against their vital interests under the command of destructive plasticity. Destructive plasticity allows them to use old collective traumas as a uniting principle which makes nations, religions and other social groups fight blindly against other groups. To put it simply, the role of authoritarian leaders remains in their support of destructive plasticity, which warrants them their power in return. It does not even matter that their enemies are only fictional. How else could one explain that anti-Semitism and Islamophobia flourish so beautifully in Central and Eastern Europe? All that matters is to avoid the constructive plasticity which could eventually heal old traumas and make possible new, spontaneous connections with other people. But solidarity and collaboration that support social diversity are unfortunately not welcomed under the dominion of destructive plasticity.

It can hardly console us that the reign of destructive plasticity inevitably erases all the differences between developed and developing countries. When it comes to collective self-destruction of society, we can see a strange equality among states and nations. For destructive plasticity is not a sign of some less developed state structures; it is no return to a more primitive form of social life. There is no evolution and dialectical development in destructive plasticity. A proof can be found in today's Russia and other post-communist countries. They are not backwards, incapable of the subtle functioning of representative democracy. They are trapped in destructive plasticity that reproduces itself through new and new traumatic events. The Belarussian Nobel Prize winner for literature, Svetlana Alexievich, shows this magnificently in her collective polyphonies of voices: The horrors of the Second World War captured from the perspective of women and children, the nuclear catastrophe in Chernobyl, the war in Afghanistan, the fall of communism which was far from an idyllic experience for people in the former Soviet Union – all those events appear as traumatic fractures in a society that cannot pull itself together (Alexievich 1992; 2005; 2016; 2017; 2019). Obviously, destructive plasticity concerns not only post-communist countries. It suffices to take just a short look at all conflicts and antagonisms that divide U.S. society today, not to mention other Western countries with their unresolved traumas.

PLACE FOR HOPE

Seeing the power of traumatic events in society, how can we then break the spell of destructive plasticity? How to escape from its antagonising tendencies, which either atomise our communities, or turn us into slaves of collective selfishness? How can we resist the promises of authoritarian leaders and avoid their paternalistic guidance?

Unsurprisingly, the answer remains again in understanding the nature of traumatic events properly. If all people are, to some extent, traumatised then it helps a great deal to see others not as adversaries and enemies, but as those who are also traumatised. This creates an honest equality of the traumatised that may break ethnic, religious or class barriers. It can open a space for community of the traumatised, where empathy would come always too late. One does not and cannot always agree with others, but it suffices to see them as those who are and can be traumatised. All self-helping and self-organising groups who spontaneously put themselves together, rather than waiting for help and mercy of state institutions know this. They all testify that mutual aid is possible.

For obvious reasons, it is necessary to come to terms with one's own traumatic traits, when making any viable alliances with others. It is necessary to deal with one's own traumas so that they do not jeopardise any new community with others. This is not possible without the power of constructive plasticity, which simultaneously heals our own traumas and makes new connections with others. Thanks to constructive plasticity it is possible to discover again our sense of society and world we create in coexistence with others, as Nancy would put it. Constructive plasticity opens collective time-spaces where all are equally important and no one is excluded. Its temporality is not simply given by the dimension of the future. Rather, constructive plasticity has the temporality of an event, which Nancy in his *Being Singular Plural* characterizes as a surprising opening where the having-been and the future meet, but the present is missing (Nancy 2000, 168 and 173). The becoming of event means that its presence is not yet at hand, but needs to be presented. Again and again, a new meaning is presented to us thanks to our coexistence with others. Unlike the broken time of destroyed worlds, displaced communities and lost individuals, the time-space of event brings together all those who share it and enjoy it. Instead of fracturing society into atomised individuals or self-enclosed groups of collective egoism, constructive plasticity heals old or recent wounds, overcomes borders and social distinctions. Constructive plasticity allows people to live together anew when it brings them back to the fact of their coexistence in the world. It opens unexpected possibilities of coexistence by making us realise that we need others, if we are to find any meaning in our lives. A true politics of plasticity is therefore obliged to act in the spirit of constructive plasticity, instead of exploiting collective traumas for political purposes. Such a politics, however, is not a utopia.

Contrary to Buber's notion of utopia, the phenomenon of constructive plasticity does not announce itself as a wish that comes out of the depth of collective unconsciousness, or as a revelation whose proper expression is the messianic eschatology (Buber 1996, 7–8). Buber grasps socialist utopias as collective dreams or secularised eschatologies (*Ibid.*, 9–10). 'What is at work here', he claims, 'is the longing for that *rightness* which, in religious or philosophical vision, is experienced as revelation or idea, and which of its very nature cannot be realized in the individual, but only in human community' (*Ibid.*, 7). One way or the other, utopia is always experienced in the dimension of future that is contrasted with the intolerable conditions of the present. Constructive plasticity, on the contrary, is no utopia. It is real. It is unchained and unchaining. Constructive plasticity is nothing but an expression of life that successfully faces accidents and surprising events which repeatedly open our coexistence with others. Therefore, there is always some chance for mutual aid that is made possible by constructive plasticity.

BIBLIOGRAPHY

Alexievich, Svetlana. 1992. *Zinky Boys: Soviet Voices from the Afghanistan War*. New York: W. W. Norton.

Alexievich, Svetlana. 2005. *Voices from Chernobyl: The Oral History of a Nuclear Disaster*. Funks Grove, IL: Dalkey Archive Press.

Alexievich, Svetlana. 2016. *Secondhand Time: The Last of the Soviets*. New York: Random House.

Alexievich, Svetlana. 2017. *The Unwomanly Face of War: An Oral History of Women in World War II*. New York: Random House.

Alexievich, Svetlana. 2019. *Last Witnesses: An Oral History of the Children of World War II*. New York: Random House.

Buber, Martin. 1996. *Paths in Utopia*. Syracuse, NY: Syracuse University Press.

Heidegger, Martin. 1962. *Being and Time*. Translated by John Macquarrie and Edward Robinson. New York: Harper Collins.

Kouba, Petr. 2015. *The Phenomenon of Mental Disorder: Perspectives of Heidegger's Thought in Psychopathology*. Dordrecht: Springer.

Malabou, Catherine. 2011. *The Heidegger Change: On the Fantastic in Philosophy*. Albany: SUNY Press.

Malabou, Catherine. 2012a. "Post-Trauma: Towards a New Definition?" In *Telemorphosis: Theory in the Era of Climate Change, Volume 1*, edited by Tom Cohen, 226–238. Ann Arbor: Open Humanities Press.

Malabou, Catherine. 2012b. *Ontology of the Accident: An Essay on Destructive Plasticity*. Cambridge: Polity.

Malabou, Catherine. 2012c. *The New Wounded: From Neurosis to Brain Damage*. New York: Fordham University Press.

Milstein, Cindy. 2010. *Anarchism and its Aspirations*. Oakland, CA: AK Press.

Nancy, Jean-Luc. 2000. *Being Singular Plural*. Stanford: Stanford University Press.

Chapter 5

The Dynamics of Plasticity

Absolute Knowing and Sympoiesis

Rasmus Sandnes Haukedal

Catherine Malabou's philosophy is a reformulation of Hegel's philosophy of nature, critically engaged with new developments within the life sciences. Her key concept, plasticity, concerns the intertwined giving and receiving of form – how organisms must be able to canalise perturbations to maintain their individuality. In this chapter, I build on her conceptualisation of Absolute Knowing to argue for an ecological understanding of plasticity. First, I outline Absolute Knowing and its implications for plasticity; I then introduce *metaplasticity* as a way of theorising an ecological view of the brain. Next, I extend this to the discussion of unity and negativity in Malabou's work and her understanding of habit and virtuality. Finally, I sketch some similarities between Malabou, Donna Haraway and Scott Gilbert and stage a discussion of autopoiesis and selfishness that is informed by the Gaia hypothesis.

In the latter respect, Lynn Margulis's concept of symbiosis – as a challenge to bounded individualism – leads me to ask whether the Gaia hypothesis provides a way of expanding the scope of Absolute Knowing. The Gaia hypothesis may extend its impact by adding a dimension of constitutive multi-species interplay. I do not, however, presume to be comprehensive on this subject matter, merely to suggest a possible theoretical overlap that should be explored further.

THE PROCESS OF ABSOLUTE KNOWING

Against misconceptions of the Absolute as a noun, I follow Burbidge (2007) in holding that Hegel applies it as an adjective. Absolute Knowing has no positive content: 'it' concerns the process of dialectics. Moreover, it cannot be relativised since it is presupposed in such attempts. While it is about truth claims, it does not concern *what* is known but *how* we know. Its content is nothing but the movement, the failed attempts to know something as true – a failure which reveals that what was perceived as other cuts through to the subject itself, making a clear delineation impossible (Radnik 2017).

Hence, *The Phenomenology of Spirit* is a process of making knowledge claims which are absolute on the face of it but turn out to be relative. Absolute Knowing is the explication of this process – and the process through which it becomes explicit. It is 'spirit knowing itself as spirit', as a process that cannot be halted. This indicates that substance is ontologically incomplete, realised through the subject which it also enables. Substance gains actuality by splitting from itself (self-alienation) and then returning. The subjective appropriation of substance is part of the latter's actualisation. But this actualisation must remain incomplete if the subject is to remain irreducible to substance.

Absolute Knowing is not about determinate objects but a knowing in which the distinction between subject and object collapses, whereby the subject becomes conscious of its processual nature. Malabou writes: 'Whether one is prior to the other is not something that can be known. This is what Absolute Knowledge *knows*' (2005, 163). Absolute Knowing is not the culmination of the system but a repetition of the former stages that retroactively change their significance, and thus their future (Comay and Ruda 2018). It is 'involved in every, even the simplest phase of consciousness; it is implied in every act of knowledge, in every subject-object relation' (Cunningham 1908, 622). In other words, it is the result of the dialectical process, but, paradoxically, a result that proves to be operative at each stage.

In Malabou's view, Absolute Knowing marks not the end of dialectics but its transformation. It concerns the absolute relativity both of all knowledge claims and the subject making the claims. Its content is nothing but the dialectical movement, sublating the concrete forms of the Absolute. This changes the notion of sublation from being the completion of the previous stages to marking how contradiction is insurmountable. The interplay between the subject and the substance is never brought to a close, which means reconciliation is not about a harmonious state but about identifying (with) the persistence of contradiction (McGowan 2019).

Absolute Knowing fails to contain itself and hereby disclose how all truth claims are transitory and in the process of being overturned. Presumed distinctions dissolve and the dialectical process is characterised by a radical openness, wherein substance is shaped by the subjective appropriation it enables. Modelled on Absolute Knowing, Malabou's concept of plasticity – giving, receiving and possibly exploding form – involves the possibility of a radical transformation of the dialectical process itself. It is absolute because it is inverted upon itself (Malabou 2005).

In summary, Absolute Knowing reveals how reasoning always fails, how our limitation is insurmountable. According to Slavoj Žižek (2012), this does not introduce solipsism because the limitation to our knowing indicates that the subjective acknowledgement of the limits of knowing is due to the ontological incompleteness that makes free subjectivity possible. As I argue in the following, this free self-grounding is not a sovereign act but emerges from interaction with the outside world and other subjects caught in the same interplay. The notion that Absolute Knowing operates throughout the process without subjective awareness, implies that the decision is not consciously made, nor made in isolation from others (see Žižek 2020).

NEUROPLASTICITY IS METAPLASTICITY

Negativity is tied to the subject's self-relation and exerts its power through formative destruction. This 'good infinity' signifies the act of self-limitation through which it produces a transient membrane. But if the self is always bound up with others – not strictly outside but partaking in the self's active delimitation – the singular individual never exists, as s/he is caught up with and dependent on others. This means that the individual is a productive tension of singularity and universality. As such, 'the notion of an "individual" does not merely apply to man, but ultimately can apply also to a nation, an artistic epoch, a philosophy, or a moment of the "substance-subject"' (Malabou 2005, 73).

Malabou extends this analysis to neuroplasticity; she argues that flexibility without negativity is the 'ideological avatar' of plasticity because it obfuscates the dialectical relation between the destructive and creative aspects of plasticity, that is, how negativity makes resistance against passive moulding possible (Malabou 2008). This aspect underscores the material effects of our actions, some of which are more irreversible and constrain our future more than others. The impossibility of returning distinguishes plasticity from flexibility. Something flexible is not constrained by its history and in a sense, it does not have a history.

From this perspective, the brain is not a command centre, controlling other processes. Nor does it adapt passively to them. Insofar as it is in a healthy state, it can resist perturbations. This exemplifies the logic of Absolute Knowing: The contradiction between maintenance and alteration within the brain casts brain development is a discontinuous process, wherein changes in the form and structure happen through formative ruptures. Destructive plasticity is the 'plasticity of transition', of interaction between the brain, body and environment. The brain is, therefore, 'a multiple, fragmented organization' (Malabou 2008, 35–36).

Chiew (2012) claims that there is a contradiction in Malabou's concept of agency and consciousness: Although its agency is delocalised, and the brain is fragmented, Malabou still seems to hold that it constitutes an agent *within us* that may reinstate its centrality as a 'site of resistance', insofar as we become aware of this agency. She thus treats it as if distinct from the outside. Conscious agency, located inside the brain, could be instantiated by becoming aware of our plastic potential.[1] Is this also what Absolute Knowing knows?

I suggest that the term *metaplasticity*, introduced by Lambros Malafouris (2013), may undermine this charge. It denotes the interaction between plastic systems – implying 'that boundaries between cognitive systems are much more vague, ephemeral and less fixed than assumed' (Kirchhoff and Meyer 2019, 187). While the brain evinces autonomy from other systems, it is not independent from them. This view converges on Malabou's focus on the interplay between different forms of plasticity – how the new 'figure of command' is the constitutive mirroring of the neuronal and the social (Malabou 2008). Thus, the idea that the brain gains centrality in certain instances does not entail that it is self-sufficient.

Malafouris regards the mind as an extended hybrid, spread out into the world. Agency is a matter of nested agents acting upon each other in a metaplastic organisation. The weight of each agent's influence is therefore not given in advance or by any agent in isolation but decided by the concrete interaction between them.

The interacting systems impose *enabling constraints* on each other, from which emerges a higher-order regime of mutual dependence, a web of entanglement subject to constant change (Longo et al. 2012; Mossio et al. 2016). On the relevant timescale, constraints are conserved, that is, unperturbed by the processes they act upon. But they are changeable on other timescales, not static. Biological autonomy is achieved when constraints attain relative closure, which means that they maintain each other through mutual dependence (Montévil and Mossio 2015). Concomitantly, a metaplastic system is a product of 'the emergent properties of the enactive constitutive intertwining between brain and culture', which means that 'we have a plastic mind which is embedded and inextricably enfolded with a plastic culture' (Malafouris 2013, 46).

---

[1] Chiew writes: 'Malabou construes the relationship between the biological and the social as a gap, a discontinuity that can be reconciled by a creative resistance to the plasticity of plasticity [. . .]. However, as a consequence of her presumption that the neurobiological and the sociopolitical are *separate* ontological registers, [. . .] Malabou's intervention by way of resistance reinstates [. . .] the binary opposition of an individual *against* an external source/cause. Her view of transition as a differentiating passage between two enclosed systems [. . .] short-changes the complexity of neuroplasticity's *involvement* in the messy entanglement of relationships.' (Chiew 2011, 39–40).

Extra-neural resources are not wholly discontinuous with the brain, although physically located outside it. The agency of the subject is not a by-product of lower-level linear mechanisms, as it constrains and thus harnesses these processes. Simultaneously, the individual is not free to do whatever. There is a distributed sense of agency, a differentiation without a central locus, which runs against mechanistic models – of decomposition and localisation – since 'metaplastic systems exhibit global or large-scale features that cannot readily be explained by the activity of local or micro-scale aspects of a system' (Kirchhoff and Meyer 2019, 188). Mechanisms cannot be neatly delimited, and causality does not run in one direction only; there is co-constitution all the way down.

Similarly, Malabou insists 'upon the community between different kinds of systematic plastic organizations' (Vahanian 2008, 6). This idea was latent in our discussion of Absolute Knowing: refuting the causal closure of the universe, acknowledging the virtual as the site of freedom, we get a grip on how subjective agency is possible. Absolute Knowing exposes the plasticity of plasticity – how the functioning of plasticity may itself be radically overturned (Moder 2015). As such, it provides a key for understanding plasticity, and Chiew's critique simply brings out its contradictory nature – how any site of resistance must *emerge from within* the system. There is no outside.

We have already seen how such an organisation should be understood: as an emergent regime of agencies constraining and enabling each other's orchestrated action. Such a community is metaplastic. By utilising the organisational perspective, we get a firmer understanding of what such a community would encapsulate. It brings out how different organisations achieve higher-order closure of constraints that regulate the involved systems.

Knowing, then, is a process through which what seems external to the individual is revealed as partaking in its constitution – and vice versa. Based on what Malabou says about biological organisation above, I claim that brain plasticity is always metaplastic. This elucidates what Malabou means by a subjectivity that 'transcends and goes beyond the "I"' (Malabou 2005, 156). As I argue below, this suggests niche construction theory, a way of theorising how organisms are extended spatially and temporally, exemplifying 'how we evolved to become phenotypically and developmentally plastic' (Menary 2014, 287).

In summary, the plasticity of the brain is entangled with other plasticities. For instance, neuroplasticity is strained if the cultural niche that the brain is related to is too rigid.[2] Such an outcome is, however, not necessary. Instead,

[2] I have recently discussed this in another article (see Haukedal 2020).

we should think of it in terms of *enablement*. We find this perspective echoed when Malabou writes:

> This structure of competing tensions creates a multiple and mobile perspective, a reciprocal mirroring [. . .] that is no longer the work of individual consciousness and no longer depends on a single centre. It is a composition of perspectives, allowing the determinate moments to be connected [. . .] even while they are in opposition, rather than simply being opposed. Each determinate moment brings the other into view through a new angle, as part of a systematic structure sparked by the establishment of contact points. (Malabou 2005, 166)

Absolute Knowing is a plastic process of concrete instantiations that moulds and is moulded by intertwined processes. It is the end and beginning of the process of individuation, knowing the contingency of any material practice. From this view, perceived negativity proves to be an externality that is shaped by the organism itself (Kisner 2014). It is a speculative identity between identity and difference, which brings forth the heteronomy of knowing.

UNITY AS PROCESS

The ideas outlined above dovetail with niche construction, whereby organisms either change the effect of the surrounding environment, or modify its effect directly through physically changing it or move away from it (Chiu and Gilbert 2015). It thus highlights how 'effects of the environment are [. . .] relative to the organism experiencing it' (Chiu and Gilbert 2015, 199), and involves all influencing agents in an organism's environment, affecting developmental processes and natural selection. This is an example of the diachronically constitutive relationships between forms of plasticity, such as that between the ecological niche and the organism.

Thomas Fuchs (2017) offers us a holistic model of the brain, explaining phenomenal experience as the products of *ongoing integral of the functional loops between organism and environment* (Fuchs 2017, xx, emphasis original). He characterises the brain as a resonance organ, reverberating between the whole organism and its environment. His idea of the brain offers a grasp of how plasticity works.[3] Reverberations between systems together produce the mind; it does not produce the mind by itself but mediates relations between the organism and the world.

[3] The resonance metaphor is found already in Paul Weiss who, like Fuchs, did not mean a specific mechanism but a systemic property (see Haraway 2004).

Fuchs speaks about how the functions of the brain are dependent on the unity of the organism. This is unity in the sense of autopoiesis, self-production, which is founded on operational closure (Hernández and Vecchi 2019). Likewise, Malafouris conceptualises the unity between mind and matter. Such unity must, however, be composite and emergent if Malafouris does not want to level down distinctions between processes. The meta-level described by Malafouris is not one where processes are harmonised at a higher level. There is no permanent 'above' in the play of different plasticities. Any regulatory meta-level is transient, and the action of the overall system is not predictable from the activity of any of the systems in isolation. Rather, it is shaped through interaction between them, together producing an emergent organisation by constraining the actions of the underlying processes.

Such constraints are themselves processes subject to change; they degenerate if not maintained. If we accept that plastic systems constrain and enable each other's development, the relations and what emerges from them cannot be stated in advance. There is no predefined space of all possible plastic interactions since these interactions give rise to new possibilities that are impossible to state ahead of time.

The brain does not *cause* mental experiences, it enables them. We hereby avoid a model of the interaction of the brain and its environment that secretly privileges the brain. The metaplastic perspective does not imply a unitary system but an ongoing dialogue of dynamic instances. Such dynamical systems 'are composed of many parts, often with different properties, that interact and interconnect in specific ways' (Kirchhoff and Meyer 2019). As such, it describes the individuation of cognitive systems without levelling the different parts into one. We are dealing with the unity of plurality. Thomas Pradeu (2011) writes that,

> development is always co-development, that is, it results from the co-construction of living things belonging to distinct species. Every organism is 'mixed', heterogeneous, and not homogenous or 'pure'. A well-understood convergence of today's microbiology, immunology, ecology and developmental biology leads us to better understanding the organism as the unity of such a plurality. (Pradeu 2011, 80)

Unity is an emergent totality that constrains its processes through downward causation. If this were not the case, the organism would be bereft of any causal power. The base would remain what it is, and the subject would be an epiphenomenon produced by the firing of neurons and the movement of particles – unable to canalise these processes. Against this, I argue that unity is impossible without the work of the subject. If retroactivity is truly causal it must concern a self-defining act that cannot be predicted at the outset (Comay and Ruda 2018).

Malabou suggests unity as an emergent product coinciding with the arrival of genuine singularity (Malabou 2005, 29). Unity marks the failed attempt at interiorising what was considered exterior. This is linked to the 'feeling of self':

> The body and the soul form a 'system' consisting of two distinct subsystems: on the one hand, that formed by the five senses ('simple system of specified corporeity'); on the other hand, that which enables the regulated functioning of the determinations originating internally and given bodily form ('system of inward sensibility'). To show the fundamental unity of these two economies, Hegel insists on the necessity of producing a science whose object would be the reciprocal relation between the physical and the psychical, a science he names 'psychical physiology'. (Malabou 2005, 33)

Here, we notice the enablement between multiple systems, which together tend towards closure and thus attain autonomy. This view intersects with an extended autopoietic approach in which the organism is entrenched in the environment in a way that makes processes outside it part of its functioning (Virgo et al. 2011).[4] Through habit formation, a transient synthesis is achieved in which the soul 'neither distinguishing itself from nor confusing itself with its specific features or expressions, comes to enjoy a position between abstraction and rigidity' (Malabou 2005, 37). This position is plasticity, a replacement (or sublation) of the first immediacy by the second, posited, immediacy.

Unity in and through difference means that the individual is self-differentiating. The subject becomes what it is by becoming other and striving to include this other in the fold. In this way, virtuality is introduced into substance (Malabou 2005):

> The process of substance's auto-differentiation [. . .] can only be possible if there is admitted within it an element of virtuality: substance possesses in itself its future actualizations. The outcome (logical and chronological) of substance's actualizations contains the principle of substance's internal differentiation, the principle without which the concept of 'spiritual development' would be unintelligible. Hegel imagines the existence of a noetic habit [. . .] inscribing within substance the very possibility of its history. (Malabou 2005, 52)

---

4 The discussion of whether the organism and its environment can achieve closure or at least tend towards closure is ongoing. See Suárez and Triviño (2019) who argue that the holobiont is an emergent individual.

As touched upon, negativity concerns the self-splitting and differentiation of substance. It reveals the restlessness of every form, which is why the truth of being is becoming. Negativity is therefore related to virtuality, as it 'preserves that which it negates' (Malabou 2005, 54). It governs substance, as the perpetual acquisitions through loss. This means that we are dealing with *voyaging systems*, that is, 'processes that require for their very existence a dynamic trajectory over time' (Kirchhoff and Meyer 2019, 187).

Each reiteration changes what is preserved. The non-linearity of entangled processes and emergent systems explains why reversion to the initial form is impossible: the initial position is itself 'virtual' – changed by any attempt at re-actualisation. There is not a one-to-one relation between input and output to be predicted at the outset because the potential is itself changed by its historical becoming. This explains why it is impossible to understand metaplastic systems in mechanistic terms.

It should be clear, then, that autodifferentiation in the above passage does not mean 'an endless iteration, a self-movement of the One and same being, differentiating itself through reflection' (Comay and Ruda 2018, 96). Development is not simply the unfolding of the given potential, but a process that produces this potential. Missing this point repeats the mistake of regarding the Absolute as a noun. Auto-differentiation is only admissible 'if there is admitted within it an element of virtuality' (Malabou 2005, 52). This virtuality, which is tied to habit, upends idealist interpretations of Hegel.

HABITS AND PROGRAMMES

To recap: Plasticity is never one, never isolated and not about a linear unfolding of a pregiven potential. Instead of oneness predating multiplicity, the opposite is more accurate. Oneness is a consequence of multiplicity crystallising, and a mere snapshot of this obfuscates its diachronic emergence (see Kirchhoff 2015). Besides, by misrecognising our primary involvement with our fellow critters we fail to see we are shaped through processes of organismic activity, of becoming-with.

Evelyn Fox Keller notes that the realm of living organisms 'required its own figurations: more a three than a chain, and as much a succession of becoming as of beings' (Fox Keller 2000, 12). Chains are made up of discrete beings, monads not modified by their interrelations. Such singular and enclosed beings enfolded in unilinear causal structures are closely connected to the notion of a *programme*, which is mechanistic and assumed to be predictable (Fox Keller 2000). The idea of 'one gene, one trait' or 'one genome, one organism' is founded on this view. By contrast, if we take the view of the organism and hold that genes are enabled and constrained by their integration with other processes, a non-linear (and multi-genomic) model is more adequate. The fact that genes are differentially activated and modulated by non-genetic factors testifies to this. Specific functions cannot be defined except in relation to the organisation in which it operates.

Habits are virtual in the sense of not being present but still changing the subject's dispositions, its space of possibilities. They function as attractors guiding individual actions and retroactively changing the subject itself. As such, it is not ready-to-hand but 'as much the result as the condition of the exercise' (Malabou 2005, 56). An organism preserves its plastic unity by 'maintaining its own unity through the synthesis of differences: the difference between the organism and its environment and the difference between the heterogeneous elements which make up the organism' (Malabou 2005, 58). The reconstruction of physical elements into a singular individual, the work of habit, decides the function of the composite parts through the relationship established between them, and the higher-order closure they seek to achieve. This is a way of grasping why no locus has a prescribed function outside the system it is part of.

The interdependence between niche construction and habit formation should be evident. Through such processes, one's cognitive load decreases and the ability to discriminate fluently increases, thus making possible the appropriation of what was perceived as external. By these means, a living being 'can transform its environment through the active power its organism acquires by developing within processes of adaptation, it is not completely a prisoner of natural circumstances' (Malabou 2005, 63).

The chain metaphor implies a preformed unity consisting of parts with pre-given functions – operative, according to Malabou, within both biology and discourse, even after the impact of Darwin, through the introduction of the biological code. It gained material reality through the discovery of the double helix. While Darwin wrote about multiple sources of variation, besides the dynamics between random mutations and natural selection, the model of competition and survival of the fittest has become the hegemonic version of Darwinism. To challenge this view, I now bring together the topics we have discussed, linking Absolute Knowing to Gaia.

ABSOLUTE GAIA

Peter Kropotkin argues that cooperation is a neglected factor in evolution, citing geographical proof of cooperation between animals and humans (Kropotkin 2006). In a way, Haraway and Gilbert radicalise this perspective by challenging the notion that separate species work on each other from the outside. Rather, organisms are symbiotic, they co-evolve with their symbionts. Organisms consist of multiple genomes, mostly microbial; for example, 90 per cent of human cells are bacterial. Accordingly, the unit of selection is the *holobiont* – an organismic host plus its persistent symbiotic communities. It 'describes the integrated organism comprised of both host elements and persistent populations of symbionts' (Gilbert et al. 2012, 327–328) and signifies 'whole beings' (Haraway 2016).

Partners in such relationships undergo extensive genomic reduction, whereby they outsource metabolically costly functions to their partner, thus achieving functional integration (see Hernández and Vecchi 2019). These symbiotic assemblages blur the dichotomy between competition and cooperation because they do not take bounded units for granted (genes, cells, organisms, etc.). An example of this interplay is the 'microbiota-gut-brain axis', which is proven a key regulator of brain development and degeneration (see Gilbert and Barresi 2016).

I argue that this symbiotic dimension complements Malabou's view, that altruistic relationships 'bear witness to a *historization of the biological*, as they render manifest the point of contact between nature and the social, which partly erases the frontiers between evolution and history' (Malabou 2020, emphasis original). She opts for an extended view of organisms and claims that they should be viewed as ecosystems, thus pointing beyond the restricted forms of agency widespread within Neo-Darwinism (Malabou 2017).[5] Would this not also be a way of understanding Absolute Knowing, as the knowing that it is neither possible to decide the ontological priority of cooperation and competition nor symbolic and biological life?

Margulis's version of Gaia – a point of view more than a theory – overlaps with this decentralised form of knowing without a singular subject position. It depicts the Earth as a self-regulating, meta-stable, complex system, perpetually evolving.[6] Margulis insists that it does not imply that the Earth is a single organism or subject. It works like a complex system that asymptotically establishes some form of stability, as an 'emergent property of interaction among organisms' (Margulis 1998, 119). Composed of multi-species interaction it is thus the 'only giant ecosystem on Earth' Margulis says.

---

[5] Cf. Calude and Longo:

> An organism is an ecosystem, inhabited, for example, by about 1014 bacteria and by an immune system which is, per se, an ecosystem [. . .]. Yet, an ecosystem is not an organism: it does not have the relative metric stability (distance of the components) nor global regulating organs, such as the neural system in animals. (Calude and Longo 2016, 269)

[6] I do not take a stand on which version of the Gaia hypothesis is most apt, and whether it is a scientifically testable hypothesis, but I will say this: The weak version of Gaia, which holds that life has had a significant effect on the earth's atmosphere, is uncontroversial and has been verified (see Kirchner 1989).

Furthermore, the approach outlined above may broaden our understanding of Gaia, since the Gaia hypothesis involves the idea that life co-evolved with its appropriate climate, viz., that organisms adjust their environment to accommodate their needs. Gaia cannot be controlled; it is not designed by an engineer to function in a preordained manner. Rather, it is the emergent product of the distributed intentionality of agents modifying their niches, without the possibility of predicting the consequences of their actions.

The complex interaction between processes undermines hierarchical order in nature. It implies co-constitutive relations between multiple agents, cutting across levels – showing how levels are themselves ephemeral products. It also suggests the term *sympoiesis* or *symbiopoiesis*: 'collectively-producing systems that do not have self-defined spatial or temporal boundaries' (Haraway 2016, 61). Taken together with what I have said about Absolute Knowing, autopoiesis is not enough. No self produces itself as a living being nor a self-forming and sustaining system.

Autopoiesis involves self-forming systems, whereas sympoiesis is a making-with (Haraway 2016). M. Beth Dempster (1998), who coined the term, argues that many systems regarded as autopoietic should rather be considered sympoietic because their borders are not internally produced. Insofar as 'autopoiesis' does not denote self-sufficiency, it does not stand in opposition to sympoiesis but is in a relation of 'generative enfolding' (Haraway 2016, 61). Autopoietic systems are autonomous, self-produced in the sense that their development is not dependent on interaction with their environment, although they are not thereby totally independent from it (Dempster 1998). This composite unity is characterised by organisational closure and central control – where changes occur through the interplay of internal elements that recursively reproduce the network of productions that produced them. But while autopoietic systems must exchange matter and energy with their environment to stay alive, environmental processes are not part of their formation. In short, they are embedded in but not constituted by their environments (Villalobos and Razeto-Barry 2020).

This means that their relationship with the environment is not a function of constitutive interplay but centrally controlled, following from their internal identity (Moreno and Mossio 2015). By contrast, if we regard the production of life as distributed across symbionts, the boundary maintenance between inner and outer is accomplished by their interplay, and thus transient. Gaia is a mediating concept that allows us to grasp why niche construction is not a chain in which Gaia is the sentient being on top of the hierarchy. The self-regulative character of Gaia is an emergent property of metaplastic processes. It is not a unified system and thus cannot be regarded as a meta-subject that steers other processes.

The living planet is not 'a unified planet, [or] a superorganism' (Latour 2017, 102), and the first-order cybernetic notion of Gaia as something that may be steered or controlled intentionally must therefore be abandoned. This move fits with Malabou's critique of the brain as a central locus of control that overdetermines other processes: As the distinctions between life and environment is jettisoned, so must the 'systemic self-regulation emerge [. . .] from the synergy of the entire ensemble' (Clarke 2020, 207).

According to Haraway and Scott, the smallest possible *patterns* – not units – of natural selection are relations. Patterns are processes of patterning, not stable entities; and they are produced not in isolation but through constitutive intra-action. Similarly, plasticity is a patterned process in constant flux, where the boundaries between systems are continually negotiated.

Francisco Varela says that Gaia 'has an identity as a whole, an adaptable and plastic unity, acquired through time in this dynamic partnership between life and its terrestrial environment' (Varela and Anspach 1991, 69). By reference to such a plastic unity, we might say that Hegel anticipates the Gaia hypothesis, as he explicitly rejects preformation and recognises the close interdependence between organism and environment (Harris 1998). Although this is a broad subject in need of more elucidation, it is worth noting that, in the *Philosophy of Nature*, Hegel characterises the earth as a geological organism. This is reminiscent of Gaia, but only if organisms are perceived as ecosystems.

Symbiosis and sympoiesis contest the entrenched notions of the individual, as organisms are extended to include their functional integration with other organisms. This not only challenges ideas of insular individuals but bears on the notion of selfishness, as in genes using organisms to perpetuate themselves. It offers a new way of understanding surprising changes, both in development and evolution, and challenges the concept of the individual as detachable from its critters, making it impossible to decide which species' genes are using the organism to proliferate. Organisms are not vehicles but agents in their own development.

So, while selfish gene theory involves a strict delineation between an agent's inside and outside – the only way to calculate zero-sum games between individuals – such delineations are rendered impossible by the concept put forward in this chapter:

> what is so implausible in the idea of the 'selfish gene' is not that genes are selfish – each agent pursues its own interest up to its sad end – but that one can calculate an agent's 'viability' by *externalizing* all the other actors in what would constitute, for a given actor, its 'environment'. In other words, the problem with the selfish gene is the definition of the *self*. (Latour 2017, 104, emphasis original)

Gains and losses cannot be calculated in isolation because the organism does not find itself in a static environment but contributes to its becoming.

Gaia is not a static background within which life happens but 'intimately related to life' (Gambarotto and Illetterati 2020, 9). No independent measure is possible because the organism and environment are co-constitutive. Genes are ecological in the sense that they produce phenotypes that have downward effects on the gene's activity by constraining it. If we are multi-species and multi-genomic beings, for whom different genomes work together to produce the holobiont, we cannot decide which genes are selfishly enhancing their fitness and which are altruistically working together; not only because lines between organisms and environments are blurred but because selection works on multiple levels that are also co-constituted.

CONCLUSION

The displacement of the individual, the idea that 'every "individual" animal is always already multi-systemic, multi-genomic holobiont host' (Clarke 2020, 205), disrupts common conceptions of individuality and freedom, just as Absolute Knowing. Gaia thus adds a dimension to the knowing at stake in Absolute Knowing by highlighting how we are active constructors of that which we adapt to and that the process of knowing is constrained by its constitutive multi-species interaction. We cannot but modify our environments, but we never do so independently.

Moreover, Gaia brings into relief how ideas of bounded and competing individuals undergird the view that organisms simply (and flexibly) adapt or die; in this view, they may react but cannot *respond* to selection pressures. They cannot mobilise their plasticity to modify the demands impinging on them. There is no room for making-with here, no constitutive cooperation across phyla. In mutualistic symbioses between composite individuals, on the other hand, there is hardly room for selfishness, although this does not exclude competition.

Finally, if normal development is a matter of interspecies communication, relationships between organisms acting as symbionts for each other – tending towards while never fully achieving closure – are not optional but mandatory (Haraway 2016). Normal development and autonomy are both premised on the ongoing dialogue with the environment and other species. Organisms are active agents in the acquisition of genomes and use their adaptive potential to exploit and shape the affordances provided by their niches. By these means, the tendency towards functional integration between organisms and environments is maintained – allowing species to thrive through cooperation.

BIBLIOGRAPHY

Burbidge, John W. 2007. *Hegel's Systematic Contingency*. New York: Palgrave Macmillan. https://doi.org/10.1057/9780230590366.

Calude, Cristian S., and Giuseppe Longo. 2016. "Classical, Quantum and Biological Randomness as Relative Unpredictability." *Natural Computing* 15(2): 263–278. https://doi.org/10.1007/s11047-015-9533-2.

Chiew, Florence. 2012. "Neuroplasticity as an Ecology of Mind: A Conversation with Gregory Bateson and Catherine Malabou." *Journal of Consciousness Studies* 19(11–12): 32–54.

Chiu, Lynn, and Scott F. Gilbert. 2015. "The Birth of the Holobiont: Multi-Species Birthing Through Mutual Scaffolding and Niche Construction." *Biosemiotics* 8(2): 191–210. https://doi.org/10.1007/s12304-015-9232-5.

Clarke, Bruce. 2020. *Gaian Systems: Lynn Margulis, Neocybernetics, and the End of the Anthropocene*. Minneapolis: University of Minnesota Press.

Comay, Rebecca, and Frank Ruda. 2018. *The Dash—: The Other Side of Absolute Knowing*. Cambridge, MA: MIT Press.

Cunningham, G. W. 1908. "The Significance of the Hegelian Conception of Absolute Knowledge." *The Philosophical Review* 17(6): 619–642. https://doi.org/10.2307/2177556.

Dempster, M. Beth. 1998. "A Self-Organizing Systems Perspective on Planning for Sustainability." MA thesis, Environmental Studies, University of Waterloo.

Fox Keller, Evelyn. 2000. *The Century of the Gene*. Cambridge, MA: Harvard University Press.

Fuchs, Thomas. 2017. *Ecology of the Brain: The Phenomenology and Biology of the Embodied Mind*. London and New York: Routledge.

Gambarotto, Andrea, and Luca Illetterati. 2020. "Hegel's Philosophy of Biology? A Programmatic Overview." *Hegel Bulletin* 41(3): 1–22. https://doi.org/10.1017/hgl.2020.21.

Gilbert, Scott F., and Mich Barresi. 2016. *Developmental Biology*. 11th ed. Oxford, UK: Sinauer Associates.

Gilbert, Scott F., Jan Sapp, and Alfred I. Tauber. 2012. "A Symbiotic View of Life: We Have Never Been Individuals." *Quarterly Review of Biology* 87(4): 325–341. https://doi.org/10.1086/668166.

Haraway, Donna Jeanne. 2004. *Crystals, Fabrics, and Fields: Metaphors That Shape Embryos*. Berkeley, CA: North Atlantic Books.

Haraway, Donna Jeanne. 2016. *Staying With the Trouble: Making Kin in the Chthulucene*. Durham, NC: Duke University Press Books.

Harris, Errol E. 1998. "How Final Is Hegel's Rejection of Evolution?" In *Hegel and the Philosophy of Nature*, edited by Stephen Houlgate, 189–208. New York: State University of New York Press.

Haukedal, Rasmus Sandnes. 2020. "Disturbance and Destruction: The Aetiology of Trauma." *Culture, Theory and Critique* 61(1): 22–36. https://doi.org/10.1080/14735784.2020.1762101.

Hernández, Isaac, and Davide Vecchi. 2019. "The Interactive Construction of Biological Individuality Through Biotic Entrenchment." *Frontiers in Psychology*. Frontiers Media S.A. https://doi.org/10.3389/fpsyg.2019.02578.

Kirchhoff, Michael D. 2015. "Extended Cognition & the Causal-Constitutive Fallacy: In Search for a Diachronic and Dynamical Conception of Constitution." *Philosophy and Phenomenological Research* 90(2): 320–360. https://doi.org/10.1111/phpr.12039.

Kirchhoff, Michael D., and Russell Meyer. 2019. "Breaking Explanatory Boundaries: Flexible Borders and Plastic Minds." *Phenomenology and the Cognitive Sciences* 18(1): 185–204. https://doi.org/10.1007/s11097-017-9536-9.

Kirchner, James W. 1989. "The Gaia Hypothesis: Can It Be Tested?" *Reviews of Geophysics* 27(2): 223–235. https://doi.org/10.1029/RG027i002p00223.

Kisner, Wendell. 2014. *Ecological Ethics and Living Subjectivity in Hegel's Logic*. London: Palgrave Macmillan UK. https://doi.org/10.1057/9781137412119.

Kropotkin, P. 2006. *Mutual Aid: A Factor of Evolution*. New York: Dover Publications Inc. https://doi.org/10.2307/2140787.

Latour, Bruno. 2017. *Facing Gaia: Eight Lectures in the New Climatic Regime*. Cambridge, UK: Polity Press.

Longo, Giuseppe, Maël Montévil, and Stuart Kauffman. 2012. "No Entailing Laws, but Enablement in the Evolution of the Biosphere." *ACM Proceedings of GECCO*: 1379–1392.

Malabou, Catherine. 2005. *The Future of Hegel: Plasticity, Temporality and Dialectic. The Future of Hegel: Plasticity, Temporality and Dialectic*. London and New York: Routledge. https://doi.org/10.4324/9780203489338.

Malabou, Catherine. 2008. *What Should We Do with Our Brain?* New York: Fordham University Press.

Malabou, Catherine. 2017. "The Brain of History, or, The Mentality of the Anthropocene." *South Atlantic Quarterly* 116(1): 39–53. https://doi.org/10.1215/00382876-3749304.

Malabou, Catherine. 2020. "Rethinking Mutual Aid: Kropotkin and Singer in Debate." *Fall Semester*, April 10, 2020. https://fallsemester.org/2020-1/2020/4/8/catherine-malabou-rethinking-mutual-aid-kropotkin-and-singer-in-debate.

Malafouris, Lambros. 2013. *How Things Shape the Mind A Theory of Material Engagement*. Cambridge, MA: MIT Press.

Margulis, Lynn. 1998. *Symbiotic Planet: A New Look at Evolution*. New York: Basic Books.

McGowan, Todd. 2019. *Emancipation After Hegel: Achieving a Contradictory Revolution*. New York: Columbia University Press.

Menary, Richard. 2014. "Neural Plasticity, Neuronal Recycling and Niche Construction." *Mind and Language* 29(3): 286–303. https://doi.org/10.1111/mila.12051.

Moder, Gregor. 2015. "Catherine Malabou's Hegel: One or Several Plasticities?" *Filozofija i Drustvo* 26(4): 813–829. https://doi.org/10.2298/fid1504813m.

Montévil, Maël, and Matteo Mossio. 2015. "Biological Organisation as Closure of Constraints." *Journal of Theoretical Biology* 372 (May): 179–191. https://doi.org/10.1016/j.jtbi.2015.02.029.

Moreno, Alvaro, and Matteo Mossio. 2015. *Biological Autonomy. Vol. 12. History, Philosophy and Theory of the Life Sciences*. Dordrecht: Springer Netherlands. https://doi.org/10.1007/978-94-017-9837-2.

Mossio, Matteo, Maël Montévil, and Giuseppe Longo. 2016. "Theoretical Principles for Biology: Organization." *Progress in Biophysics and Molecular Biology* 122(1): 24–35. https://doi.org/10.1016/j.pbiomolbio.2016.07.005.

Pradeu, Thomas. 2011. "A Mixed Self: The Role of Symbiosis in Development." *Biological Theory* 6(1): 80–88. https://doi.org/10.1007/s13752-011-0011-5.

Radnik, Borna. 2017. "The Absolute Plasticity of Hegel's Absolutes." *Crisis and Critique* 4(1): 352–375. http://crisiscritique.org/2017/march/Borna Radnik.pdf.

Suárez, Javier, and Vanessa Triviño. 2019. "A Metaphysical Approach to Holobiont Individuality: Holobionts as Emergent Individuals." *Quaderns de Filosofia* 6(1): 59–76. https://doi.org/10.7203/qfia.6.1.14825.

Vahanian, Noelle. 2008. "A Conversation with Malabou." *Journal for Cultural and Religious Theory* 9(1).

Varela, Francisco J., and Mark Anspach. 1991. "Immuknowledge: The Process of Somatic Individuality." In *Gaia 2. Emergence, the New Science of Becoming*, edited by W.I. Thompson, 68–85. Hudson, NY: Lindisfarne Books.

Villalobos, Mario, and Pablo Razeto-Barry. 2020. "Are Living Beings Extended Autopoietic Systems? An Embodied Reply." *Adaptive Behavior* 28(1): 3–13. https://doi.org/10.1177/1059712318823723.

Virgo, Nathaniel, Matthew D. Egbert, and Tom Froese. 2011. "The Role of the Spatial Boundary in Autopoiesis." In *Advances in Artificial Life: Darwin Meets von Neumann*, edited by George Kampis, István Karsai, and Eörs Szathmáry, 240–247. Dordrecht: Springer. https://doi.org/10.1007/978-3-642-21283-3_30.

Žižek, Slavoj. 2012. *Less than Nothing: Hegel and the Shadow of Dialectical Materialism*. London: Verso.

Žižek, Slavoj. 2020. *Hegel in a Wired Brain*. London: Bloomsbury Academic.

Chapter 6

Ethics of the Care for the Brain

Neuroplasticity with Stirner, Malabou and Foucault

Tim Elmo Feiten

Shortly after Max Stirner published his only book, *The Unique and Its Property*,[1] late in 1844, Ludwig Feuerbach published an astonishing response. Feuerbach had been one of the main targets of Stirner's scathing attack on humanism, liberalism and socialism as all unwittingly continuing in the footsteps of religion and dragging along its mistakes and misdeeds in their wake. According to Stirner's diagnosis, the different philosophical and social projects rapidly emerging from the dissolution of Hegel's system shared one fatal mistake: they merely swapped out the ideological content of Christianity for something new, while retaining and even strengthening its structures of oppression and exploitation. In response to Stirner's anti-essentialism, Feuerbach asked: 'Can you sever masculinity from what is called mind? Isn't your brain, the most sacred and elevated organ of your body, definitively masculine?' (cited in Stirner 2012, 89).

It is striking how closely this line of argumentation – the interface between gender as the truth of the self and the brain as the truth of the self – mirrors the situation today in which an unholy alliance between evolutionary psychology (cf. McKinnon 2005) and neuro-determinism seeks to naturalise gender differences as fixed by evolution in the deep history of our species and manifested in male and female brains, our gendered essence rendered on the

I would like to thank the editors of this volume, especially Dan Swain and Petr Urban, whose helpful and critical comments greatly improved this paper. Further, I am grateful to all participants of the Politics of Plasticity conference for their feedback and suggestions, in particular to Catherine Malabou. I owe special thanks to Adam Christopher Jones for his insightful remarks on an earlier draft and to Wolfgang Essbach for his continued encouragement of my work.

[1] I use the 2017 translation by Wolfi Landstreicher, the first new translation in English since Stirner's book was first rendered as *The Ego and His Own* by Steve Byington in 1907. In addition to the anachronistic Freudian associations of the term, Byington also uses 'ego' to translate a range of German words rendered more precisely as 'I', 'individual' and 'unique' (cf. Landstreicher 2017, 8–9).

screen by the wonders of neuroimaging. In the 'so-called age of the brain', the brain has become firmly established as a cultural locus of the truth of the self (Pitts-Taylor 2012). While during the twentieth century the structure and function of the post-adolescent brain were considered to be largely static and subject mostly to degenerative change, the twenty-first century has seen a dramatic shift towards the notion of the brain as a fundamentally plastic organ (cf. Rees 2016). This turn from determinism to plasticity has opened up possibilities for emancipatory interventions that consider the plastic brain, as well as the discourses surrounding it, as a site of struggle against reactionary essentialisms. Alongside the 'struggles among scientists, doctors, patients, advocates, ethicists, and activists over what the brain is, should be, and can be', philosophers and theorists have taken up the brain and its plasticity as a new lens to provide insight into old problems (Pitts-Taylor 2012). In light of 'the inextricability of neuronal matter with its bodily, social, and historical surroundings', the brain becomes a site of political interventions, contested by a multitude of actors (Pitts-Taylor 2012). Catherine Malabou is among those who have taken up the fight against oppression and exploitation on this terrain, by working towards a 'culture of neuronal liberation' (Malabou 2008, 30) and a 'politics of plasticity' (Malabou this volume).

The central appearance of the brain in the heated debate between Stirner and Feuerbach is an exception, it plays no larger role in Stirner's writing. Nevertheless, my claim is that Stirner's account of an insurrection against essentialism as a radical act of self-empowerment constitutes a valuable resource for the project of developing a politics of plasticity, and for answering the question that is the title of Malabou's book: *What Should We Do with Our Brain?*

In order to give such an answer, we have to make Stirner speak in a language other than his own. I will attempt to lift Stirner's thought from the Young Hegelian debates of the 1840s into the context of contemporary theories of embodiment, plasticity and self-shaping. Developing this entirely new reading of Stirner and putting it to work for a politics of plasticity is a large task, and I will only be able to lay the groundwork for it in this chapter. I will focus on four aspects:

In the following section, I will motivate the need for a new reading by highlighting the shortcomings of the earliest and latest reactions to Stirner, by Marx and post-anarchism, respectively. I will also situate this new reading of Stirner roughly in the context of recent empirically informed continental theory as a way out of the false choice Malabou identifies 'between *essentialism* and *discursivity*' (Malabou this volume, 17).

In the third section, I will show that the structures of religion have not 'melt[ed] into air', but are still operative in the form of ideology and through a mechanism that is profoundly embodied. We internalise ideological norms and materialise their effects in and through our own bodies. Similarly, our rejection of ideology and our self-assertion against it start with bodily exertion.

In the fourth section, I show that Stirner's notion of 'property' has nothing to do with legal ownership (which he rejects along with the whole realm of legality),[2] but instead matches very closely Jakob von Uexküll's concept of *Umwelt.* It describes the phenomenal world of each living subject, and by treating it as one's property, Stirner means relating to the affordances in our environment without the limitations of what Iris Marion Young calls the self-imposed 'I cannot' (Young 1980, 146).

Neuroplasticity wards off the spectre of neurodeterminism, but it opens up the challenge of the neoliberal neuronal self: How do we avoid merely internalising the pressures of the market when we shape ourselves? Critically following up on existing comparisons between Stirner and the later thought of Michel Foucault, in the fifth section I will show that Stirner's self-empowerment matches Malabou's challenge of thinking resistance to oppression and exploitation 'without falling back into sociobiological ideology on the one hand, ultra-liberal philosophy on the other' (Malabou this volume, 17).

A NEW READING OF STIRNER

If, as Etienne Gilson says, '[p]hilosophy always buries its own undertakers' why do we need to dig up Stirner again? (Putnam 1983, 303, as cited in Malachowski 1990, xi) Even though Stirner has undergone several periodic revivals since his death, I argue that this perpetual revenant still has unfinished business on this earth. I will lay the groundwork for a new reading of Stirner, to make him rise from his shallow grave in the history of thought once again, this time to help answer Malabou's question: *What Should We Do with our Brain?*

Stirner's thought has always elicited strong reactions – repelling to some and alluring to others, but frustrating and confusing to most. Stirner's radical rejection of religion, humanism, morality, as well as marriage, the state and the family, is often considered to be merely the 'self-destructive endpoint' of Young Hegelianism (Laska 1994, 5; translation mine). He sought to throw off ideology through insurrection and to avoid any essentialism by speaking not of humans, women and men or citizens, but only of 'unique ones', a phrase which has no conceptual content and thus does not impose any expectations

[2] For this reason, one might prefer the translation as 'own' instead of 'property' that is used in some translations. However, the misleading legal-economic connotations of 'property' are the same as for the German "Eigentum", so I follow the translation by Wolfi Landstreicher that I generally rely on.

on its referents (Stirner 2017, 216). He sought to dissolve and posit his own identity in every moment and live as a 'creative nothing', in voluntary associations with others called 'union[s] of egoists' (Stirner 2017, 377 and 233). My claim is that reading Stirner through and alongside different theories of embodiment, we can understand his thought in a way that is both more adequate to his text and more useful to us today, including as a resource for a politics of plasticity. I will first show that we have good reason not to follow Marx's rejection of Stirner, but also that we should not be fully satisfied with the recent readings of Stirner as a forerunner of post-anarchism.

In reaction to the publication of Stirner's only book, *The Unique and Its Property,* Marx penned a vitriolic tirade against him. Even though this indictment was only edited into a book along with other texts in the 1930s, this extremely negative reading of Stirner has shaped his reception so that the most common view of him today is still that of a petty-bourgeois individualist obsessed with hoarding property, cynically dismissive of all social relations. That this is a misreading will become clear when I explain Stirner's notion of property, but Marx also includes Stirner in a more general critique of the Young Hegelians. He mocks them for setting all their hopes on ideas and ignoring material reality, comparing them to a man who thinks he can save himself from drowning if he just gets rid of his belief in the force of gravity (Marx and Engels 2010a, 24). Strategically, Marx and Engels set up the attack on the Young Hegelians to ridicule critique of ideology as a useless and misguided activity (Marx and Engels 2010, 23–24). They were surely right to reject 'the critique of religion as the Alpha and Omega of radical leftism', as Adrian Johnston puts it, but they also threw out the baby with the bathwater (Johnston 2020, 3 and 7). They believed that history had destroyed ideological illusions better than any theorist could: 'for exploitation, veiled by religious and political illusions, it has substituted naked, shameless, direct, brutal exploitation' (cited in Johnston 2020, 8). However, 'subsequent history has been [. . .] unkind to Marx and Engels's 1848 heralding and celebration of economically-driven profanation' (Johnston 2020, 9). The continued necessity of critically analysing the structures and contents of ideology is well-represented in Marxist thought since the twentieth century, but its implication – that one of the main reasons for rejecting Young Hegelian thought has turned out to be invalid – has not led to a reconsideration of those thinkers belittled in *The German Ideology.*

In contrast to Marx's rejection, a positive reading of Stirner has been developed within post-anarchism since the 1990s. This largely academically inflected variant of anarchism brought the conceptual apparatus of Foucault, Deleuze and Lacan – among others – to bear against the perceived essentialism of classical nineteenth-century anarchism. In this context, Stirner's anti-essentialist project has been compared favourably to the works of all three thinkers and Stirner has taken on the role of a forerunner, if not a patron saint, of anti-essentialist anarchism (cf. Newman 2001a; Newman 2001b; Newman 2011a; Koch 2011; Feiten 2014; and Feiten 2019). This narrative itself and the role Stirner plays in it are problematic in subtle ways that I have pointed out elsewhere (Feiten 2013). One weakness of the post-anarchist reading of Stirner should be pointed out here because it illustrates very well how Stirner's project lines up with Malabou's dissatisfaction with the 'discursive paradigm' (Malabou this volume, 21). Saul Newman, the most prominent and prolific post-anarchist reader of Stirner, summarises his commitment to the discursive paradigm thus:

> We live in a symbolic and linguistic universe, and to speculate about an original condition of authenticity and immediacy, or to imagine that an authentic presence is attainable behind the veils of the symbolic order or beyond the grasp of language, is futile. There is no getting outside language and the symbolic. (Newman 2011b, 156)

The problem is that this is completely incompatible with Stirner's project. Stirner dethrones thinking through the insurrection of embodied experience, and he invents a way of speaking that is meant to prevent discursivity from ever usurping power again, by emptying it of its representational content. In the fight against ideology, 'only thoughtlessness really saves me from thoughts. It isn't thinking, but my thoughtlessness, or I, the unthinkable, inconceivable, that frees me from possession' (Stirner 2017, 165). Self-empowerment requires a relation to oneself that is grounded in pre-linguistic bodily self-experience. Referring to ourselves and each other as unique pays tribute to the fact that we are not reducible to discourse. The unique is in this sense an empty phrase, 'the unspeakable, and therefore not merely something thought' (Stirner 2017, 357). Newman's view might be an extreme example, but post-anarchist readings of Stirner are generally limited by this problem.[3]

The reading of Stirner I will start to develop here bears some resemblance to a movement in philosophy that has been called 'continental naturalism' or 'post-continental naturalism', of which Malabou's politics of plasticity is one example (Mullarkey 2009, 259–276 and 263; Erkan 2020). One of its defining features is a way of thinking nature that cannot be reduced to the theoretical horizon of post-structuralism. Even though the post-anarchist readings of Stirner have done important work in reviving interest in him and highlighting

[3] Depending on their primary source of inspiration, they might have other problems with Stirner, I will comment on the ones that arise for Deleuzian readings of Stirner below, as well as the shortcomings of post-anarchist comparisons between Stirner and late Foucault.

important aspects of his work, we now have to move beyond the 'very limited opposition' that Malabou diagnoses in the post-anarchist 'opposition between essentialism and discursivity' (Malabou this volume, 17). It is exactly this problematic that informs Stirner's entire project and his engagement with the question of nature.

Stirner's philosophical relationship to nature is complex: On the one hand, he forcefully rejected the idea of human nature, particularly in the form of Feuerbach's *species being*, as a mere abstraction over concrete individuals that is illegitimately turned into an ideal and a normative constraint. On the other hand, the vision of self-empowerment and the free play of creative agency itself seem to suggest a kind of natural state that is unearthed from the garbage heap of ideology, quoting Goethe: 'I sing as the bird sings' (Stirner 2017, 309). The crucial difference between the two appeals to nature is that Feuerbach's species being posits a human essence by which each individual is represented back to themselves in a state of perpetual inadequacy, while Stirner merely seeks poetic illustration for the free development of autonomous creativity. Feuerbach's *species being,* at least on Stirner's reading, is a kind of knowledge that claims both epistemic authority over nature and the normative authority of nature over each individual, whereas Stirner leaves nature undetermined, leaving it to express itself. Importantly, Stirner's appeal to nature, like his reference to the unique, is not conceptual. Just as much as he rejects essentialism, Stirner refuses to be caught up in discursivity: 'the content of the unique is not thought content, the unique cannot be thought or said' (Stirner 2012, 57). His naturalism is one that rejects essences and discursive representations alike: 'Only when nothing is said about you and you are merely named, are you recognized as you' (Stirner 2012, 58). By merely naming the individuals, nothing is predicated of them that could be held up against them as a normative standard – as it is when we call someone a human, a Christian, a woman or a man, a citizen and so forth.

STIRNER'S EMBODIMENT

Stirner's analysis of ideology was formulated as a direct provocation against his contemporaries: 'Our atheists are pious people' (Stirner 2017, 198). He saw the budding liberalism, socialism and humanism of the German *Vormärz* period as mere continuations of the religious mystifications that had propped up the *ancien regime:* 'Man, your head is haunted' (Stirner 2017, 61). Marx rejected Stirner's preoccupation with ideology as ineffective and misguided, as an idealist method to which he opposed the materialism he developed together with Engels. But modern neuroscience has changed our appreciation of the material reality of thought and ideology in a way that complicates the dichotomy between idealism and materialism and prevents some of the more direct moves of the debate in the 1840s. The ideological palimpsest that 'weighs like a nightmare on the brains of the living' has a material existence in the neuronal pathways of our brains and the surrounding tissues that enable and modify their operation, in what Malabou calls an 'indissociable unity between matter and meaning' (Marx 2010, 103; Malabou this volume, 25). But already in the 1840s, Stirner's account of the individual's insurrection against ideology could not be rejected simply as a matter of fanciful ideas. It is not just the head that is haunted, but the entire body. I will demonstrate this central point of my reading, that in Stirner's analysis ideology takes a hold of us through our bodies, and that our struggle against ideology is also a bodily activity, in two key passages.

Stirner links the way in which we are complicit in our own subjugation to the way that ideology works through our bodies. This relation is illustrated in explicitly libidinal terms. Stirner describes one of the 'victims of self-denial' policing her own bodily desires and preventing their expression when the 'the rich forces of youth' come into conflict with the internalised prohibitions of ideology:

> When your head burrowed into the soft pillows, how awakening nature quivered through your limbs, blood swelled your veins [. . .]! Then the specter of the soul and its salvation appeared. You were frightened, [. . .] you – prayed. Nature's storms were silenced, quiet glided over the ocean of your desires. Slowly the weary eyelids sank over the life extinguished under them, the tension crept unnoticed from the exuberant limbs [. . .], and – *the soul was tranquil.* You fell asleep, to awaken in the morning to a new battle and a new-prayer. [. . .] The soul is saved, let the body perish! (Stirner 2017, 78–79)

What we see in this passage is the body acting as an interface between the demands of ideology which the woman has internalised and the bodily desires and forces that are properly her own. Ideology works in and through the body, and its effects are directly opposed to the fulfilment of our needs and desires. The body is the altar on which we sacrifice our happiness to the gods of introjected normativity. But the body in Stirner's analysis is not just the place at which ideology takes a hold of us, but equally the site of our struggle against it:

> A jerk does me the service of the most careful thought, a stretching of the limbs shakes off the torment of thoughts, an upward leap hurls the nightmare of the religious world from my breast, a hurrah shouted out with joy throws off years of burdens. (Stirner 2017, 165)

Just as our complicity in our own subjugation to ideology is enacted through the body, so is our insurrection against it. The logic of ideology seeks to represent the individual back to itself as an instance of the normative categories of the human, female (or male), citizen and so on. Against this, Stirner's unique asserts its self-ownership in a rebellion that is described with reference to concepts, but is carried out primarily as a bodily activity. By exerting the capacities of our bodies and inhabiting the world through our bodies without mediating this relationship through any form of representation, we short-circuit the functioning of the ideological device that has been inserted between our desires and our actions and which serves to reroute our energies from their original role in the fulfilment of our desires towards the propagation of this very parasitic structure.

Stirner's project, both in its critical and in its positive dimensions, is deeply embodied. No reading that strives to do it justice and capture its full scope can afford to dismiss it as a rebellion in thought alone, as Marx does. Stirner describes the lived experience of the individual subject as fundamentally embodied, so it can neither be reduced to its anti-essentialist commitments, nor considered as a set of events and processes that can be described without privileging the subject and its relation to the world, as would be required by the interpretive horizon of post-anarchism.

THE UNIQUE AND ITS *UMWELT*

A second set of provocations consists in Stirner's claims that he is the centre of the world and that the world is his property. Taken out of context, Stirner sounds like a megalomaniac, and Marx made ample use of the extreme character of Stirner's rhetoric in ridiculing him as such. Specifically, the notion of property drew Marx's ire and led him to portray Stirner as nothing more than a petty bourgeois individualist, a label that has unfortunately stuck through the centuries. But Stirner's use of the term 'property' has nothing to do with legal ownership, as should be clear from Stirner's detailed critique of laws in general and the idea of legal ownership in particular, both of which he firmly rejects (Stirner 2017, 186–198). What Stirner means by 'property' is something completely different: 'Your world extends as far as your capacity, and what you grasp is your own simply because you grasp it. You, the unique, are "the unique" *only together with "your property"*' (Stirner 2012, 63). This notion has more to do with theoretical biology than legal ownership, and the thought of Jakob von Uexküll can help us understand what it means. Comparing Stirner's notion of property to Uexküll's concept of *Umwelt* also makes clear why Stirner's claim to be the centre of the world is not the product of intense hubris or delusion, but simply a description of how the world is given to each living subject.

A forerunner of biosemiotics and cybernetics, Jakob von Uexküll was a biologist working primarily on the physiology of sea creatures, who developed a theory of organismic subjects and their environments that was both deeply inspired by and very influential on philosophy (cf. Feiten 2020; and Feiten et al. 2020). He believed that organisms are not merely complex machines, but living subjects, and that each of them lives in their own world. He illustrates this by inviting us to imagine a stroll on which we encounter each animal enclosed in their own phenomenal world, or *Umwelt,* as in a soap bubble:

> We begin such a stroll on a sunny day before a flowering meadow in which insects buzz and butterflies flutter, and we make a bubble around each of the animals living in the meadow. The bubble represents each animal's environment and contains all the features accessible to the subject. As soon as we enter into one such bubble, the previous surroundings of the subject are completely reconfigured. [. . .] A new world arises in each bubble. (Uexküll 2010, 43)

Uexküll developed the concept of *Umwelt* to refer to the environment of a living creature as it is experienced from the first-person perspective, in contrast to its physical surroundings considered in an abstract view from nowhere (Feiten 2020, 2–4). What this means is simply that the world I experience and inhabit is my own because its existence as phenomenal experience is brought forth through my own existence and activity. This is what Stirner means when he writes that 'no one lives in any other world than his own, and [. . .] everyone is the center of his own world' (Stirner 2012, 63).

Stirner says that your 'world extends as far as your capacity' because the Umwelt of an animal is made up only of those aspects of its environment that are capable of affecting it in some way. For most animals, those are only those objects that provide a direct opportunity for action in the service of satisfying some organismic need. In ecological psychology, these properties of the environment which provide an opportunity and invitation for goal-directed action are called *affordances*, 'equally a fact of the environment and a fact of behavior' (Gibson 1979, 121; see also Chemero 2009).

The affordances that make up an Umwelt depend on the abilities of a subject, its power, but the subject also has to be attuned to the match between the information about features of the physical world available in its sensory array and its own powers. This attunement is not a conscious mental act or content, but instead an achievement of the nervous system that makes it possible for affordances to appear in the conscious experience of the subject. Uexküll took his theory to be a continuation of Kant's first *Critique,* but it constitutes a radical departure from Kant: instead of categories and forms of sensible intuition, Uexküll describes a kind of embodied a priori: the semicircular canals in our inner ear make possible our experience of three-dimensional space. The nervous system, for those animals that have one, plays an absolutely crucial role in the constitution of their *Umwelt.* Uexküll's view anticipates aspects of different contemporary views on the brain, even where these views are generally opposed: like Thomas Metzinger, Uexküll sees the brain as projecting a world of experience (Metzinger 2009). Even though Thomas Fuchs is radically opposed to Metzinger's position, he adopts Uexküll's view that the brain 'provides open loops of possibility that are closed by suitable complements in the environment and thus become functional cycles of interaction' (Fuchs 2020, 5).

For Uexküll, as for Stirner, each living subject inhabits a world of their own. A central tenet of Uexküll's view is that there are 'as many worlds as there are subjects', and Stirner agrees that 'no one lives in any other world than his own, and [. . .] everyone is the center of his own world' (Uexküll 1926, 70; Stirner 2012, 63). This brings them into conflict with two different strands of post-anarchism, those who adopt a Deleuzian view and those who adopt realism (Rousselle 2013, 157–165). Despite Deleuze's positive use of Uexküll at different points, his mode of thinking rules out that every subject is contained in their own world. Instead he emphasises the Spinozist motifs in Uexküll's *Bedeutunglehre* and develops a kind of non-constructivist reading of Uexküll (cf. Feiten et al. 2020, 10–16; Uexküll 2010; Deleuze 1988, 122–130).

Besides Uexküll, Stirner's radically self-centred account of existence also resonates very strongly with the starting point[4] of Maurice Merleau-Ponty's *Phenomenology of Perception*:

> I am, not a 'living creature' nor even a 'man', nor again even 'a consciousness' endowed with all the characteristics which zoology, social anatomy or inductive psychology recognize [. . .] – I am the absolute source, my existence does not stem from my antecedents, from my physical and social environment; instead it moves out towards them and sustains them, for I alone bring into being for myself [. . .] the horizon [. . .]. (Merleau-Ponty 2002, ix)

[4] The starting point, but not the end point. Importantly, Merleau-Ponty and other phenomenologists also emphasise the inter-subjective nature of our experience. What exactly the methodological and ontological consequences of this commitment are and whether they are as incompatible with Stirner's view as the term 'inter-subjective' suggests cannot be discussed here in detail. I do not claim that Stirner agrees with the phenomenologists I cite here in every regard, only that important aspects of their work can help us understand Stirner better.

Stirner has been described as an 'an early, generic practical phenomenologist', with the caveat that terms like 'phenomenal' cannot be taken to describe a fixed method in Stirner but merely point out that he is dealing with 'non-conceptual experiences' that exceed and occur independently of 'symbolic concepts' (McQuinn 2012, 36 and 7–8). However, some general points from phenomenology can highlight the specificity of Stirner's project. Likely drawing on Husserl's then unpublished writings, which he accessed in the archives at Leuven, Merleau-Ponty writes that '[c]onsciousness is in the first place not a matter of "I think that" but of "I can"' (Merleau-Ponty 2002, 159; cf. Bernet 2013, 44). This matches Stirner's valuing of bodily action over thought as the primary mode of being in the world, where 'grasping' in the intellectual sense becomes merely one modulated variant of the more general embodied grasp that the subject has on its world.

Iris Marion Young in her analysis of '[f]eminine bodily existence' adds to Merleau-Ponty's 'I can' the case of an 'inhibited intentionality' which 'withholds its full bodily commitment [. . .] in a self-imposed "I cannot"' (Young 1980, 146). This is also a strikingly apt analysis of Stirner's episode of the young woman outlined above. Ideology works through the body in the form of a self-imposed 'I cannot', and Stirner's project is to show us ways out of this self-imposed misery. This also helps us understand Stirner's clarification of what he means by 'egoism': '[not] forgetting that the world is "ours", [not] forgetting that one is the center or *owner* of this world, that it is our property' (Stirner 2012, 64). Property here has nothing to do with legal ownership, in fact quite the opposite: The world is my property if I stop self-imposing an 'I cannot' that turns abstract ideological, moral and legal norms into real limits to my own embodied intentionality. Stirner's 'property' consists in an active relation to my environment that is not mediated and constrained by the specious authority of these concepts, one of which is legal property.

In Uexküll's account of animals, the functional cycles that link a given animal's nervous system to its environment through a loop of perception and action are prespecified in the grand plan of Nature (Feiten 2020, 7). For humans, the situation is different: facing nature with a lack of claws, poison or instinctual reactions reliably fitted to our environment, our survival hinges on the ability to adapt to the situations we find ourselves in. In this way, we have always been creatures and creators of our own plasticity. A new reading of Stirner's project as an embodied insurrection against the way that we limit ourselves by imposing ideological limits on our bodily intentionality thus provides a starting point for developing a politics of plasticity. Such a reading of Stirner's self-empowerment as traversing multiple dimensions of change through the coupling of brain, body and behaviour – and against the way in which ideology interfaces with all of them – highlights also the 'conceptual bridge between neural and cultural plasticity', what Lambros Malafouris calls 'metaplasticity' (Malafouris 2015, 352).

THE PROBLEM OF THE CARE FOR THE SELF

An embodied reading of Stirner's self-empowerment gives us the first step of a politics of plasticity: the decision to take control of the process whereby we are shaped and shape ourselves. But it can also help us think productively about the challenges involved with the second step: Once we have made this decision, what is the form we give ourselves? Once we control our plasticity, what is the shape we mould ourselves into? Critical commentators on neuroplasticity have clearly pointed out a danger here: instead of a progressive or liberatory effect, the 'neuronal subjects' are pressured to shape themselves into ever more productive, flexible and resilient workers and citizens through a 'neoliberal ethic of personal self-care and responsibility' (Pitts-Taylor 2010, 639). Even though the agency of shaping the subject is transmitted from ideological state apparatuses to the subjects themselves, the form in which they are shaped is still determined by the vectors of their oppression and exploitation. The neuronal subject would then merely internalise the pressures of the market in the same way that when Stirner was writing '[e]very Prussian carrie[d] his gendarme in his breast' (Stirner 2017, 37).

The difference between a self-shaping which frees the subject from external authority and one that merely places the responsibility for maintaining its conformity to ideology with the subject itself can be illustrated by the difference between Stirner's project and the ethics of the concern for the self as a practice of freedom in the later work of Michel Foucault (Foucault 1997). Post-anarchists have read these two accounts as describing at heart the same form of self-empowerment. Highlighting the crucial difference between the two will then also show how my reading moves beyond the constraints of the post-anarchist reception of Stirner.

Comparisons between Stirner and Foucault have been drawn since at least the 1980s (Marti 1988). In terms of Foucault's later work on ethics of the care for the self, two major commentators make largely identical, although ultimately somewhat superficial, arguments for a link with Stirner's notion of self-empowerment. Both Jürgen Mümken and Saul Newman look to Foucault and Stirner for concrete practices of resistance against the ideological forces that shape us into docile subjects (Mümken 2004; Newman 2001a). Two questions reveal the weaknesses of this approach:

a) What are the concrete practices we should adopt?
b) What exactly are we cultivating by adopting these practices?

The problem with the first question is that Foucault is 'not looking for an alternative; you can't find the solution of a problem in the solution of another problem raised at another moment by other people' (Foucault 1984, 343). He is not interested in a 'history of solutions' but a 'genealogy of problems' (Foucault 1984, 343). The point of Foucault's analysis is to show that 'the emergence of new thought, the motion of practice, is contingent upon the problematic that precedes it' and that each such 'problematization [. . .] is capable of supporting contradictory responses' (Koopman 2016, 107). It is tempting to read Foucault's work on this 'technology of the self' as a direct source for practices of self-empowerment, but it is also clear that the text does not provide this (Foucault 1984, 342).

The second, perhaps even more pressing issue with the 'concern for the self as a practice of freedom' concerns the question of what is meant by 'freedom' (Foucault 1997, 281). Stirner criticises the ideal of 'freedom' at length and forcefully rejects it: rather than orienting us towards improving our situation, the concept of freedom is somewhat of a red herring, an empty phrase that waits to be filled with content by cultural and political projects which then yoke the individual to their goals, rather than enabling them to pursue their own. In Stirner's analysis, the ideological structures, both doctrinal and institutional, which produce subjects ready to collaborate in their own exploitation and oppression, are shorn of their religious contents, but retained basically intact and even entrenched more deeply in the quest for secularisation.

The 'technology of the self' described by Foucault must equally be seen in its historical context. In general, the techniques described by Foucault were used only by privileged and powerful members of the relevant societies, that is, free men. What it meant for them to practice care for the self is to ensure that they conduct their lives the way a free man would. This includes controlling one's passions to a certain degree, inflicting only the correct amount of violence on one's wife, children, slaves and so on. Freedom in this context means the degree to which one conforms to an existing social ideal, and the practices that Foucault describes in antiquity serve this goal (Miller 1997, 176–178). It is easy to see how a politics of plasticity could fall prey to this danger and result in individuals actively shaping themselves to conform to a neoliberal conception of what it means to be free. This is all diametrically opposed to Stirner's project and highlights precisely the reasons why he rejected freedom as an ideal in favour of *Eigenheit*, or ownness, which describes not any particular state of being, so not just another new ideal, but a way of relating to oneself that is not mediated by ideals (cf. Feiten 2014).

The pressing question then is whether Stirner's project can escape the fate of such a 'practice of freedom'. Some might think that the pressures of a capitalist environment would still lead the Stirnerian to shape themselves into a docile citizen and a good consumer. His rhetoric certainly enables such views: 'To me, objects are only material that I consume' (Stirner 2017, 306). However, Stirner's consumption cannot be equated with the consumption of commodities, and he makes it clear that he does not think that pursuing one's desires unhindered by ideology will be compatible with capitalism. First, he is not interested in material gain or social status: 'Perhaps I can make very little out of myself; this little, however, is all, and is better than what I allow the power of others to make out of me, through the training of custom, religion, law, the state, etc.' (Stirner 2017, 195). Stirner also rejects the free market and argues for '[a]bolishing competition', favouring instead free associations that work together to meet their common needs (Stirner 2017, 287). He advocated for workers to unite to fight scabs and bargain for better wages, leading Plekhanov to praise him for 'attacking bourgeois reformers and utopian socialists who thought the proletariat could be emancipated by the virtuous acts of the propertied class' (Feiten 2013, 123). Despite his otherwise critical stance, Plekhanov acknowledges Stirner as preaching class struggle (Plekhanov 2001, 47–52).

Stirner's radical rejection of all external authority starts with oneself, but it does not end there. Taking ownership of one's lifeworld and agency does not entail a diminishing of social relations. On the contrary, almost all of our desires directly require that we fulfil them socially. Stirner's concept of insurrection is not 'aimed at new arrangements', it aims to 'no longer let ourselves be arranged, but rather to arrange ourselves' (Stirner 2017, 398). Stirner is 'not against love, but against sacred love, not against thought, but against sacred thought, not against socialists, but against sacred socialist' (Stirner 2012, 81–82). It seems plausible that a successful embodied insurrection against ideology could only succeed as a collective effort, because that would create the social space necessary for free association to occur and hence for the unique ones to live their lives according to their desires. The processes of self-empowerment and self-shaping that Stirner describes for a single individual become even more complex once they involve others. Stirner's own thought does not take us very far towards a detailed image of what these forms of social cooperation might look like. In one sense, his position is opposed to the very idea of determining them in advance, because this would prevent them from emerging spontaneously from the creative collaborations of unique individuals. In terms of the project for developing a politics of plasticity, this seems like an impasse at first.

THE INDIVIDUAL AND THE SOCIAL

Is Stirner's 'egoism' not a doctrine of isolation, at odds with the notions of solidarity and mutual aid? This common accusation led Stirner himself to complain that '[n]o one gives Stirner credit for his global intercourse and his association of egoists' (Stirner 2012, 82). These are voluntary associations that only exist as the active process of organising and do not constitute institutions with a separate existence of their own. These relations are not mediated by any representations of its members as belonging to a particular gender, nationality, religion or even as being human, they are enacted purely on the ground of the participants' common interest and joined powers. As Stirner puts it, 'the "exclusiveness" of the egoist, which some want to pass off as isolation, separation, loneliness, is on the contrary full participation in the interesting', what is excluded are only the obligations and limitations that go along with various ideological representations of subjects (Stirner 2012, 82). A core aspect of this 'full participation' is the 'voluntary and reciprocal exchange of resources and services' that Malabou identifies as mutual aid (Malabou this volume, 15).

On Stirner's account, solidarity and mutual aid do not arise out of a sense of obligation, but that does not mean that no obligations are ever involved. Once a 'union of egoists' is formed to pursue some common goal, obligations arise. By cooperating freely and organising, they are generating and accepting obligations within the context of their association. Although the association is voluntary, it thus also limits the freedom of its participants: Every 'society to which I adhere takes many a freedom away from me, but grants me other freedoms in return' (Stirner 2017, 319). '[W]ith respect to freedom, state and associating are subject to no essential difference', but the state denies also my ownness when 'it demands that those who belong to it subject themselves to it' (Stirner 2017, 320). What the associating egoists eschew is the creation of an institution that exists above and beyond the living human beings whose agency it usurps.

It is crucial to understand that Stirner's book is not a screed against pro-social behaviour, but against the ideological formation of humanism: 'Yes, the book actually is written against the human being, and yet Stirner could have gone after the same target without offending people so severely if he had reversed the subject and said that he wrote against the inhuman monster' (Stirner 2012, 74). Stirner's critique cuts through a sentimental essentialist altruism the same way as through a libertarian essentialised competition. Stirner is not opposed to feelings of solidarity or their expression in behaviours of mutual aid, but only to their symbolic representation as abstract duties. Once we learn to associate without mediation by these ideological constructs, our mutual aid will have become unchained in this way. It is not a chain of signifiers – citizen, Christian, man, human – that produces or encodes pro-social behaviour, but the voluntary creation of 'horizontal relationships that [. . .] exclude any feeling of guilt or debt' (Malabou this volume, 15).

But is the idea of individual agency not an illusion, is the behaviour of individuals not determined by their material reality, that is, by social and/or biological factors beyond their control? Is Stirner's notion of empowerment an idealistic voluntarism, the idea of a self-positing will totally independent of matter and history? Not so. In his early essay '*Das unwahre Prinzip unserer Erziehung*' ('The Untrue Principle of Our Education', Stirner 1986), Stirner emphasises that individual agency is not somehow separate from the material realities of the social world, but that the will is something that develops over the course of a lifetime. The conditions which enable an individual to develop their will are social, and different contexts can support or stifle this development.

And what about social and biological determinations? Stirner does not attempt to deny material reality, he merely attacks normative representations that lead us to rush ahead and shape our actions in the way we have been told they are determined. If there really is some natural force or tendency in us that produces our feelings of love and solidarity with others, Stirner's egoists will act on them, since these feelings are their own. However, they will reject feelings of obligation that are induced by representations of human nature. Similarly, if class interest describes a material reality, it will coincide with the self-interest of Stirner's egoists and they will act in their class interest on their own volition, without guidance by a party.

This being said, we would also be misled in expecting Stirner's thought to give us a system of thought that solves all our problems. Instead, the value of his work for us in the present will likely lie in the productive combinations with other schools of thought. Many positions that partially resonate with Stirner's attention to subjective experience, such as phenomenology, gestalt therapy or enactivism, have developed rich accounts of intersubjectivity that can provide us with useful perspectives on social life where Stirner falls short. If we manage to move beyond historical misunderstandings, we might also develop a productive dialogue between the views of Marx and Stirner – a possibility that was suggested early on by Engels, Plekhanov and Max Adler, but quickly rendered anathema by the dominant Marxist reading of Stirner (cf. Laska 1996, 23–24 and 60–62). An embodied reading of Stirner can help us see old conceptual problems in a new light, and opens up new directions for exploring conceptual ties and tensions that have been ignored because of Stirner's status as a pariah in the history of thought.

CONCLUSION

We have seen that Stirner's project is not exhausted by the post-anarchist readings that have popularised his thought in recent decades, but that it is fundamentally embodied in a way that escapes the discursive paradigm. Neither is it vulnerable to the central points of Marx's attack: First, ideology is alive and well today as it was in the 1840s – insofar as something can be said to be alive that has no life of its own, but exists in and through our bodies and brains. Stirner traces the way it works on our bodies, and how our bodies flex their muscles when we try to throw it off. Second, Stirner's notion of property has nothing to do with a petty bourgeois fixation on legal ownership. Instead, it refers to the phenomenal world each of us inhabits and the way we relate to it once we stop imposing ideology's 'I cannot' on ourselves and our bodies. We have seen that Stirner's self-empowerment is different from the concern for the self that Foucault investigates in antiquity, and that it has at least a fighting chance at avoiding the danger of a neoliberal plasticity, in which we would take control of our lives merely in order to mould ourselves in the shape of productive workers and prolific consumers. And yet, a lot remains to be done before this new reading of Stirner can really be put to work for a politics of plasticity.

BIBLIOGRAPHY

Bernet, Rudolf. 2013. "The Body as a 'Legitimate Naturalization of Consciousness.'" In *Phenomenology and Naturalism: Examining the Relationship between Human Experience and Nature*, edited by Havi Carel and Darian Meacham, 43–65. Cambridge: Cambridge University Press.

Chemero, Anthony. 2009. *Radical Embodied Cognitive Science.* Cambridge, MA: The MIT Press.

Deleuze, Gilles. 1988. *Spinoza: Practical Philosophy.* San Francisco, CA: City Lights Books.

Erkan, Ekin. 2020. "Post-Continental Naturalism: Equipollence between Science and Ontological Pluralism." *Rhizomes: Cultural Studies in Emerging Knowledge* 36 [online] doi:10.20415/rhiz/036.r04.

Feiten, Tim Elmo. 2013. "Would the Real Max Stirner Please Stand Up?," *Anarchist Developments in Cultural Studies* 1: 117–137.

Feiten, Tim Elmo. 2014. "Ethik in der Stirner-Rezeption Saul Newmans." In *Der Einzige: Jahrbuch der Max Stirner Gesellschaft*, vol. 6, 53–61. Leipzig: edition unica.

Feiten, Tim Elmo. 2019. "Deleuze & Stirner: Ties, Tensions, and Rifts." In *Deleuze & Anarchism,* edited by Chantelle Gray van Heerden and Aragorn Eloff, 120–135. Edinburgh: Edinburgh University Press.

Feiten, Tim Elmo. 2020. "Mind after Uexküll: A Foray into the Worlds of Ecological Psychologists and Enactivists." *Frontiers in Psychology* 11: Article nr. 480. doi.org/10.3389/fpsyg.2020.00480.

Feiten, Tim Elmo, Kristopher Holland, and Anthony Chemero. 2020. "Worlds Apart? Reassessing von Uexküll's Umwelt in Embodied Cognition with Canguilhem, Merleau-Ponty, and Deleuze." *Journal of French and Francophone Philosophy* 28(1): 1–26.

Foucault, Michel. 1984. "On the Genealogy of Ethics: An Overview of Work in Progress." In *The Foucault Reader,* edited by Paul Rabinow, 340–372. New York: Pantheon Books.

Foucault, Michel. 1997. "The Ethics of the Concern for Self as a Practice of Freedom." In *Ethics: Subjectivity and Truth*, edited by Paul Rabinow, 281–302. New York: The New Press.

Fuchs, Thomas. 2020. "The Circularity of the Embodied Mind." *Frontiers in Psychology* 11: Article nr. 1707. https://doi.org/10.3389/fpsyg.2020.01707.

Gibson, James J. 1979. *The Ecological Approach to Visual Perception.* Boston, MA: Houghton-Mifflin.

Johnston, Adrian. 2020. "The Triumph of Theological Economics: God Goes Underground." *Philosophy Today*, 64(1): 3–50.

Koch, Andrew. 2011. "Post-Structuralism and the Epistemological Basis of Anarchism." In *Post-Anarchism: A Reader*, edited by Süreyyya Evren and Duane Rousselle, 23–40. London and New York: Pluto Press.

Koopman, Colin. 2016. "Critical Problematization in Foucault and Deleuze: The Force of Critique without Judgment." In *Between Deleuze and Foucault,* edited by Thomas Nail, Daniel W. Smith, and Nicolae Morar, 97–119. Edinburgh: Edinburgh University Press.

Landstreicher, Wolfi. 2017. "Introduction." In Stirner, M. *The Unique and Its Property*, translated by Apio Ludd aka Wolfi Landstreicher, 7–21. Baltimore, MD: Underworld Amusements.

Laska, Bernd. 1996. *Ein dauerhafter Dissident.* Nürnberg: LSR-Verlag.

Laska, Bernd. 1994. *Ein heimlicher Hit.* Nürnberg: LSR-Verlag.

Malabou, Catherine. 2008. *What Should We Do with Our Brain?* New York: Fordham University Press.

Malafouris, Lambros. 2015. "Metaplasticity and the Primacy of Material Engagement." *Time & Mind* 8(4): 351–371.

Malachowski, Alan R. 1990. "Preface." In *Reading Rorty: Critical Responses to Philosophy and the Mirror of Nature (and Beyond),* edited by Alan R. Malachowski, x–xii. Oxford: Basil Blackwell.

Marti, Urs. 1988. *Michel Foucault.* Munich: C.H. Beck.

Marx, Karl, and Friedrich Engels. 1970. *Manifest der Kommunistischen Partei.* Berlin: Dietz Verlag.

Marx, Karl, and Friedrich Engels. 2010. "The German Ideology." In *Marx & Engels Collected Works, Volume 5,* edited by James S. Allen et al., 19–581. London: Lawrence & Wishart.

Marx, Karl. 2010. "The Eighteenth Brumaire of Louis Bonaparte." In *Marx & Engels Collected Works, Volume 11*, edited by James S. Allen et al., 99–197. London: Lawrence & Wishart.

McKinnon, Susan. 2005. *Neo-liberal Genetics.* Chicago, IL: Prickly Paradigm Press.

McQuinn, Jason. 2012. "Clarifying the Unique and Its Self-Creation: An Introduction to 'Stirner's Critics' and 'The Philosophical Reactionaries'." In *Stirner's Critics*, 5–45. Oakland, CA: Little Black Cart.

Merleau-Ponty, Maurice. 2002. *Phenomenology of Perception*. New York: Routledge.
Metzinger, Thomas. 2009. *The Ego Tunnel: The Science of the Mind and the Myth of the Self*. New York: Basic Books.
Miller, Paul Allen. 1997. "Catullan Consciousness, the 'Care of the Self,' and the Force of the Negative in History." In *Rethinking Sexuality: Foucault and Classical Antiquity,* edited by David H. J. Larmour, Paul Allen Miller, and Charles Platter, 171–203. Princeton: Princeton University Press.
Mullarkey, John. 2009. "The Future of Continental Philosophy." In *Continuum Companion to Continental Philosophy,* edited by John Mullarkey and Beth Lord, 259–276. London: Continuum.
Mümken, Jürgen. 2004. *Freiheit, Individualität und Subjektivität: Staat und Subjekt in der Postmoderne aus anarchistischer Perspektive*. Bodenburg: Edition AV.
Newman, Saul. 2001a. *From Bakunin to Lacan: Anti-Authoritarianism and the Dislocation of Power*. Lanham: Lexington Books.
Newman, Saul. 2001b. "War on the State: Deleuze and Stirner's Anarchism." *Anarchist Studies* 9(2): 147–164.
Newman, Saul. 2011a. "Stirner's Ethics of Voluntary Inservitude." In *Max Stirner,* edited by Saul Newman, 189–209. London: Palgrave Macmillan.
Newman, Saul. 2011b. *The Politics of Postanarchism.* Edinburgh: Edinburgh University Press.
Koch, Andrew M. 2011. "Post-Structuralism and the Epistemological Basis of Anarchism." In *Post-Anarchism: A Reader,* edited by Süreyyya Evren and Duane Rousselle, 23–40. London and New York: Pluto Press.
Pitts-Taylor, Victoria. 2012. "Neurocultures Manifesto." *Social Text.* Accessed on 31st October, 2020. https://socialtextjournal.org/periscope_article/neurocultures-manifesto/.
Pitts-Taylor, Victoria. 2010. "The Plastic Brain: Neoliberalism and the Neuronal Self." *Health* 14(6): 635–652.
Plekhanov, Georg. 2001. "Anarchismus und Sozialismus." In *Texte (1892-1894): Heft 3*, edited by Kurt Fleming, 47–52. Leipzig: Max-Stirner-Archiv.
Putnam, Hilary. 1983. "Beyond Historicism." In *Realism and Reason: Philosophical Papers, Volume 3.* Cambridge: Cambridge University Press.
Rees, Tobias. 2016. *Plastic Reason: An Anthropology of Brain Science in Embryogenetic Terms.* Oakland, CA: University of California Press.
Rousselle, Duane. 2013. "Max Stirner's Post-Post-Anarchism: A Review Essay." *Journal for the Study of Radicalism* 7(1): 157–165.
Stirner, Max. 1986. "Das unwahre Prinzip unserer Erziehung." In *Parerga, Kritiken, Repliken*, edited by Bernd Laska, 75–97. Nürnberg: LSR-Verlag.
Stirner, Max. 2012. *Stirner's Critics*. Translated by Wolfi Landstreicher. Oakland, CA: Little Black Cart.
Stirner, Max. 2017. *The Unique and Its Property*. Translated by Apio Ludd aka Wolfi Landstreicher. Baltimore, MD: Underworld Amusements.
von Uexküll, Jakob. 1926. *Theoretical Biology*. New York, NY: Harcourt, Brace & Company, Inc.

von Uexküll, Jakob. 2010. *A Foray into the Worlds of Animals and Humans, with A Theory of Meaning*. Minneapolis: University of Minnesota Press.

Young, Iris Marion. 1980. "Throwing Like a Girl: A Phenomenology of Feminine Body Comportment Motility and Spatiality." *Human Studies* 3: 137–156.

Chapter 7

Materialisms, Old and New

Individuation and Anarchy in Gilbert Simondon and Catherine Malabou

Arianne Conty

Subjects and objects, the infatuation of modernity, have gone out of fashion. Scholars today see agency, events, lines of flight and entanglements where they used to see subjects and objects, often leading to an indiscretion between the two that is celebrated as having finally overcome the anthropocentrism responsible for justifying a human subject over and against a world of things. Instead of separating the active human subject from a world of passive objects, the world of human culture from a background of brute nature and the human being from all non-human life-forms, new materialism is the name that has been given to the scholarship devoted to replacing modern dichotomies with a processual and contextual understanding of the human being as part of a unified theory of life. Though the scholars grouped under this heading are extremely diverse, they all seek to celebrate the materiality of our world, a materiality understood no longer as inert and passive, but rather as vibrant and full of agency.

Integrating natural science into their research in the human sciences, new materialist scholars use physics, biology, ethology, geology and other natural sciences to enrich our understanding of the human being and its history on the earth. Inspired by the work of physicists such as David Bohm and Ilya Prigogine, and biologists such as Jacob von Uexküll and Lynn Margulis, many anthropologists, historians and philosophers[1] have shown how environments and other species are essential to human identity and survival.

[1] Such anthropologists include Gregory Bateson, Anna Lowenhaupt Tsing, Elizabeth Povinelli, Tim Ingold, Philippe Descola, Viveiros de Castro and Eduardo Kohn. Regarding historians, I am thinking here in particular of historians of consciousness Karen Barad (also a physicist) and Donna Haraway (also a biologist). Philosophers working in this direction include Raymond Ruyer, Alfred

Studies in symbiogenesis have shown, for instance, that many forms of life, including the human form, depend upon foreign organisms for their survival. This is the case with gut bacteria for all animals possessing digestive tracts, and for the mitochondria in animal cells, which have their own RNA and a separate existence within the cell. The ecosystem is thus constituted by sets of interdependent relations, none of which exist intrinsically outside of these relations. Such interdependent material relations allow New Materialists to question the focus of the Western tradition in anthropocentric essentialism and patriarchal scorn for all things ephemeral, material, bodily and earthly. It has become a priority for New Materialists to undermine modern ideologies that were ignorant of evolution and introduce interdisciplinary research that understands the contributions of brain science and of quantum mechanics, for such sciences undermine unchanging ontological essences, just as they undermine human exceptionalism and predeterminism. Such interdependence belies the boundaries of academic isolation that separates the human sciences from the natural sciences, since the human being is of course natural, and all of nature culturally invested.

Though her work is indebted to continental philosophers George Friedrich Hegel, Martin Heidegger and Jacques Derrida, none of whom were particularly interested in materiality, philosopher Catherine Malabou is often understood as belonging to this eclectic group of new materialists in her attempts to integrate biology and especially brain science into her philosophy in order to highlight the plasticity of human identity. Thus Brenna Bhandar and Jonathan Goldberg-Hiller claim that Malabou 'has pioneered a distinctive mode of reading the Continental philosophical tradition, revealing a new materialism' (Bhandar and Goldberg-Hiller 2015, 1) and Deborah Goldgaber claims that 'Malabou is one of the most influential 'new materialist' Continental philosophers' (2018, 39). Indeed, Malabou has understood herself in these very terms, claiming that only such new materialist scholarship is capable of overcoming the dichotomies of modernity and replacing them with a continuous and reversible understanding that she calls a 'new philosophy of spirit'. In her book *Les nouveaux blessés,* she writes: 'I continue to defend the thesis that the only valid philosophical path today lies in the elaboration of a new materialism that would precisely refuse to envisage the least separation, not only between the brain and thought but also between the brain and the unconscious' (Malabou 2017, 342).

Similarly, in her book coauthored with Adrian Johnston, *Self and Emotional Life: Philosophy, Psychoanalysis, and Neuroscience,* she repeats this call to elaborate a New Materialism that could build a bridge between biology and the humanities: 'The time has come to elaborate a new

---

North Whitehead, Gilbert Simondon, Jane Bennett, Catherine Malabou and Isabelle Stengers, among many others.

materialism, which would determine a new position of Continental philosophy vis-à-vis neurobiology, and build or rebuild, at long last, a bridge connecting the humanities and biological sciences' (Johnston and Malabou 2013, 72).

For Malabou, taking matter seriously and undermining the modern division between nature and culture entails integrating the results of research in the natural sciences into philosophy, and adapting our understanding of the human species in accord with the major advances that have occurred in the discipline of biology. Focusing on the concept of plasticity, Malabou is able to show how an encounter between philosophy, biology and brain science can lead to a far more relevant understanding of the human animal, not as unchanging soul substance but as plastic potentiality.

Though his theories considerably predate the coining of the term 'new materialism', this chapter will claim that philosopher Gilbert Simondon (1924–1989) should also be considered a 'new materialist' scholar, one whose work has considerably influenced that of Malabou. Such a statement implies two things:

First, it implies that Simondon would find himself much more at home in the contemporary context of new materialist scholarship than in the context of his own time, when his putting into question of what Barthélémy calls 'the anthropological break' separating the human being from the rest of the animate world was largely ignored. Barthélémy writes: 'To the subject of the living being, along with the non-living and psycho-social life, Simondon brings a mode of questioning that does not exactly belong to his epoch, but whose initial strangeness makes more sense today' (Barthélémy 2015, 16).

Second, it implies that new materialism is not so new. It is perhaps the growth of feminist scholarship, coupled with the urgency of the Anthropocene Age which impels us to look clearly at the toxic after-effects of modernity that have given this movement its impetus and its widespread appeal today. But it is important to trace such contemporary materialisms back to their earlier forebears, in order to avoid defending the fad of the new that has beset academic writing and that often testifies to an ignorance of the past. Though it is certainly the case that such interest in material relations is more widespread today and has reached a stage of maturity, attempts to study the human being as dependent upon and inseparable from a non-human context are not in fact new. Theories seeking to overcome the nature/culture, human/non-human divide have been developed and argued for quite some time. They have simply not been given the attention they deserve. The plasticity of the brain, for example, was already being theorised in the embryo-genetic theory of philosopher Raymond Ruyer (1902–1987), in the 'genetic epistemology' of psychologist Jean Piaget (1896–1980), the 'psycho-civilized' theory of physiologist José Delgado (1915–2011), and the ontogenetic theory of

Simondon himself, whose influence on Malabou will be the subject of the present chapter.

In the hopes of developing a form of resistance against the fetishism of the new so widespread in postmodern culture, and connecting new materialisms to materialisms not so new, this chapter will elucidate Catherine Malabou's epigenetic theory of plasticity by placing it into dialogue with Simondon's ontogenetic theory of individuation. Just as Simondon develops an ontogenetics that seeks to trace the genesis of life forms and thereby unify nature and culture, Malabou similarly develops what she calls an epigenetics that seeks to show how the symbolic and the biologic, human history and natural history, coincide. Such ontogenetic and epigenetic genealogies refute biological determinism by revealing the psychic content of genetic development while at the same time elucidating the biological substrate of all mental content. Inheriting from Charles Darwin and Sigmund Freud an interest not in already constituted ontological entities, but in their formation, both Simondon and Malabou are interested not in what the human subject is, but in how such a subject comes into being. Just as Darwin's principle of adaptation entails an interiorisation of external conditions, it is the interiorisation of cultural memory that creates what Freud calls the psyche. There is thus a correlation between the biological development of the human body, and the process of individuation through acculturation. Rather than focusing on *what* the human being is, as though it were born fully constituted, both philosophers are interested in *how* a subject develops from a pre-subjective matrix, and how the subject internalises external forces in order to individualise society. Taking for granted the neoteny of the human being at birth, such a processual approach understands the development of stem cells into individuated and differential organs and the psychic process of acculturation via parenting, education and ideology as parallel indeterminate processes that mirror each other and reveal the relational nature of psychic and biological life. The human being is thus shown, in both thinkers, to be constituted by its relation to a past that remains its founding principle of potentiality, a past that exceeds the boundaries of cognition and individuated identity.

Because the unlived potentialities of both the individual and its brain cells await a 'germ of contingency' to become realised, the theories of both Simondon and Malabou also provide us with a methodology for thinking time materially and envisioning an open future. Because material forms evolve in time, thinking this pre-material matrix of potential allows for a reconceptualisation of futurity. Because Simondon's 'reservoir of becoming' (Chabot 2013, 86) exceeds the individual in its pre-individual origin, the unlived potentiality of the past can always be individuated in the future, revealing a reversibility of time that belies chronological cultural history. Individuated potentials are always trans-individual since they can transcend a biological life-span in the form of cultural transmission, thanks to technological resources. Similarly, in understanding biology and history as interdependent, Malabou is able to develop what she calls a 'new ethics' that reveals reason itself to be plastic, and hence open to the future. Such an epigenesis of reason situates the transcendental a-priori not as a pre-constituted judgement given from without, nor as an innate and hence determined subjective ability within, but rather as the very immanent possibility of reason to create a future that is neither predetermined nor placed in a radically transcendent alterity. In their attempt to integrate evolution into philosophy proper, both Simondon and Malabou develop a philosophical theory of subject formation that provides a new interpretation of human freedom and its ability to construct an open future, constituting what we will call a psycho-genetic revolution for the twenty-first century.

GILBERT SIMONDON: ONTOGENETICS

The title of Simondon's book *L'individuation à la lumière des notions de forme et d'information* itself testifies to the ways that Simondon deconstructs modern conceptions of human identity. Instead of beginning with a preformed and fully constituted individual, Simondon uses the term *ontogenesis* to describe the process of individuation from potential energy into individuated form. In the words of Pascal Chabot, 'Simondon sought a philosophy that could account for evolution' (Chabot 2013, 73). Individuation thus translates Darwinian evolution into a framework that takes into account psychic development, and ontogenesis translates adaptation into a philosophical framework that can take into account the birth and development of individuated entities: 'Adaptation' Simondon writes, 'is a permanent onto-genesis' (Simondon 2005, 235).[2]

Such a psycho-biological ontogenesis is meant to replace the substantialism and hylomorphism that for Simondon plague philosophy and limit its ability to understand human identity as a process of becoming rather than of stable being. Instead of 'the hylomorphic path, (which considers) the individual as engendered by the encounter between form and matter" (Simondon 2005, 23), Simondon replaces such stable distinctions with "the concept of a formed matter and a material form' (Chabot 2013, 76). Since for Simondon there are no first substances, no atoms that are irreducible to alterity, relationality itself becomes the foundation. Rather than isolating each entity as an autonomous and individual substance, Simondon studies the relations in the natural and

[2] Citations are from the French edition and translations are my own, unless otherwise indicated.

cultural world that allow for the genesis of distinct psycho-biologic forms of life, and once this context is taken into account, the relational nature of all entities becomes evident. In the words of Chabot: 'The relation is not an accidental feature that emerges after the fact to give the substance a new determination. On the contrary: no substance can exist or acquire determinate properties without relations to other substances and to a specific milieu. To exist is to be connected' (Chabot 2013, 77).

Just as hylomorphism is to blame for ignoring context, Simondon will blame substantialism for ignoring the history and development of being, or as he puts it, for 'considering being as consisting in its unity, given to itself, founded in itself, uncreated, resisting to all that is not itself' (Simondon 2005, 23). Rather than understanding the human being as having an essence that places it at the pinnacle of nature, or else outside of nature altogether, for Simondon, 'nature is not opposed to Man, but rather the first phase of being' (Simondon 1995, 196). Extending the concept of subject to include other animals, Simondon seeks to understand the process of hominisation from primate development to the trans-individual instantiations of techno-cultural transmission. Instead of beginning with the individual as if it were somehow pre-fabricated, ontogenesis explains how pre-individual life individualises itself in order to become subjective. He writes:

> If, on the contrary, we were to suppose that individuation did not only produce the individual, we would not seek to rapidly pass over the phase of individuation to arrive at the last reality that is the individual: we would seek to grasp ontogenesis in the full development of its reality, and to know the individual by means of individuation rather than individuation by means of the individual. (Simondon 2005, 24)

Because both the substantialist and the hylomorphic theories presuppose 'a principle of individuation anterior to individuation itself' they present a 'reverse ontogenesis' by working backwards from a constituted individual to its conditions of existence. When the subject is understood as already constituted, and being already the being of the individual, the question is always regarding the 'what' of its constitution – its properties and ontological status. When instead the focus is placed on the process of individuation, the question shifts to a 'how', which emphasises the relationality of subjectivation to a pre-subjective world. Ontogenesis thus substitutes for ontology in Simondon's work, and replaces the ontological focus on substance with a biological focus on processual development. Because the material world is a flux of energy in constant evolution, there can be no such thing as an individual, since such an entity ignores the process of evolutionary time. Rather, there is only a process of genesis, of always incomplete individuation. Simondon writes:

> Strictly speaking, we cannot speak of the individual, but only of individuation; we must get back to the activity, to genesis, rather than trying to grasp the already given being in order to discover the criteria by which we can know whether or not it is an individual. The individual is not a being but an act, and being is an individual as the agent of this act of individuation by which it shows itself and exists. Individuality is an aspect of generation, is explained by the genesis of a being, and consists in the perpetuation of this genesis. (Simondon 1995, 191)

Such an interdisciplinary philosophy of life capable of accounting for subjective and collective individuation, as well as nature and culture as a unified whole constitutes what Jean-Hugues Barthélémy has called an 'encyclopedic genetics' (2008). As philosopher Gilles Deleuze has pointed out in his review of Simondon's book *The Individual and Its Physico-Biological Genesis*, such a principle of individuation 'must be truly genetic, and not simply a principle of reflection' (Deleuze 2001, 115). Such a genetics must be understood in the literal sense of a genesis, in that Simondon seeks a unified theory that takes into account the physical, biological and psychosocial elements of being, by retracing life-forms back to their generation, or, similar to Anaximander's *apeiron,* to what he calls the pre-individual. As 'a reservoir of becoming' (Chabot 2013, 86), the pre-individual entails that chaos is merely a bath of potentiality, awaiting the germ that will transform it into a crystal.

Instead of the relation between variation and selection as per Darwin, Simondon will focus on the relation between pre-individual potential and transduction, the crystallisation of a particular potential into an individuated form with a particular duration and psychic energy: 'Evolution', he writes, 'is a transduction more than it is a continual progress or a dialectic' (Simondon 1995, 163). Transforming Freud's notion of instinct into his own concept of transduction, Simondon explains the vital energy channelled from the pre-individual matrix into the process of individuation as 'the irreversibility of creative nature' rather than as a pre-determined drive. Thus, rather than the life drive of *eros* opposing the death drive of *thanatos* as in Freud's theory, Simondon understands transduction as the duration of a particular actualisation of pre-individual potential energy, which always has a limited duration. Like the process of formation of a crystal, the process of individuation is the living out of a selective potential or 'structural germ' that will eventually exhaust itself. Sean Bowden clarifies as follows: 'transduction is the name given to the ongoing actualization or structuring of the potentials of a metastable system whose constitutive heterogeneous orders have been brought into communication by a singularity functioning as a "structural germ"' (Bowden 2012, 141).

Because the process of individuation can actualise several vital potentials, and not just one, an individual can change, and is capable of becoming other to itself and transmitting, post mortem, its unlived potentials. The individual is thus constituted by discontinuity, rather than continuity, and death, rather than opposing life, becomes its very condition of possibility.

Thanks to the role of the pre-individual in Simondon's theory, the individual takes on a sense of dignity quite different from that of Humanism, for such dignity lies in its ability to face the unknown potential of becoming, and in particular, that of becoming other to itself. The metastability of the process of individuation means that the subject is never fully constituted, and that it can always return to a pre-individual reserve of potentials that enable it to remain in movement, open to transformation and self-difference. Like the Freudian unconscious,[3] the individual is thus always more than itself, always harbouring the potential to become other, always constituted by these unlived potentials that lie in wait. This is what Muriel Combes has called 'an impersonal-molecular zone of affective life held immediately in common with other individuals and thus constituting a transindividual commons, or collective potential' (2013, 110).

By reversing the ontological privilege of being over becoming, the process of individuation is meant to replace the ontological category of the individual with a longer history, a genealogy that reveals such an individual to be merely what Simondon calls 'a phase of being' developing out of a pre-individual matrix of potential, and growing in a trans-individual or psycho-social context. The individual is not coextensive with being, but rather a moment in a process that includes both a pre-individual phase, and a trans-individual or psycho-social phase. Simondon writes: 'The psychosocial is the transindividual: it is this reality that the individuated being transports with him, this charge of being for future individuations' (Simondon 2005, 303). It is precisely the difference between these states that is fundamental to the process of individuation, for, as Deleuze explains, it is such 'a difference of potential' that is capable of alternating between 'intensive quantities' in a metastable system that allows for an infinite order of gradations. In this sense, the individual, for Simondon, is a self-differing entity, in relation with its pre-individual substrate and its trans-individual context. Rather than a self-contained subject, such auto-alterity allows the individual to be understood as a relation

[3] Though Freud posits a principle of genesis prior to the individual, and instinctive drives that constitute individuation as a process, he remains hylomorphic by reducing all psychic activity to a homeostatic biological mechanism, thereby positing individuation as a binary struggle between id and superego, repression and social norm. Instead, for Simondon, transduction is the channelling of potentials that each have a particular duration and energy in a metastable system that is both psychic and biological.

to its own instantiations, and to a time and a place that exceed it. The individual is thus, as Simondon puts it, 'always more than one'. He writes:

> To think individuation, being must be considered not as a substance, or matter, or form, but as taut system, oversaturated, above the level of unity, consisting not only of itself and incapable of being thought by means of the excluded middle; concrete being, or complete being, in other words pre-individual being, is a being that is more than a unity. (Simondon 2005, 25)

If transduction is a process of necrosis, it also allows for the individuated phase to 'integrate a problematic that is greater than its own being' (Simondon 1995, 11) that of the trans-individual that lives on after the death of the individual and carries forward its information. Simondon focuses on the role of the cultural and biological environment in order to trace how unformed potential energy becomes informed during the process of transduction. In this sense, culture, and in particular what he calls technological resources, allow the social collective to gain control of the process of biological individuation by rendering autonomous its symbolic information. Understood by Simondon as an extension of nature, or what he calls 'nature in man', culture is shown to be a means of controlling and continuing the biological process of individuation. Relinquishing its separate individuation, each potential can thus live on in the collective at the level of symbolic information. Such symbolic information, transmitted by means of technological resources, allows humanity to take responsibility for its process of individuation, and to control its transmission. Though human reality is but one among myriad incarnations of being, it is unique precisely because of this autonomy whereby it can itself control the transmission of its potential through externalising the duration of the process of individuation by technical means.

Simondon's philosophy integrates an understanding of evolution and adaptation with a theory of psychic and technological development in order to explain individuation as a particular phase of being. By placing being into a temporal relation with a pre-individual unconscious potential and a trans-individual sociology, Simondon restores the human being as a process of individuation to the natural history of material evolution. Though the process of transduction is indeed one of necrosis, as each potential has a finite life span, Simondon's theory focuses on the ways that being exceeds the individual in both its pre-individual origin and trans-individual destiny. Such a temporality, by means of which the unlived potentiality of the past can always be individuated in the future, reveals a reversibility of time that belies chronological cultural history and replaces it with a biological history that respects the cycles of life of the natural world and the reversibility of time as developed in physics. Deleuze has called this temporal reversibility a 'carnal or vital topology', one that brings past and future 'into confrontation at the limit of the living present' (Deleuze 2006, 97). Not only does such a theory undermine the unity and isolation of the atomic and unchanging modern individual, but it also opens a path to help us understand how individuated potentials can transcend a biological life-span in the form of cultural transmission, thanks to technological resources. In this sense, our cultural transmission can be understood as a continuation of biological and psychic individuation, one that we can control and thus that provides a new interpretation of human freedom and its ability to construct an open future.

CATHERINE MALABOU: EPIGENETICS

Advances in biology and neurology, chemistry and physics have shown the centrality of plasticity to the scientific disciplines, which can no longer be reduced to a deterministic ideology. In her research, philosopher Catherine Malabou has traced the many ways the creativity and plasticity traditionally attributed to the humanities has migrated to the scientific disciplines, and because it is essential today for humanistic disciplines to centre their development in scientific discovery, she has called for a similar migration of scientific ideas to the humanities.[4] Overcoming the dichotomies of modernity that separated the academic disciplines into subjective and objective, material and metaphysical and symbolic and biological, Malabou claims that we cannot understand human identity in a contingent and immanent world until we cease to separate the psychic and material content of our embodied nature. She states:

> If we are able to admit that the difference between 'material' and 'psychic' is very thin and even perhaps non-existing, if we agree on the absurdity of regarding the brain and the psyche as two separate and distinct instances, then we will have moved forward a great deal [. . .]. (Vahanian and Malabou 2008, 8)

Following Simondon's example in developing a theory of individuation capable of replacing a stable and unchanging a-priori conception of the self with an indeterminate, plastic understanding of psychic and material development, Malabou reduces the scope of Simondon's research by focusing on the brain. Indeed,

4 However promising such an engagement between philosophy and cognitive science may be, it is important to point towards some shortcomings that require caution in adopting the naturalisation of consciousness too readily. Great attention must be taken to not reify the brain as some cognitive scientists tend to do, essentialising it (as was done with the 'selfish gene') outside of its symbiotic relationality to the entire organism and its environment. Furthermore, experience should not be reduced to brain function, as has become typical of much reductionist science. Reducing experience to behaviour entails a significant loss of reality as it is actually lived.

thanks to the recent development of brain science and neurobiology, the brain is often recognised as the hub of human identity, the ontic and ontological entity responsible for the human sense of self. Both body and soul, both material and psychic, in Malabou's research the cellular development and plasticity of the brain have come to stand in for Simondon's process of individuation.

Though Malabou nowhere speaks of Simondon as a direct influence on her work, she develops a historical analysis from epigenesis to epigenetics, just as Simondon moves from ontogenesis to develop an ontogenetics. As Malabou explains, epigenesis is the term used to differentiate a biological theory of gradual development of the embryo from the preformationism that held the embryo to be wholly constituted from conception in the seed. Malabou traces the study of epigenetics back to the development of the organism from undifferentiated cells, drawing an interesting parallel to Simondon's analysis of the pre-individual potential that is channelled into the individuating process of transduction. Epigenesis thus relies on advances in the study of the cell that reveal the indetermination of the cells constituting the embryo, and the ways that a particular context at a particular time will select cells to be developed into specific functions in ways reminiscent of Simondon's explanation of transduction. Thus, just as being enters into a phase of individuation, so too do cells. Malabou describes the cells in advanced mammals as having undergone what we can call a process of individuation that selects, from an open matrix of stem cells, one potential and develops it into a single function.

Malabou develops the theory of epigenesis into a theory of epigenetics in order to explain the changes to the organism that are not determined by genetic heredity, and thus to explain the relation between genotype and phenotype as processual and co-dependent. It is precisely the relation between the material and psychic, the biological and cultural, that defines the subject as constituted by both genotype and phenotype, heredity and experience. Focusing, just as Simondon did before her, on the process of individuation rather than taking for granted a fixed unchanging conception of self, Malabou will trace such a development back to the cell, and then compare the plasticity of the cell to that of the brain as both a material and psychic structure. And just as Simondon described the relation between individuation and pre-individual potentials as open, so will Malabou focus upon a reversible temporality in her analysis of cell development. At the cellular level, individuation is not only a process of necrosis, but represents the repression of potentiality necessary in order to develop specific functionality. Under Malabou's pen, epigenetics thus becomes a biological deconstruction that traces the cell from a particular function back to its status as open potential, for instance that of asexual reproduction and regeneration. As biology develops stem cell research in order to regenerate human tissue and organs, such future-oriented research could also be called 'back to the future' or 'before tomorrow' to cite the title of one of her recent books (Malabou 2014a), since it is primarily interested in redeeming the open, undifferentiated status of the stem cells prior to 'individuation'. Rather than creating new organisms in order to cure diseases and fight entropy, cellular research has redoubled its interest in prehistoric organisms that have remained undifferentiated such as the planarians and starfish, composed of auto-regenerating cells that never individuate and that allow for an organism 'to duplicate and repeat itself' (Malabou 2015, 70). This is also the case with stem cells, which 'dedifferentiate themselves' and 'self-renew to produce more stem cells' (Malabou 2015, 70). Malabou cites biologist Jean-Claude Ameisen to explain how such cellular potentiality is repressed to create determinate functions: 'The innumerable innovations of the living [. . .] are built on the – temporary – repression of most of their potentialities. And the wealth of these potentialities that sleep in the depths of our body no doubt surpass by far anything that we can yet imagine' (Malabou 2014a, 438).

This reference to Freudian repression is far from fortuitous, for Malabou's work seeks to establish more than just an analogous relation between genetic and psychic repression. Just as the indetermination of the cell can be reclaimed with a reversible history or return of the repressed that seeks the future in the past, so should we understand the plasticity of the brain as a process of psychic repression and retrieval. By pointing to Freud's inability to take into account brain trauma due to the limitations of his pleasure principle, her book *The Ontology of the Accident* (2012) uses recent research in neurobiology to map the reversibility of the psyche onto the plasticity of the material brain. Just as we return to a long-forgotten past each night when we dream, and the development of mental life allows for 'regression' or 'involution', since primitive stages of mental development can always return (Malabou 2014a, 438), so the plasticity of the brain allows for adaptability to new contexts, but also for regression, as is often the case in aging, and for becoming radically other in the case of brain lesions that incur loss of memory. Malabou deconstructs attempts to understand the brain as a deterministic mechanical structure by showing that the plasticity of the brain entails an ability to transform itself beyond recognition, to repair itself, to improvise and to regress.[5] Rather than a hierarchical and centralised system, the body is a decentralised network or web of relations that exceed the closed

[5] Jairus Grove (2015) has critiqued Malabou for not taking into account the dangerous potential of brain plasticity, particularly regarding government and marketing attempts to control, brainwash and influence individuals and ensure their cooperation. Perhaps in response to Grove, Malabou has recognised such dangers in her last book *Morphing Intelligence,* where she duly takes note of attempts to manipulate and control brain plasticity. She writes: 'Brain plasticity is a spring as much as it is a living coral; it is an ideological norm as much as it is a resource for epigenetic potentialities. While it appears to be the sign of biological indeterminacy, it also serves to legitimize new modes of standardizing psychosomatic expressions' (Malabou 2019, 98).

structure of genetic programming. As she puts it in her book *What Should We Do with Our Brain?*: 'The representation of the center collapses into the network' (Malabou 2008, 35). Such indetermination is required in order to explain the role of experience in phenotypic transformation of our genetic inheritance. Experience gradually effaces the notion of model or archetype, since synaptic growth or decline depends upon individual experience (playing the piano increases such ability, whereas repetitive labour decreases it). She writes: 'By extension, epigenetics studies also the changes that are due, as is the case in the brain, to experience or education. Nongenetic changes include these kinds of modifications, caused by cultural influences. In a sense, plasticity and epigenetics may be regarded as identical or synonymous' (Malabou 2014b, 214).

Building upon Simondon's development of the pre-individual as a phase of being that pre-dates individuation and is constituted by as yet undeveloped potentials, Malabou seeks to rehabilitate lost psychic and cellular possibilities in order to defend the open status of the human body and psyche. We saw that for Simondon transduction cannot exhaust the pre-individual potentials that remain as latent possibilities of future individuation. Similarly, Malabou develops a reversible history of biologic and psychic life capable of finding the future in the past and human potential in a starfish. Such a continuous understanding of life allows the focus to move from the given life forms to the process of formation, and thus from an ontology to a new conception of temporality.

Because of its plasticity and the epigenetic character of an important part of its development, the brain is not a mere biological organ. It can also be considered a historical organ. The in-between space between history and biology is the space in which we live today, in the neurobiological age. Which means that the frontier between history and biology, between historical genesis and biological epigenesis tends to erase itself, thus opening the issue of a new kind of truth that amounts to a new kind of ethics (Malabou 2014b, 216).

For Malabou, such an understanding of the open indetermination of our bio-historical origins is necessary in order to conceive of the notion of futurity. It is such a futurity that opens up 'a new kind of ethics' (2014a), since the future depends upon a pre-individuated past, and is thus not the fruit of the autonomous will or of Kantian reason. Or so one might have assumed. Yet rather than providing a critique of the will or of Kantian reason, Malabou will find plasticity even in Kant's reason, just as her dissertation had previously found plasticity in Hegel's will.

Indeed, in her recent book on Kant, *Avant Demain: Epigénèse et rationalité*, Malabou develops a new interpretation of the Kantian a priori through a re-reading of a passage from §27 of the Transcendental Deduction in the first *Critique,* where Kant mentions the 'epigenesis of reason'. Such an epigenesis of reason situates the transcendental a-priori not as a pre-constituted judgement given from without, nor as an innate and hence determined subjective ability within, but rather as the very immanent possibility of reason to create a future that is neither predetermined nor placed in a radically transcendent alterity. Through understanding the transcendental as itself plastic, Malabou is able to transfer a psychoanalytic understanding of time as psychic history to the very heart of philosophy. Not only is the brain plastic, but reason itself as a temporal self-regulating process must be understood historically.

Such an epigenetic rationality, based in a biological analogy, will allow Malabou to provide an alternative to the rejection of Kant by Speculative Realists like Quentin Meillassoux. Rejecting correlationism, the human perspective on reality that is required by Kant's categories of the mind, Meillassoux claims that correlationism makes it impossible for the human being to take into account a non-human past. In order to 'pierce a hole in the wall constructed by he who separated thought from the great outdoors' (Meillassoux 2006, 98). Meillassoux seeks to rehabilitate what he calls the 'arch-fossil' (*Ibid.*, 167), the scientific certainty in a world anterior to human evolution. Rather than such a stark dichotomy between human and non-human reality, Malabou's interpretation of Kant's 'epigenesis of reason' reveals how reason itself evolves in a natural environment over time. Though immanent and embodied, such reason is neither fully determined by its context, nor contingent as Meillassoux would have it, for its epigenetic development allows it to influence its environment in order to shape the future. Such an immanent, yet non-deterministic understanding of reason provides a necessary alternative to Meillassoux's reliance on mathematics as the language of a radically non-human and transcendent reality.

Likewise, in an article titled 'The Future of Derrida: Time between Epigenesis and Epigenetics', Malabou (2014b) uses this re-reading of Kant to give a future to deconstruction, one that is not forced into the dead-end of messianic alterity as its only way to envision a future. Her reinterpretation of Kant allows her to replace the faith in a messianic future developed by Derrida with an immanent understanding of futurity based in the plasticity of reason. After her research on the plasticity of the brain, she is here interested in showing that reason is itself plastic, and hence capable of influencing an open future by 'fashioning its own possibility. Understood from this perspective, the future coincides with the self-shaping of reason' (Malabou 2014b, 216). Just as she is critical of Meillassoux's need to replace Kant with the transcendent contingency of mathematics, so is she critical of Derrida's need to found the possibility of justice in an indeconstructible messianic future. Rather, for Malabou, history is always deconstructible, and a future ethics can only be developed when such a deconstruction is applied to our psychobiologic identity. Such a future is built upon the immanent structure of our plastic history, and needs no radical messianic temporality to set it free from its deconstructability. It is the deconstruction of our psycho-biological identity that reveals the meaning of time and the sufficiency of human reason to enact the necessary reversals required of our future. Malabou writes:

> we are responsible for the formation of our rational productions, beliefs, and values and we know that all of them are deconstructible. We have to know how to inhabit the space that opens between nature and history, which is the new space for deconstruction. We are responsible for this invention, because nobody else than us will tell or teach us how to become the subjects of our time. (Malabou 2014b, 217)

Such a re-reading of Kant in order to salvage a philosophic futurity by reinterpreting the transcendent as the possibility of immanent change, allows us to make a final comparison between Malabou and Simondon. We might understand the role that reason plays in Malabou's book on Kant as comparable to Simondon's understanding of symbolic transmission by means of technological resources, since both are situated within the subject and without, and both allow for the autonomy of the human animal over the process of individuation. Just as Simondon describes techno-symbolic transmission as allowing individuated potentials to live on after the individual and to replace a biological evolution with a symbolic one that humans can control, so Malabou situates the a-priori reason of the Kantian enlightenment back into the immanent framework of human bio-history, giving to reason the capacity to construct an open future. Understanding the plasticity of reason as the mark of this indetermination, Malabou's theory gives the individual a sense of freedom that does not oppose materiality with a transcendentality that lies within or without, but unveils the transcendental as the very immanent potential of the future. It is such an attention to the past and the process of individuation to which it gives rise that allows both philosophers to delineate an open future, one that transcends the individual by allowing it to transmit its symbolic potential to future generations, through reason and its technological hybrids.

BACK TO THE FUTURE: ANARCHY

Through studying our pre-individual past, both Simondon and Malabou develop 'new operations'[6] that make an important contribution to new

---

[6] We hope to have shown that the 'new operations' that Gilles Deleuze praises Gilbert Simondon for apply equally well to Catherine Malabou:

materialist scholarship. If the modern paradigm was built on dichotomies that have set the natural and human sciences against each other, and separated the human being from its own unconscious and pre-human past and its dependence on non-human nature-cultures, Simondon and Malabou enable us to envision a future where the sciences necessarily inform each other, so that we are able to ensure that they work together instead of creating a future divided against itself. Understanding that the relationship between the symbolic content of our technological resources and the use of our reason depends upon a pre-individual matrix of psycho-biologic potential can help us to enlarge our understanding of the human being from an isolated *cogito* to a more inclusive and plastic material being in constant relation to alterity. Such a psychogenetic understanding of how the human is constituted by what transcends the conscious mind is essential if we hope 'to think beyond what we are' (Malabou 2017) in order to become responsible for what we may become.

Just as Lynn Margulis's work on symbiogenesis has disproved the 'selfish gene' and shown the interdependent relationality of all forms of life, perhaps Simondon and Malabou's 'new operations' can similarly be used to disprove the predominant autonomous individualism of capitalist ideology founded in a biological determinism convinced that nature is 'red in tooth and claw'. If our psycho-genetic future involves redeeming the unlived potentials of our past, perhaps it is time to apply the advances of New Materialist scholarship to free ourselves from what Malabou calls the 'chains' of political determinisms. What possibilities would reveal themselves if we were to use our transductive reason to think of developing pre-individual potentials from a political perspective? Though it appears as though we are locked in an exploitative capitalist worldview with no other alternatives, this is the case only from the perspective of an autonomous substantial individual subject. If individualities and collectivities cannot be separated, and if politics is the fruit of our mutable and reversible processes of individuation, then there must be a politics better able to reflect the process of transductive becoming. Understanding our biologic and genetic plasticity as a process from a pre-individual matrix to a post-individual transduction could allow us to overcome the divisions of modernity and learn to share human potential, and even, human reason, for the benefit of all.

If nature is indeterminate, as Simondon holds, then the reality of being is always saturated by pre-individual potential. By interpreting the Greek

---

Few books, in any case, make us feel the extent to which a philosopher can take inspiration from scientific actuality while at the same time linking them to the great classical problems by transforming and renewing them [. . .]. And what Simondon elaborates is an entire ontology, according to which Being is never One: pre-individual, it is meta-stable, superposed, simultaneous to itself; individuated, it remains multiple, because 'poly-phased', 'the phase of becoming that will lead to new operations'. (Deleuze 2001, 118).

apeiron as a pre-individual reserve of being, Simondon claims that each being is always carrying an infinity of possible beginnings, waiting to be awakened by the right conditions, the right encounters. Such an open ontology of human becoming would always find itself shackled and deformed by deterministic ideologies that do not allow for spontaneous transformation. So, perhaps, such a psycho-genetic revolution does indeed carry political repercussions. This is the position defended by philosopher Daniel Colson, in an essay that traces correspondences between the thought of Simondon and anarchism. Colson compares Simondon's *apeiron* to the *arché* of anarchy, in order to show that this lack of first principles should itself be understood as the source of all spontaneity, an originary chaos that contains all potential becomings within itself like seeds waiting for water and sunlight. Like Simondon's *apeiron,* anarchy, Colson writes,

> is thought as the incessant construction of new subjectivities, as the capacity of beings and collective forces to express and to order, by means of always new association, the infinite and chaotic power of the forces that create and carry them. (Colson 2002, 79)

By allowing pre-individual potentials to actuate themselves, anarchy could be understood as the system that best represents human plasticity.

In her chapter in this volume, Malabou explicitly seeks to re-elaborate community outside state policy, in what she called 'a shift in the morphology of democracy' (Malabou this volume, 15). In her attempts to avoid the chains of essentialism and discursivity (*Ibid.*, 19), Malabou is seeking a way of using New Materialist scholarship, and particularly the unity between biology and the symbolic, to think an unchained philosophy of mutual aid. Indeed, we might claim that plasticity is a way for Malabou to seek an exit from the deterministic closures that 'chain' us to stasis and the 'symbolic grip' of sovereignty. In this sense, political plasticity could be understood as representing a *fil conducteur* of her work, and a way of taking political responsibility for the consequences of New Materialist scholarship. In an article titled 'Whither Materialism? Althusser/Darwin', Malabou asks:

> Whether the destiny of social selection is a fatality, or if selection could, in the political realm, join in any way the natural plastic condition. How can we ensure, within the realm of community and culture, the equilibrium between variation and selection, the future of difference, the promise of unexpected forms? (Malabou 2015, 55)

Seeking 'the unassignable place in a global world where every place is assigned' (*Ibid.*, 58) Malabou has had the courage to deconstruct all forms of sovereignty, and seek to protect what she calls the fragile '"open fields" of singularity, surprise, nonanticipatable selection, recognition of aptitudes, the capacity to welcome new forms without expecting them' (*Ibid.*, 58–59). Might not anarchy represent the best political expression of the plasticity her work seeks to elucidate by providing guidance 'without chains'?

If community can be reconstituted, outside the bounds of nation-state exclusions and political determinisms of all sorts, anarchy appears to be the best candidate for such a reconstitution. Indeed, we might hypothesise that the rising manifestations of local anarchist governance that are sprouting up across the globe to contest globalisation may be the result of this new materialist thinking and the instantiation of such a psycho-genetic future. Signs of such 'non-hegemonic' solidarity are easy to see. From permaculture coalitions to Extinction Rebellion Groups, from informal networks of citizens concerned to protect the commons, to the ZAD, local terrains have become the theatre where we witness the solidarity of those unchained from the logic of party politics and pyramidal structures. It is the power of such instances of mutual aid that will allow us to re-discover unlived potentials and avoid an unliveable future. Commenting on this possibility, Malabou writes: 'I think the ecological crisis can help us develop this sense of a common benefit that urges us to act together without any essentialist or symbolic security [. . .] something like a second nature perhaps' (Malabou 2018, 17).

Voluntary association, self-organisation and forms of direct democracy are the growing response to the deterministic 'chains' that are destroying our earth in the name of corporate growth. These small, local, anarchist groups are learning from indigenous peoples that never developed pyramidal hierarchies how to protect the good life, the *buen vivir* and how to cherish the hope that a better future lies waiting in the unlived potentials we all harbour. It is essential today, if we hope to survive on a plastic and rapidly transforming earth, that we learn from Simondon and Malabou how to develop such a second nature.

BIBLIOGRAPHY

Barthélémy, Jean-Hugues. 2008. *Simondon ou l'encyclopédisme génétique*. Paris: PUF.

Barthélémy, Jean-Hugues. 2015. *Life and Technology: An Inquiry into and beyond Simondon,* Translated by Barnaby Norman. Luneburg: Meson Press.

Bhandar, Brenna, and Jonathan Goldberg-Hiller. 2015. *Plastic Materialities: Politics, Legality and Metamorphosis in the Work of Catherine Malabou.* Durham, NC: Duke University Press.

Bowden, Sean. 2012. "Gilles Deleuze, a Reader of Gilbert Simondon." In *Gilbert Simondon: Being and Technology,* edited by Arne de Boever, Alex Murray, Jon Roffe, and Ashley Woodward, 135–153. Edinburgh: Edinburgh University Press.

Chabot, Pascal. 2013. *The Philosophy of Simondon: Between Technology and Individuation.* London: Bloomsbury Press.

Colson, Daniel. 2002. "Crise collective et désaisissement subjectif: la notion de pré-individuel chez Simondon à la lumière de la littérature anarchiste au XIX siècle." In *Gilbert Simondon: Une pensée opérative,* edited by Jacques Roux, 63–80. Saint-Étienne: Université de Saint-Étienne.

Combes, Muriel. 2013. *Simondon, Une philosophie du transindividuel.* Paris: Éditions Dittmar.

Deleuze, Gilles. 2001. "Review of Gilbert Simondon's *L'individu et sa genese physico-biologique* (1966)." *Pli* 12: 43–49.

Deleuze, Gilles. 2006. *Foucault.* London: Continuum.

Johnston, Adrian, and Catherine Malabou. 2013. *Self and Emotional Life: Philosophy, Psychoanalysis, and Neuroscience.* New York, NY: Columbia University Press.

Malabou, Catherine. 2017. *Les nouveaux blesses: De Freud à la neurologie, penser les traumatismes contemporains.* Paris: PUF.

Malabou, Catherine. 2008. *What Should We Do with Our Brain?* New York, NY: Fordham University Press.

Malabou, Catherine. 2012. *The Ontology of the Accident: An Essay on Destructive Plasticity.* Cambridge: Polity Press.

Malabou, Catherine. 2014a. *Avant demain: Epigenèse et rationalité.* Paris: PUF.

Malabou, Catherine. 2014b. "The Future of Derrida: Time between Epigenesis and Epigenetics." In *The Future of Continental Philosophy of Religion,* edited by Clayton Crockett, Keith B. Putt, and Jeffrey W. Robins, 209–218. Bloomington: Indiana University Press.

Malabou, Catherine. 2015. "Whither Materialism? Althusser/Darwin." In *Plastic Materialities: Politics, Legality, and Metamorphosis in the Work of Catherine Malabou,* edited by Brenna Bhandar and Jonathan Goldberg-Hiller, 47–60. Durham, NC: Duke University Press.

Malabou, Catherine. 2018. "Mutual Aid Beyond Discursivity." Conference presentation, February 23rd, 2018, Prague.

Malabou, Catherine. 2019. *Morphing Intelligence: From IQ Measurement to Artificial Brains.* New York: Columbia University Press.

Meillessoux, Quentin. 2006. *Après la finitude: Essai sur la nécessité de la contingence.* Paris: Seuil.

Simondon, Gilbert. 1995. *L'Individu et sa genèse physico-biologique.* Grenoble: Million.

Simondon, Gilbert. 2005. *L'individuation à la lumière des notions de forme et d'information.* Paris: Million.

Simondon, Gilbert. 2012 [1968]. *Du mode d'existence des objets techniques.* Paris: Aubier.

Vahanian, Noëlle, and Catherine Malabou. 2008. "A Conversation with Catherine Malabou." *Journal of Culture and Religious Theory* 9(1): 1–13.

Part II

'THE WAR OF EACH AGAINST ALL IS NOT THE LAW OF NATURE' – MUTUAL AID, ANARCHISM AND EVOLUTIONARY BIOLOGY

Chapter 8

The Anarchist Impulse

A Factor of Human and Non-Human Nature

Gearóid Brinn and Georgina Butterfield

Anarchism is notoriously subject to misunderstanding and misrepresentation. Aside from misrepresentations by opponents from all sides, academic accounts of anarchism that attempt to corral the irrepressible variety of anarchist thought have also contributed to a widespread, simplistic and reductive image of anarchism as based on an essentialist and naïvely optimistic account of human nature. Many have challenged this representation of anarchism as inaccurate, and held that anarchists have tended towards more complex and nuanced visions of humanity than given credit for (e.g., Marshall 1989; Morland 1997; Franks 2012). This chapter contributes to this challenge to reductive accounts of anarchist views of humanity, but does so with a focus on one aspect of anarchist perspectives that is generally overlooked. Essentialist views of human nature usually share an implicit characteristic in common: they are assertions regarding the singular quality (essence) that most represents the distinctiveness of humans in comparison to non-human animals. A peculiar feature, however, of at least some historic and contemporary anarchist thinkers, is that their conceptions of human nature are situated explicitly in the animal world, and are multi-faceted rather than singular accounts. These anarchists ask us to recognise the multi-faceted and variable expressions of our nature, and our similarity with other animals, drawing attention back to the inescapable fact of our embeddedness in the material natural world, and how that awareness might inform our ideas of, and approaches to changing, human social organisation.

While the question of the anarchist conception of human nature has in recent decades been re-invigorated by the development of 'postanarchism' and debates over the veracity of postanarchist claims about the essentialist constructs of 'classical' (i.e. nineteenth-century) anarchists, this debate has both limited and complicated a broader understanding of anarchist accounts of human nature. In both the critique of classical anarchism by postanarchists and the defence against those critiques, the scope of difference and disagreement in anarchist thought is often obscured.[1]

The anarchist perspective outlined here challenges the sense of linear development implied by the classical/post distinction, as this strain of anarchism existed in the classical era and has continued to exist and develop in anarchist theory and movements since. And while it also rejects humanist essentialism, that it does so by way of a focus on similarity rather than distinction with non-human nature also transcends the still anthropocentric humanist framework of poststructural discursive approaches. It therefore offers an anti-essentialist approach to radical politics that provides an alternative to both the simplistic essentialism of the standard image of classical anarchism and the approaches of postanarchists and other poststructural radical theories such as Ernesto Laclau and Chantal Mouffe's radical democratic theory (Laclau and Mouffe 1985).

This alternative standpoint sees human nature as irreducibly multi-faceted and situated within nature more broadly – within biological animal nature and the systems within which the animal world is in turn embedded. It therefore rejects the reductively mechanistic visions of nature, humans and evolution 'shaped by the Enlightenment narratives of emancipation, progress and rationalism'[2] (Newman 2015, 7) – which are attributed by postanarchists to all forms of anarchism (May 1994, 12, 95–96). Rather than seeing all of nature and humans' place within it as a single coherent machine that could be scientifically known and measured in its entirety, anarchists (even 'classical' anarchists) have tended towards interpretations that come closer to the contemporary view of nature as constellations of fluid, chaotic, inter-related and mutually influencing complex systems.[3]

This chapter outlines this alternative anarchist conception of human nature and nature more broadly, its alignment with contemporary scientific conceptions of the natural world, and the political implications therein. The chapter proceeds in four sections. The first introduces the standard treatment of anarchism in political theory, the debate over human nature in 'classical' and 'post' anarchisms, and the relation of this discourse to the largely unrecognised status of the particular anarchist perspective considered here, which we refer to as 'realist anarchism'. This anarchist perspective on humans and nature is realist not only in the sense that it accords with the disposition referred to as realism in political

[1] For more on this see: Cohn and Wilbur (2003).
[2] That this is a reductive simplification not only of anarchism, but also of the Enlightenment, is a larger issue that we must leave aside here.
[3] See e.g. Malatesta's 'Liberty and fatalism, determinism and will', in Malatesta (2014, 363).

theory,[4] but also in that it is largely confirmed by developments in scientific research in a variety of fields since the nineteenth century, such as particle physics, systems theory and evolutionary biology, and therefore arguably reflects a realistic, materialist understanding of existence beyond the human species.

The second section sketches an introductory outline of this realist anarchist perspective with particular focus on its approach to human nature and how this approach contrasts with other anarchist perspectives. In the third section we argue that the validity and realism of this perspective is reinforced by various developments in scientific understandings of humans and with complementary philosophical conceptions of the world in which we live, including ecology, systems theory and biosemiotics.

The fourth and final section considers the implications of this perspective for radical social and political action in the context of looming catastrophic climate change, and argues that it offers an anti-essentialist approach that resonates strongly with contemporary scientific understandings of both human and non-human nature.

CLASSICAL, POST AND REALIST ANARCHISMS

One of the most persistent elements of the standard representation of anarchism is that it is based on a naïve, optimistic and humanist vision of human nature as essentially good and co-operative (e.g., Adams 1993, 172; Gamble 1981, 109). Despite the fact that this perspective is not actually discernible on close reading of any influential anarchist thinkers (Franks 2011, 173), this reputation has been widespread enough to affect developments in anarchist theory. For instance, it forms the basis of the development of 'postanarchism' which claims to supplement and supersede 'classical anarchism' by correcting the latter's supposed essentialism with a poststructural anti-essentialist perspective (Newman 2001, 47–48; May 1994, 61–64).

It has been argued by many that the representations of classical anarchism upon which the postanarchist claim of novelty is based are either misreadings or misrepresentations (e.g., Cohn 2002; Franks 2011; 2012; Jun 2012; Swann 2010). Put simply, it is claimed that the postanarchist representation of classical anarchism, usually with reference to only a handful of theorists,[5] as wholly and uncritically committed to an essentialist, humanist view of human nature is incorrect, and that classical anarchists had a much more nuanced view of human nature than they are given credit for. So, for instance, Peter

4 We leave this aside here as it is addressed in detail elsewhere, see: Brinn (2020).

5 Usually a narrow 'canon' of three or four 'influential thinkers', Cohn and Wilbur (2003); Call (2002, 14); Newman (2015, 12–13); May 1994, 87.

Kropotkin is often put forward as the epitome of the classical anarchist who sees human nature as essentially cooperative and 'good' (e.g., Newman 2015, 6; Call 2002, 14). Critics of postanarchism then often argue that, despite the fact that there is indeed a spectrum of classical anarchist positions on human nature and that Kropotkin might be seen as one of those closest to the humanist representation, even he does not hold to the simplistic view postanarchists attribute to him (Swann 2010, 237, 241).

The value of such an approach is clear – if even the most supposedly essentialist anarchist is actually not so, then the postanarchist claims of anarchism as a wholly essentialist body of thought is clearly false. And the implication is also clear: if postanarchism is based on the claim that it advances anarchism by freeing it of assumptions that it does not in fact hold, then postanarchism adds nothing that was not already established in anarchist thought (Cohn 2002).

While the simplistic reduction of classical anarchism represented in postanarchism is unfortunate (and problematic for postanarchism), this particular mode of defence of classical anarchism also has some unintended implications. For instance, the claim that postanarchism adds nothing implicitly suggests that 'postanarchism is just anarchism' and that classical anarchists had already 'added' all that postanarchism could hope to. This position does disservice to the nuance and variety in anarchism in the classical era and since. It represents anarchism as 'a kind of postmodernism' (Jun 2012, xvi), which might be true in the sense that anarchists generally anticipate the poststructural critique of essentialist conceptions of human nature but obscures the fact that anarchists have generally taken this critique in very different directions; both compared to that of the poststructuralists, as well as from each other. In this sense the representation of anarchism as 'already post' also obscures the scope of disagreement on these issues amongst anarchists and, perhaps unintentionally, positions classical anarchism as a homogeneous collection that was merely a precursor of a political perspective that finds its full, coherent expression in poststructural philosophy.

Therefore, our aim here is not to retrace the debate over postanarchist claims regarding the view of human nature accepted within the problematic construct of 'classical anarchism', but instead to explicate a perspective within anarchist thought that disrupts this simplistic binary. While accepting that postanarchist claims do not accurately apply to any 'classical' anarchist theorist of the nineteenth century, we resist the homogenisation of the field and emphasise that it contained a variety of different perspectives on human nature. Though no classical anarchists are guilty of the charge of naïve, optimistic, essentialist humanism, some are more easily misinterpreted as such than others. Our focus then is on one of the perspectives in anarchism that is less easily mistaken or misread as based on a simplistic, essentialist conception of human nature. This strain of anarchism, while not a distinct school or movement such as anarcha-feminism, anarcho-syndicalism or eco-anarchism, is discernable in anarchist theory across eras and so is present in both classical and contemporary anarchism, further disturbing the assumptions of linear progression accepted by the classical/post binary.

Therefore, the existence of this 'realist' strain of anarchism demonstrates that classical anarchism is not unified and that there are anarchists who decisively reject an essentialist conception of human nature. But it also shows that this perspective has continued across eras and so is also an example of an anti-essentialist perspective that differs from, but exists and develops contemporaneously with (i.e. it is not superseded or made obsolete by), post-structural anti-essentialists. This perspective, as we will argue in the third section, goes further in its rejection of anthropocentric humanist essentialism than the discursive focus of poststructuralism and its political mobilisations in approaches such as postanarchism or the radical democratic theory of Laclau and Mouffe.

HUMAN NATURE IN REALIST ANARCHISM

While it is erroneous to charge classical anarchism with the essentialism generally attributed to it, some anarchists have taken particular effort to explicitly challenge both this impression and the tendency in anarchist thought that has, perhaps unwittingly, encouraged or perpetuated this interpretation. Kropotkin's friend and fellow anarchist theorist and militant Errico Malatesta expended much energy in his remarkably long political life challenging such views, or the appearance of them, in other anarchists. Despite their friendship the two often disagreed and Malatesta criticised those who 'luxuriated in that blessed Kropotkinian optimism' (Malatesta 2014, 453), decrying the 'evil effect' (*Ibid.*, 520) that he saw this perspective as having on the anarchist movement. This he saw particularly as the lack of critical preparedness that is encouraged by the view that revolution essentially consist of removing the fetters from humans' fundamentally natural altruistic cooperativeness, and the subsequent implication that there would be spontaneous resolution of all social problems 'on the morrow of the revolution'. Though Kropotkin believed that 'man [*sic*] is nothing but a resultant, always changeable, of all his diverse faculties' (Kropotkin 1993, 102), Malatesta argued that his work invited interpretation as wedded to an essentially cooperative and benign view of human nature. Malatesta found the influence of this interpretation of Kropotkin so pervasive in the anarchist movement that it was the primary element of his legacy criticised by Malatesta in the wake of his friend's death (Malatesta 2014, 511).

Malatesta's alternative casts any attempt to define human nature by a single essence or 'explain everything according to the same principle' (*Ibid.*, 514) as on the one hand an expression of the unrealistic idea that one person could 'comprehend the whole truth' (*Ibid.*, 511) of such complex issues, and on the other, patently contradicted by the 'terrible and murderous disharmonies' (*Ibid.*, 520) of human history – 'violence, wars, carnage (besides the ruthless exploitation of the labour of others) and innumerable tyrannies and slavery' (Malatesta 1965, 76). Such a 'simplistic notion of human nature' that attempted to reduce all to a single essence or historical drive could not account for 'love as well as hate, passions good and bad, the condition of women, ambition, jealousy, racial pride, any sort of relations between individuals and peoples, war and peace, mass submissiveness or rebelliousness, sundry forms of family and society, political regimes, religion, morality, literature, art, science' (Malatesta 2014, 445). Instead, it should be recognised that human nature is 'multi-faceted' (*Ibid.*, 41); that 'man [*sic*] is the product of physiological heredity and of his cosmic and social environment' (*Ibid.*, 53); and that

> between man and his social environment there is a reciprocal action. Men make society what it is and society makes men what they are, and the result is therefore a kind of vicious circle. To transform society men must be changed, and to transform men, society must be changed. (*Ibid.*, 284)

So rather than a single natural cooperative essence, for Malatesta, human nature includes both (at least) a 'harsh instinct of wanting to predominate and to profit at the expense of others' as well as 'another feeling' an 'anarchist impulse' to resist the imposition of coercive authority, and which draws us closer to each other and fosters cooperation: 'the feeling of sympathy, tolerance, of love' (Malatesta 1965, 74). Though this capacity for cooperation exists as but one capacity among many, with its ascendency over other traits by no means assured, Malatesta argues that our hopes for the future of humanity depend on the fact that it does *exist at all,* and as such can develop, and importantly, can either be encouraged or discouraged by the environment and social conditions in which we are implicated and embedded (*Ibid.*).

Malatesta is not alone in expounding such views on human nature. This perspective has continued to exist and develop across the various eras of anarchism since the classical era of the nineteenth century. It is discernible in twentieth-century anarchist thinkers such as Noam Chomsky (e.g., Chomsky 2015, 62) and Murray Bookchin (e.g.: Bookchin 1979, 27), among others,[6]

[6] For more see Marshall (1989).

as well as in contemporary anarchist thinkers such as David Graeber (e.g., Graeber 2011b, 71), and in existing anarchist movements.[7]

Like Malatesta, Chomsky's view is of a multi-faceted human nature that is grounded in a biological reality that is itself both changeable and a force for change. The anarchist impulse is not an essence that is the key to our 'true' selves, or which points to our 'natural' disposition or which is necessarily more influential than other impulses such as those towards competition, domination and voluntary servitude, or which can serve as a deterministic guide to social reorganisation, or which can be expected to simply flourish 'after the revolution', or indeed which will inevitably lead to revolutionary change. It is but one trait among many present in humans (Chomsky 1998).

Graeber similarly regards attempts to reduce human nature to a singular drive as unrealistically simplistic, and indeed sees the tendency to cast all human action between the poles of 'egoism and altruism' as an erasure of the complexity of human nature which reflects the influence of particular environments – the state and market – rather than any particularly important natural drives. Rather than traits which are 'natural' to humans in the sense that they are present across cultures and eras, in stateless, non-market–based societies, action on the basis of either pure greed or completely selfless generosity is vanishingly rare, often nonsensical according to the prevailing norms, and so many such cultures do not have terms to describe the concepts (Graeber 2011b, 71). As social species however, all human societies are made possible to an extent by various forms of small-scale informal cooperation so ubiquitous that they are usually taken for granted, but which Graeber sees as pointing to the potential of radically alternative social relations (Graeber 2011a, 96).

While Bookchin (tentatively) endorses a natural sociality in humans (Bookchin 1979, 21), he also argues that the tendency to see anarchism as based on a belief in '"natural man" and "instincts for mutual aid" [. . .] is to grossly misread anarchism as a historical movement' (*Ibid.*, 27) and to treat it (as postanarchists do) as an ahistorical philosophical discourse fully captured in the writings of a handful of individuals. Still, among influential anarchist theorists there do exist those such as Bookchin, Malatesta, Chomsky and Graeber who very explicitly reject a simplistic and overly optimistic naturalism that see humans as essentially good, cooperative, resistant to coercion and so on, recognise the complexity and multi-faceted nature of being-human, and do not reduce human essence to the anarchist impulse. All however take solace in the fact that this impulse does indeed *exist at all*, and that therefore,

7 See Gordon (2007, 65).

as we argue below, there can at least be some hope that it can be encouraged and serve in some ways to inform social and political organisation.

NATURE, HUMAN NATURE AND REALITY

The realist anarchist view of human nature then is one which relies on a universal biological base, but which is defined not in relation to one natural 'essence' or single most important element, but instead by its very variety of expression and by its capacity for adaptation, evolution and recursive plasticity. Here, Catherine Malabou's usage of the term 'plasticity' is particularly useful for situating the realist anarchist perspective on nature and humans. First we mean, following Malabou, 'the capacity to give, receive, and obliterate form' (Dalton 2019, 238), that is, its tendency to change its environment and susceptibility to influence and change itself (in response to environmental or social conditions or indeed to sudden change, as in the case of brain injury) in response to its environment. However, as Malabou notes, plasticity does not merely imply flexibility or elasticity – the ability to change shape and then return to the initial state – but instead connotes a recursive changeability (Malabou 2005, 9). That is, plasticity implies the capacity to respond, change, adapt to sometimes explosively destructive change, but it does not suggest a return to 'true form'. Something plastic can only ever change 'forwards' (Malabou 2012, 36). And so it is with realist anarchist conceptions of humans and nature. There is no idealised state of nature which we can recover or re-establish. We have changed our environment and ourselves to an almost inconceivable extent, and there is no ability to return to any original, foundational or essential state for either humans or our environment (Malatesta 2014, 110, 473; Chomsky 2015, 60–61; Bookchin 2015, 39–42, 133–134). We can however recognise in our dramatic transformations thus far a capacity which can be further applied in the future, with the past standing merely as evidence of potentialities which might be exercised in new circumstances and in new ways.

This is far from an essentialist view of a singular and immutable human nature, such as liberal perspectives that see the human 'essence' as rationality or our 'propensity to truck and barter' or the claim that anarchists see humans as naturally good or cooperative. For one, the realist anarchist perspective is not that of any singular element. As shown in the previous section it is instead a view of human nature as multi-faceted and variable. Realist anarchists are careful to avoid the suggestion that humans have any single most influential element, but emphasise the complexity and variability of expressions of 'human-ness', and especially our responsiveness to environment and conditions as well as the capacity to modify these.

However, there is arguably a more consequential difference between realist anarchist conceptions of human nature and standard essentialist accounts. One of the constant features of conceptions of human nature in political thought, from liberal accounts of our rational self-interest to Marxist views of creative production or optimistic anarchist images of humans as naturally altruistic, is their identification of that element that supposedly most clearly distinguishes humans from other animals. Therefore one of the distinctive qualities of realist anarchist conceptions of human nature is that it is focused on challenging rather than reinforcing the idea of human exceptionalism. In contemporary language it is an ecological account of human nature. In this sense, realist anarchism not only resists the humanism attributed to anarchism by postanarchists and other anti-essentialists, but also resists anthropocentrism – the claim of the existence of an anarchist impulse towards co-operation and against coercion is not defended on the basis that they are exclusively human qualities, but rather precisely on the grounds that they are not.

Kropotkin of course famously based his claims about mutual aid and its role in evolution on observations of various creatures – insects, birds, deer and wild horses, among others – in the harsh conditions of Siberia and Northern Asia (Kropotkin 2006 [1902]). Likewise, anarchists and frequently noted anarchistic philosophical precursors[8] often appeal to the existence of an anarchist impulse in non-human animals, and the fact that humans' animal nature explains or at least suggests the existence of the same tendency (e.g., Goldman 1911, 7). Indeed, this view of 'human nature' aligns closely with that of German theoretical biologist and biosemiotician Jacob von Uexküll (1864–1944), for whom a human (like any other animal) is 'a system embedded in the environment of other systems' (Uexküll in Favareau 2010, 279).

Biosemiotics seeks to 'explain how life evolves through all varieties of forms of communication and signification (including cellular adaptive behavior, animal communication, and human intellect)' (Kull et al. 2011, 167). It is an attempt to provide new philosophical foundations for a theoretical biology seeking to employ the explanatory benefits of taking semiotic interpretations of biological activity as *literal* rather than *metaphoric*. Indeed, it is very difficult to explain biological phenomenon without resorting to semiotic 'metaphors'. While we communicate largely (but not solely) through language, gesture and so on other living organisms might communicate largely through chemical messages, for example. In this view, signs are anything that *means* anything to or for an organism – whether speech, sunlight, a virus

[8] For example, on Taoist narratives situating humans' rejection of coercion and tendency towards cooperation in the context of similar impulses recognisable in wild animals, see, Marshall (2010, 54, 58).

or a chemical. We do not respond to veridical perceptions of 'reality' but to what an organism responds to as *meaningful* in their environment – whether it be biological, chemical, linguistic or otherwise. These interactions are often discussed by the use of communicative metaphors, 'cues', 'signals' and 'codes', for example (Kull et al. 2011, 170). However, when we take these same phenomena and insist that these identified sign relations are truly only metaphors, and not literal descriptions of interaction between elements, we find significant gaps in our conceptual models which leave us at a loss to explain what is actually occurring and how the processes these interactions underpin are possible.

To take them *literally* is both parsimonious and useful. First, it is parsimonious because it allows for realistic and coherent understanding of these processes without falling back on these metaphorical models and intuition-pumping proxy concepts to fill gaps in mechanistic conceptions of material reality. And second, it is useful in that it provides a scaffold for making sense of ourselves in the world released from the constraints of seeing ourselves as fundamentally different from the non-human world by our use of language and its presumed counterpart 'rationality'. Instead of language being understood as a 'higher-order' cognitive process that only humans are capable of, biosemiotics frames human language as one of many forms of sign relations that are integral to biological life. Taking a biosemiotic worldview seriously also allows us to make sense of many of the ways in which communication can go awry, and the ways in which 'rational', 'linguistic' humans can behave in ways so contrary to their own interests. Interpretation of signs in the non-linguistic world is just as open to misinterpretation as language – the consequences of such misinterpretation are called 'ecological' or 'evolutionary' traps (Schlaepfer et al. 2002). The evolutionary trap of artificial light ensnares a moth that has evolved to use light from the distant sources of the sun or moon for navigation – the signal is misinterpreted to the moth's detriment. We might similarly see the rapacious greed of the powerful of our species and the authoritarian political systems that protect them as kinds of evolutionary trap – as our drive towards maintaining sustenance and security gone awry.

While we are not claiming that most realist anarchists are adherents of a biosemiotic position on theoretical biology, or defending here that a biosemiotic view is ultimately correct, we can clearly see how these perspectives align, and how when combined we create a space for a non-anthropocentric, naturalised conception of our context and responsibility in a more-than-human world. Human exceptionalists argue that some human quality not present in other animals is that essence which makes humanity the particular and unique species of animal that is apparently clearly and obviously apart from the rest. Realist anarchists instead emphasise the qualities that humans share with non-human animals thereby rejecting the dogma of human exceptionalism, and the biosemiotic point of view is in line with this perspective on interrelationality and cooperation in non-human or 'more-than-human' systems.

This naturalist tendency to situate humans as animals, and to draw attention to similarities rather than differences with non-human animals, might be considered as problematic and 'idealist' as humanist essentialism. However what this criticism misses is that this framing explicitly situates humans within a complex, interrelated and inescapable material reality that forms the basis of existence. What realist anarchism offers that is absent from both essentialist humanism and anti-essentialist, discourse-focused approaches is recognition of the unrealistic nature of abstract considerations of the exceptionalism of humans disconnected from their existence in a material environment and in relation to a multitude of non-human entities. Both approaches are purely anthropocentric and problematically 'humanist' in their abstract and disconnected focus on humans, regardless of whether this is a biologically or discursively essentialist focus.

The anarchist impulse towards cooperation then is not a unique feature of human nature but instead a quality that we share with other non-human animals, and which is sometimes even present between species.[9] In this sense the realist anarchist image of humans is even less humanist than anti-essentialist discursive approaches to human identity as it is not limited to the implicit anthropocentric contexts than the utterly anthropocentric focus on human language and discursive forms of communication.

Anarchism's opposition to all forms of domination has inevitably tended towards a facilitation of numerous strains and sub-tendencies. Despite the common contemporary inclination towards seeing nineteenth-century anarchism as a workers' movement and downplaying more 'lifestylist' expressions, 'anarcho-naturism', vegetarianism, spirituality and so on has been a continuous presence throughout anarchist history.[10] Early anarchist movements included those that extended the critique of domination to non-human relations and so advocated vegetarianism and forms of ecologically sensitive social organisation and food production. These perspectives derive from the recursive application of the anarchist principle to various previously unconsidered forms of domination, and from the view of humans as 'still an animal' (Malatesta 2014, 38), and inescapably embedded in myriad natural systems (Springer 2016, 6). The work of renowned French geographer and anarchist Élisée Reclus is particularly influential in this area, and is considered by some

[9] For an example of altruistic cooperation between species see Pitman et al. (2017).

[10] According to Bookchin, worker-based anarchism is an historical 'meandering' and these perspectives are actually anarchism's 'true home' (2015, 134), the return to which he perceived in the anti-civilisational tendencies in late twentieth-century U.S. anarchism, and which so chagrined him that he eventually rejected the label 'anarchist' as a form of disassociation. See Bookchin (1995) and Biehl (2015, 300–302).

a precursor to modern ecology, bioregionalism and systems theory (Clark, 8; Marshall 2010, 344; Springer 2016, 47–48; Toro 2017, 92–93). Like von Uexküll, Reclus believed that every aspect of nature, including humans and their systems, are interconnected and that 'it is only through an act of pure abstraction that one can contrive to present a particular aspect of the environment as if it had a distinct existence, and strive to isolate it from all the others, in order to study its essential influence' (Reclus cited in Springer 2016, 48). Reclus also saw the process of social change as one of both evolution and revolution, or in the contemporary language used to describe change in complex systems, of linear, predictable change punctuated by sudden unpredictable non-linear events of upheaval (Marshall 2010, 344; Toro 2017, 92). Similarly, when considering the possibilities of radical social change realist anarchists seek to understand humans as entities within a vast and complex inter-woven and inter-related process of life, its evolution and revolutions.

As Graeber notes, philosophers have long resisted situating humans within the animal world (Graeber 2014). Philosophers of consciousness (and evolutionary biologists) are often content to assert that all animals but humans are essentially automatons mindlessly pursuing naked self-interest and the competitive propagation of their genes. Such a perspective is so ingrained in the hegemonic worldview that any other approach is widely considered plainly unscientific (Graeber 2014). But when attempting to explain the supposedly unique existence of human consciousness the very assumptions of human nature underpinning their search – especially the rational, calculation of self-interest and advantage – precludes recognition of the very attributes that unite humans and other animals, and possibly all other levels of life. Those seeking the answer to the 'hard problem of consciousness' (Why are we aware of anything at all, rather than it all going on 'in the dark'?) are left to either assert that it emerges by a kind of magic present only in humans or to accept that the process that produces the 'I' behind our eyes is not that different to those that lead to the formation of systems and entities from the interaction of particles through the organisation of plants, insects and animals, including humans.[11] From this perspective cooperation and communication are present at the very foundation of material reality, and the important task is not to explain or defend the existence of cooperation, but to understand how we have devised a form of social organisation so in conflict with this basic quality of material systems, and how, given that, how we might change course.

For Graeber, one cause for hope is that, despite the fact that we have constructed a world ostensibly driven by cutthroat self-interest, it is impossible to

[11] This perspective is also resonant with contemporary accounts explaining the organisation of particles at a quantum level, see Conway and Kochen (2009).

eradicate the cooperation, or 'everyday communism'[12] that is woven through the entirety of human social existence, and underpins, to an extent, all collective action. From giving directions or holding an elevator for a stranger; helping a person who is drowning, or has fallen on train tracks; to the remarkable spontaneous cooperation that often emerges in disasters such as floods or economic collapse, there is a basic assumed cooperativeness in human relations without which society, or indeed any collective activity, could hardly function. In the absence of overt hostility between parties, if the need is great enough or the request reasonable enough then the maxim 'from each according to their ability, to each according to their need' will be assumed to apply. And regardless of the common rhetoric that communism 'just doesn't work' the 'scandal of capitalism' is that this principle is so 'immanent in everyday life' that it is still the basis of action even in the most competitive, capitalist enterprises – 'if someone fixing a water pipe says "hand me the wrench" their co-worker will not usually say "and what do I get for it", even if they work for Exxon-Mobil' (Graeber 2011a, 95–96). Even in the military-style top-down chains of command of corporate capitalism, 'if you want to get something done, allocating tasks by ability, and giving people what they need to do the job, is the most effective way to go about it' (Graeber 2011a, 96). Of course the extent to which the principle applies is dependent on context – in small societies and within close-knit groups it can apply to almost anything, and in larger, more impersonal cultures it may not extend much further between strangers than directions or a cigarette or a hand in an emergency, but while 'this might not seem like much [. . .] it founds the possibility of larger social relations' (Graeber 2011a, 98).

REALIST RADICAL POLITICS AND THE THREAT OF EXTINCTION

Radical politics continues to be primarily founded on either essentialist (or quasi-essentialist) or discursive anti-essentialist, accounts of humanity, both of which reproduce the 'antibiological bias' in contemporary philosophy which asserts 'the primacy of symbolic life over biological life' (Malabou 2016, 431). This abstraction and disconnectedness from biological and environmental conditions, which dominates the logic of political philosophy, implicitly ignores our embeddedness in myriad complex natural systems (as well as the existence, and thus ethical relevance, of non-human forms of life).

---

[12] Graeber somewhat provocatively uses the term 'communism' to refer to any situation, even between only two people, where the principle 'from each according with their ability, to each according to their need' is applied. See Graeber (2011a, 94).

While the legacy of classical nineteenth-century radical political theory still has a significant and influential presence in contemporary radical thought and movements, the other most prevalent radical perspectives in the contemporary radical milieu are those broadly founded on a poststructuralist base. Advocates of radical democratic agonism, autonomism and various subtypes of 'postanarchism' all implicitly reproduce the binary image of radical thought as either simplistically essentialist, or anti-essentialist from a discursive, poststructuralist perspective. Both of the still dominant perspectives on radical politics are based, therefore, on views of humans and nature that do not reflect the intricate complexity represented in contemporary understandings of humans and nature and their inter- and intra-relations. Realist anarchism however offers an alternative perspective that is non-essentialist but grounded in a conscious recognition of our biological, ecological, climatological and social material realities in a way that escapes the disconnected transcendental standpoint of abstract idealistic humanism which still characterises both essentialist and discursive approaches. In doing so, it is what we might call an *ecological* account of human and non-human nature, that takes sign relations and as such, communication in its many forms, as fundamental to, rather than in opposition to, understanding ourselves biologically, and thus ecologically.

Humans have changed our environment and ourselves to the point where we are threatening our own survival (as well as the survival of much else). We can no longer afford to treat our environment as a generally ignored 'background'. Nor can we see human or non-human nature as 'stable'. The conceit that radical political thought and action could be based on visions of an essentially unchanging human in a timeless landscape that do not centre our embeddedness in and reliance on non-human nature, whether a timeless essentialist or a floating, disconnected discourse-based approach, is, in the shadow of looming catastrophic climate change, a disastrously myopic and defiantly self-indulgent separation of ourselves from material reality. Malabou notes that the challenge of the Anthropocene 'necessitates a study of the profound interaction between the sociological and the ecological, understanding them as parts of the same metabolism' (Malabou 2017, 39). This is what an ecological, biosemiotically informed realist anarchism allows us to do; in a manner which escapes the disconnectedness of exceptionalist approaches, and which situates human potential for cooperative social reorganisation in embeddedness in a natural material environment that is complex, contingent and plastic in both wonderful and devastating ways.

The extent to which humans have reshaped our material and social environments, and in turn ourselves, evidenced by the scale of threat posed by catastrophic climate change suggests a truly incredible capacity for plastic mutation. Indeed, from the perspective that sees interpretation of sign relations as meaningful for everything from self-organising biological and ecological systems to the coherence of matter on a sub-atomic level, it represents a hubristic attempt to defy (for a time at least) the underlying logic of existence.

We are multi-faceted and plastic to the extent that we have created a society based on ruthless competition not only with each other but also with the environmental systems that make our existence possible, and more, some of us have convinced ourselves that this is in harmony with the driving force of the universe. Even discussions that seek to push against this prevalence and centre co-operation, for instance sympathetic treatments of Kropotkin's contributions to evolutionary biology, often reinforce the idea that ruthless, self-interested competition is the norm and mutualism, cooperation and 'altruism' are the aberrations in need of explanation. Both tendencies of course exist, but if we alter our view to recognise the prevalence of systems of cooperation and communication at every level then our ruthless competitiveness becomes somewhat exceptional. Just as the anarchist impulse is a standing challenge to all impositions of authority, coercion and control, a permanent stance of scepticism towards power, so too is it an acceptance of the reality, possibility and desirability of cooperation and mutual aid, and suspicion of self-interested competition.

The attempt to reduce the complexity of material and social reality to the outcomes of a single drive is unrealistic and obfuscatory. Cooperation exists. And competition exists. But some form of cooperation, broadly conceived, appears to be a precondition for the existence of life and even matter itself. Cooperation and communication, broadly conceived, are mutually dependent at every plane of existence (between atoms, neurons, trees, people) without which we need 'magical' theories to explain how we could exist at all. Without some, even rudimentary forms of communicative cooperation and cooperative communication, neither collective organisation or self-organising systems could exist and humanity must be positioned alone in a dead universe, an aberration from all existence. Cooperation's very existence need not be continually defended with the implicit assumption that ruthless self-interest is the norm. Recognising the presence of both, and many other factors as aspects of human 'nature' that can be cultivated and repressed, human-created systems that are based on competition and self-interest should be viewed with suspicion – they are not the default position, the natural order of things, they are contingent like all other systems of human organisation and as such they are never self-justifying. For the realist anarchist, like power or authority they must be presumed illegitimate unless proven otherwise with overwhelming evidence. If they cannot meet this challenge such systems should be dismantled and, if they serve some genuine need, replaced with systems which can mobilise and reinforce – that is, which can be shaped by and in turn shape in their participants – the potential for organised cooperation and mutual aid that humans share with much of non-human nature.

All this is not to say of course that cooperation is *the single most* fundamental drive, as that would be to assert its singular 'essential' status underlying all others as the 'essence' of existence. Cooperation broadly construed exists as but one fundamental and necessary drive across all levels of existence. However, merely to affirm its existence as one fundamental drive among many, as we do here, goes counter to the practically inescapably dominant perspective that situates cooperation as aberration and even then usually as the expression of some underlying competitive self-interest. It is to assert, as with the realist anarchist conception of human nature, that nature is multi-faceted and complex, that both cooperation and competition exist, and that our frameworks that situate ruthless self-interest as the default should be viewed with suspicion. Cooperation is not a rare aberration in a universe otherwise completely driven by ruthless self-interest. As Kropotkin puts it, it is 'A Factor of Evolution' – it is another fundamental drive discernible at every level of existence that we perceive.

The existence of the capacity for cooperation provides ground for some hope in the eco-precarious situation in which we and other species find ourselves. There appears in us, as in all life and arguably much of material non-living existence, the capacity for cooperation. In a sense it is natural, but not in the sense that it will 'win out in the end' in the ways that we might wish. Success is not guaranteed – we can destroy ourselves despite the anarchist impulse. Both our malleability and plasticity can provide impetus for radical change but are also the basis of the threat we face. Our ability to create a problem does not entail our ability to overcome it – this is the threat of plasticity – and catastrophic failure is a real and looming possibility. To centre the issue of climate change in radical strategy we must recognise our embeddedness in natural material reality – a world in which all actions are communicative and as such have consequences, whether 'good' or 'bad' for us or others.

In addition to changing our institutions in order to shape ourselves towards a species and society more cooperative with each other as well as the natural systems upon which our existence depends, taking seriously the threat of catastrophic climate change would also entail recognition that we, like many if not most species currently on this planet, face the very real threat of extinction. And while we of course should endeavour to survive, actually taking the issue seriously would mean also accepting the real possibility of failure, and considering how we might respond to that possibility. However, if it is true, as some argue (e.g., Bendell 2018), that it is already too late to prevent the collapse of human civilisation and possibly the extinction of our species (and countless others), then the need for radical change might be seen as driven as much by the desire to influence how we die as how we live.

The real threat of extinction, much like a potentially terminal diagnosis, can of course provoke various responses, from a turn to desperate denial and extreme, high-risk attempts at survival, or nihilistic hedonism, or perhaps a reasonable pursuit of treatment while putting one's affairs in order and preparing and acting with a view to prioritising a good death. Existence is not just about survival – on an individual level a good death might entail, among other things, the attempt to make amends and heal fractured relationships in order that the person might be able to die well and that their departure itself was not the cause of more ongoing trauma and damage to those left behind. A realist anarchist approach informed by a perspective which accepts the possibility of a capacity for communication and cooperation at all levels of existence and that seeks to mobilise and make use of our plastic adaptability to shape ourselves and our environment towards sustainable, cooperative relations with each other and our environment, must also recognise that such a task has an ethical imperative – it is not something worth undertaking only in order to have some chance at survival but regardless of whether it leads to our survival or not. Humans have had an immeasurable impact on survivability on this planet, for ourselves and for all other living species and systems with which we share this state of 'eco-precarity'. Human systems based on competition and unfettered self-interest – both on an individual and species level – have such deep and wide reach and impact that they are capable of continuing their destructive effects long after our departure.

CONCLUSION

There is of course no reason to believe that cooperation will 'win out in the end' – the existence of the anarchist impulse does not guarantee that it must overcome other (competitive, coercive or destructive) impulses. The fact that human systems of competitive self-interest are so pervasive that they threaten to destroy much of the life on this planet suggests that we can resist the anarchist impulse and reinforce others to the point of our own destruction. However, our creation of such systems that so comprehensively constrain cooperation and drive us towards certain impulses over others, points towards a remarkable capacity in humans for plasticity, in this case, in potentially catastrophic way.

To have a chance of survival it is this capacity to shape and be shaped by our environment that we must mobilise in order to create systems and institutions which encourage and guide us towards cooperative sustainable relationships with each other and the natural systems upon which we rely. But even if it is already too late to secure our survival, establishing such relationships might still be seen as imperative if we are to reduce the chances that our departure in itself would continue and even exacerbate the destruction to other life that we have set in motion, and is perhaps the minimum requirement for us to exit with dignity and salvage some self-respect as a species.

BIBLIOGRAPHY

Adams, Ian. 1993. *Political Ideology Today*. Manchester: Manchester University Press.

Bendell, Jem. 2018. "Deep Adaptation: A Map for Navigating Climate Tragedy." *Institute For Leadership And Sustainability*, Occasional Papers Volume 2. http://www.lifeworth.com/deepadaptation.pdf, accessed on 27th April, 2021.

Biehl, Janet. 2015. *Ecology or Catastrophe: The Life of Murray Bookchin*. New York: Oxford University Press.

Bookchin, Murray. 1979. "Anarchism: Past and Present." In *Reinventing Anarchy, Again*, edited by H. J. Ehrlich, 19–30. San Francisco: AK Press.

Bookchin, Murray. 1995. *Social Anarchism or Lifestyle Anarchism: An Unbridgeable Chasm*. Oakland: AK Press.

Bookchin, Murray. 2015. *The Next Revolution: Popular Assemblies and the Promise of Direct Democracy*. New York: Verso Books.

Brinn, Gearóid. 2020. "Smashing the State Gently: Radical Realism and Realist Anarchism." *European Journal of Political Theory* 19(2): 206–227.

Call, Lewis. 2002. *Postmodern Anarchism*. Lanham: Lexington Books.

Chomsky, Noam. 1998. "On Human Nature." Interview by Kate Soper. *Red Pepper*, August 1998. https://chomsky.info/199808, accessed on 27th April, 2021.

Chomsky, Noam. 2015. *What Kind of Creatures Are We?* New York: Columbia University Press.

Clark, John. 1997. "The Dialectical Social Geography of Elisée Reclus." *Philosophy and Geography* 1: 117–142.

Cohn, Jesse. 2002. "What is Postanarchism 'Post'?" *Postmodern Culture* 13(1). http://doi.org/10.1353/pmc.2002.

Cohn, Jesse, and Shawn Wilbur. 2003. "What's Wrong with Postanarchism?" *The Anarchist Library* [online]. http://theanarchistlibrary.org/library/jesse-cohn-and-shawn-wilbur-what-s-wrong-with-postanarchism.

Conway, John H., and Simon Kochen. 2009. "The Strong Free Will Theorem." *Notices of the AMS* 56(2): 226–232.

Dalton, Benjamin. 2019. "What Should We Do with Plasticity? An Interview with Catherine Malabou." *Paragraph* 42(2): 238–254.

Favareau, Donald. 2010. *Essential Readings in Biosemiotics: Anthology and Commentary*. Dordrecht: Springer.

Franks, Benjamin. 2011. "Post-Anarchism: A Partial Account." In *Post-Anarchism: A Reader*, edited by Duane Rousselle and Süreyyya Evren, 168–180. London and New York: Pluto Press.

Franks, Benjamin. 2012. "Anarchism and Analytic Philosophy." In *The Continuum Companion to Anarchism*, edited by R. Kinna, 140–161. New York: Continuum.
Gamble, Andrew. 1981. *An Introduction to Modern Social and Political Thought*. London: Macmillan.
Goldman, Emma. 1911. *Anarchism: What It Really Stands for*. New York: Mother Earth Publishing Association.
Gordon, Uri. 2007. *Anarchism and Political Theory: Contemporary Problems*. PhD Thesis, University of Oxford.
Graeber, David. 2011a. *Debt: The First 5,000 Years*. New York: Melville House.
Graeber, David. 2011b. *Revolutions in Reverse: Essays on Politics, Violence, Art and Imagination*. New York: Autonomedia.
Graeber, David. 2014. "What's the Point If We Can't Have Fun?" *The Baffler* 24: 50–58.
Jun, Nathan. 2012. *Anarchism and Political Modernity*. New York: Continuum.
Kropotkin, Peter, 1993. *Fugitive Writings*. Montréal: Black Rose Books.
Kropotkin, Peter, 2006 [1902]. *Mutual Aid: A Factor of Evolution*. Mineola, NY: Dover.
Kull, Kalevi, Terrence Deacon, Claus Emmeche, Jesper Hoffmeyer, and Frederik Stjernfelt. 2011. "Theses on Biosemiotics: Prolegomena to a Theoretical Biology." In *Towards a Semiotic Biology: Life Is the Action of Signs*, edited by Clause Emmeche and Kaveli Kull, 25–41. Singapore: World Scientific.
Laclau, Ernesto, and Chantal Mouffe. 1985. *Hegemony and Socialist Strategy: Towards a Radical Democratic Politics*. London and New York: Verso.
Malabou, Catherine. 2005. *The Future of Hegel: Plasticity, Temporality, and Dialectic*. London: Routledge.
Malabou, Catherine. 2012. *Ontology of the Accident: An Essay on Destructive Plasticity*. Cambridge: Polity Press.
Malabou, Catherine. 2016. "One Life Only: Biological Resistance, Political Resistance." *Critical Inquiry* 42(3): 429–438.
Malabou, Catherine. 2017. "The Brain of History, or, The Mentality of the Anthropocene." *South Atlantic Quarterly* 116(1): 39–53.
Malatesta, Errico. 2014. *The Method of Freedom: An Errico Malatesta Reader*. Oakland: AK Press.
Marshall, Peter. 1989. "Human Nature and Anarchism." In *For Anarchism: History, Theory, and Practice*, edited by David Goodway. London: Routledge.
Marshall, Peter. 2010. *Demanding the Impossible: A History of Anarchism*. 4th ed. Oakland: PM Press.
May, Todd. 1994. *The Political Theory of Poststructualist Anarchism*. University Park, PA: Pennsylvania State University Press.
Morland, David, 1997. *Demanding the Impossible?: Human Nature and Politics in Nineteenth-century Social Anarchism*. London: Cassell.
Newman, Saul. 2001. *From Bakunin to Lacan: Anti-authoritarianism and the Dislocation of Power*. Plymouth: Lexington Books.
Newman, Saul, 2015. *Postanarchism*. Cambridge: Polity Press.

Pitman, Robert L., Volker B. Deecke, Christine M. Gabriele, Mridula Srinivasan, Nancy Black, Judith Denkinger, John W. Durban, Elizabeth A. Mathews, Dena R. Matkin, and Janet L. Neilson. 2017. "Humpback Whales Interfering When Mammal-eating Killer Whales Attack Other Species: Mobbing Behavior and Interspecific Altruism?" *Marine Mammal Science* 33(1): 7–58.

Schlaepfer, Martin A., Michael C. Runge, and Paul W. Sherman. 2002. "Ecological and Evolutionary Traps." *Trends in Ecology & Evolution* 17(10): 474–480.

Springer, Simon. 2016. *The Anarchist Roots of Geography: Toward Spatial Emancipation*. Minneapolis: University of Minnesota Press.

Swann, Thomas. 2010. "Are Postanarchists Right to Call Classical Anarchists 'Humanist'?" In *Anarchism and Moral Philosophy*, edited by Benjamin Franks and Matthew Wilson, 226–242. Basingstoke: Palgrave Macmillan.

Toro, Francisco. 2017. "The Thought of Élisée Reclus as an Inspiration for Degrowth Ethos." In *Historical Geographies of Anarchism: Early Critical Geographers and Present-Day Scientific Challenges*, edited by Federico Ferretti et al., 89–112. London: Taylor & Francis.

Chapter 9

Mutual Aid Armature

Plasticity All the Way Down

Eugene Kuchinov

The works of Peter Kropotkin, undoubtedly one of the most famous and powerful theorists of mutual aid, are today in the grip of a double (mis)reading: one critical and one conservative. The first exposes him as an essentialist and rejects him on that basis, the second presents him as a thinker whose ideas can be used without radical reworking. Both readings take Kropotkin for granted, overlooking the tension of his ideas. In this chapter, I try to unleash mutual aid by freeing Kropotkin from this grip and (re)reading him, first, from the anarchist position of the utilisation of the history of philosophy through the maximal modification proposed by Gilles Deleuze, and second, by orienting Kropotkin's ideas towards ontological extremes of plasticity, rebellion and animation. Ultimately, I intend to view mutual aid as a panpsychistic armature that unfolds all the way down, traversing the orders of organic and non-organic life.

UNRECOGNIZABLE KROPOTKIN

As a tribute to an influential researcher who left this world unexpectedly, let's start with a small quote. In their Introduction to the forthcoming edition of *Mutual Aid: An Illuminated Factor of Evolution* David Graeber and Andrej Grubačić write that Kropotkin's book is that rare case when an 'argument against reigning political common sense presents such a shock to the system that it becomes necessary to create an entire body of theory to refute it'. The depth of the *shock* caused by Kropotkin's challenge is due to the fact that

I would like to express my sincere gratitude to Jesse Cohn for his responsiveness and help in working on the manuscript, and Immanuel Kant Baltic Federal University for support.

'it's not just about the nature of government, but the nature of nature – that is, reality – itself' (Graeber and Grubačić 2020). Several important points can be noted here. First, it is the radicalism and novelty of Kropotkin's thought, which literally *forces* us to think. This radicalism and novelty cause shock, the depth of which is proportional to how deeply the object under study lies. Second, one consequence of shock is idle chatter about the 'radical object': the creation of special theories to explain it away or simply reject it. But there is also a danger here: the discourse of someone who fully supports a radical theory, *recognises* himself in it and finds in it the answer to his own questions and a guide to action can become the most insidious form of idle chatter. Kropotkin shocks (our) 'enemies', but not us, he is our friend, he is on our side. If we adhere to this opinion, we are protected from shock, Kropotkin does not threaten us with anything. But if so, then we lose a chance to *encounter* him, he becomes an 'object of recognition'. Let us listen to Deleuze: 'Something in the world forces us to think. This something is an object not of recognition but of a fundamental encounter. What is encountered may be Socrates, a temple or a demon' (Deleuze 1997, 139). A little further, he writes that an object of a fundamental encounter cannot be a friend. Can Kropotkin take the place of Socrates here, can he become a demon? For Kropotkin to become a demon that dodges both enemies and friends, he must be driven to the *extreme*. So the line that runs through these three points will be one of pushing to extremes and will form the guiding thread of our study of mutual aid. We must retain or rediscover the radical, shocking nature of this concept, bearing in mind that the only way to save it from idle chatter is an approach that makes it even *more radical*. Perhaps – and it is necessary to be ready for this – Kropotkin will appear before us as an unrecognisable monster, as one who will force us to think. 'Thinking' here ceases to coincide with 'recognition', becoming its complete opposite. We will try to develop the most radical aspects of his thought – to develop so much that Kropotkin himself, perhaps, would not recognise himself in them. Unlike Graeber and Grubačić, I will look at Kropotkin not in the usual context of social theory, but in the context of speculative ontology. To do this, we need to find the ontological *vector* of his thoughts (and try to draw it further than Kropotkin did), as well as find explosive ontological *details* in his writings (and try to detonate them). Let's call this direction a speculative unchaining of mutual aid.

Considering mutual aid as plastic *armature* (Kropotkin himself often refers to mutual aid using the word 'arm' – a weapon, a tool, an organ – so, a split-level set of tools and movable units constitutes mutual aid armature), we will take it to its *extreme* forms – *all the way down*. The term 'extremity' (or extreme forms) is borrowed from Deleuze's dictionary, where it indicates novelty, metamorphosis and even orgiasticity, and is opposed to *average* forms (stable organic identities and representations) (Deleuze 1997, 42).

In philosophical use, the notion of armature is often associated with extreme formality, but in Deleuze's vocabulary, extreme formality is used 'only for an excessive formlessness', and the formless is 'the product of the most extreme formality' (Deleuze 1997, 91 and 115). Extreme formality does not coincide with either rigidity or flexibility; it is rather plastic. Roughly the same can be said about armature, the concept of which could combine in itself both mobility (in electrical engineering) and hardness of the frame (in sculpture), both the outer and the inner; and – unlike ('structuralist') scaffolding – armature is inseparable from elements that it binds. So with these conceptual tools we intend to follow Catherine Malabou's call for ontological, biological and discursive unchaining through plasticity, which 'is the plastic explosive that destroys both the essence and the floating signifier. It breaks the chains' (Malabou 2021, 25).

THE NATURE OF NATURE ITSELF

The concept that contains the greatest ontological charge in Kropotkin is the concept of *Nature*. Despite the warnings of Kropotkin himself, who called for avoiding the optimistic (Rousseau) and pessimistic (Hobbes) extremes in its understanding, insisting on realism, in which neither of these two extremes has a decisive voice, it is the Rousseauian note that predominates in the reading of this concept. To answer the question, what is the 'nature of nature', Kropotkin offers several methodological orientations. Note that these orientations do not imply a middle way – between the extremes of optimism and pessimism – to achieve the *average form* of realism. Rather, the optimistic and pessimistic poles of nature are only half-hearted extremes, while nature itself is the total *extremity* for Kropotkin. Heading towards the nature of nature itself, Kropotkin seeks not a calm ontological h(e)aven, but a mobile insurgent ground from which irreconcilability and rebellion grow.

Orientation 1. Unity in Plurality (Extremum of Plasticity)

Kropotkin assumes that his ideas are obvious 'to a mind accustomed to the idea of unity in nature' (Kropotkin 2018, 49). The principle of natural *unity in plurality*, which he probably borrowed from Alexander Humboldt, is guiding for him. He constantly insists that there is nothing supernatural that could intervene in the course of natural processes from the outside, break or disrupt them, introducing into nature what is absent in it. There is nothing external to nature – nothing above, nothing below (and there is no *other* nature). This means that all possible oppositions, among which the most important for Kropotkin is the opposition of life and death, are revealed inside nature – as its ossifications and as explosions of these ossifications. It should be noted that opposition here does not mean a sharp negative confrontation, but presupposes a gradient of differences in the degree of 'naturalness', the scope and extent of which we penetrate when we 'ask Nature' and listen to its 'voice' (Kropotkin 2018, 11 and 48).[1] Differences are differently communicated among themselves, building among themselves a dynamic resulting unity. It is also important to understand that Kropotkin thinks of difference itself as growth, as positivity. In short, nature itself produces its own distinctive *excess*, the excess of excess of excess and so on. Nature abounds in its own variations. That is why Kropotkin can say: 'Nature is variety itself, offering all possible varieties of characters, from the basest to the highest' (Kropotkin 2018, 27). It is precisely the gradient of gradual growth that escapes our attention here, the fact that nature differs from itself to a superlative degree, but without a negative gap, without a 'war'.

The presentation of nature as permanent war is the result of an aberration of research optics (in a sense, it is a delusion of nature itself). Speaking about the distorted logic of describing the development of human societies, Kropotkin notes: 'all historical documents bear the same character; they deal with breaches of peace, not with peace itself'. This verdict is also true for the description of prehistoric natural life, in which 'the bright and sunny days are lost sight of in the gales and storms' (Kropotkin 2018, 70). When Kropotkin points out the invisibility of nature and the inaudibility of its voice, he ascribes to it the properties of a background that is not noticeable behind the figures. Together with Heraclitus, he could have observed: nature loves to hide; and specified: to hide behind figures of breaches. We can detect two such figures. On the one hand, the natural disaster, an explosive unforeseen (or creeping) change in the background, calling into question the sociability of individuals, this is a *macrofigure* of breach. On the other hand, an individual, especially as an isolated life, is an exemplary *microfigure* of breach. Isolated individuals appear in breaches of peace, filling them with themselves, appearing as the debris of such breaches. These fragments are characterised by the uncertainty of the future, the presence of the question of future sociability, which (1) can be restored in its previous form, (2) can persist in crystallisation and solidification of the decay state – or (3) can be reinvented in a new form. At this point, two categories are important for Kropotkin – memory and initiation. Memory without initiation gives the first outcome (preservation, repetition of a form before the catastrophe), initiation without memory gives the second

[1] However, the word 'voice' is absent in the English-language original, only 'the watchword' appears there. The 'voice' (голос) appears in the Russian translation by V. P. Baturinsky, published in 1907 under the editorship of Kropotkin, who 'took advantage of this to thoroughly revise the entire text, correct minor errors'.

outcome (repetition of the catastrophe itself, but by means of *sociability as such*), reciprocity of memory and initiation gives the third outcome (repetition as a new form of sociability).

This scheme is suitable both for describing 'a migration of fallow-deer [. . .] during which scores of thousands of these intelligent animals came together from an immense territory, flying before the coming deep snow', and for 'the great migrations of barbarians which put an end to the West Roman Empire' (Kropotkin 2018, 2, 70–71). In both the first and second cases we are talking about a certain movement of nature itself – at different levels. The principle of the unity of nature is ensured by the principle of sociability, which, like nature, loves to hide, coinciding with nature as the background. The nature of nature itself is sociability, we might say. Why? In a speculative preface to *Anarchism: Its Philosophy and Ideal* Kropotkin makes it clear: because the unity of nature is not just a unity *in* plurality, but it is a unity *of* plurality itself, in which 'the center, the origin of force [. . .] turns out to be scattered and disseminated: it is everywhere and nowhere'. Unity is only 'a resultant of all these numberless movements uniting, completing, equilibrating one another' (Kropotkin 1897, 3). Therefore, the new conditions of nature (or nature as becoming) cannot be grasped individually – and in an individual form. Unity (in and of) nature is grasped and held only collectively and in the reciprocity of its elements. To emphasise the non-essentialist improvisational character of this unity, I have to add that grasping and holding are indistinguishable from invention here.

It may seem that now we are running ahead (this haste will be justified later): I would immediately like, using the key concept of Catherine Malabou, to declare the *plasticity* of this natural unity, which is 'situated between two extremes: on the one side the sensible image of taking form [. . .], and on the other side that of the annihilation of all form' (Malabou 2008, 5). Unity (in and of) nature is the unity (in and of) plasticity. Indeed, we can consider unity as a repetitive excess of nature over nature in different forms, as being fraught with the future that free themselves in explosions and freeze in crystallisations. It can be said with all certainty and confirmed by many of Kropotkin's examples that the plastic nature 'explodes its own reserves [. . . in . . .] a process of formation and of the dissolution of form' (Malabou 2005, 186). Perhaps, the plasticity of natural unity is best reflected in the following orientation.

Orientation 2. Free Nature (Extremum of Rebellion)

This is a common thread running through *Mutual Aid* and many other works of Kropotkin: the need to turn to 'free' nature, to 'the life [. . .] (at liberty)', to consider evolutionary processes 'in the face of free Nature' (Kropotkin

2018, 15 and 32). Nature itself should be unchained by those who turn to it. However, what makes nature unfree, what fetters it? On the surface lies an answer about 'laboratories and museums' (Kropotkin 2018, 11), in which the debris of nature are violently isolated as fragments of a catastrophe originating from human intervention. Such isolation reproduces the forms of political metaphysics which reflect the existing political forms of human society, which are based on amnesia (initiation *without memory*, as discussed above). Sometimes it is too hasty to state, with reference to Kropotkin, that 'there is no scientific theory of evolution whose philosophical frame and basic concepts are not inflected by politics. After all, nature is political' (Willet 2014, 64). But in a sense, the politicisation of nature is not an effect, but a cause of the political inflection of 'frames and concepts'. If, guided by the previous orientation, we proceed from the fact that every political form of community has a natural origin, and also keep in mind the function of memory, then we can say that a constitutive element of any theory of nature is a certain historical form of attitude towards it. In this regard, a more radical thesis can be formulated: the nature of nature itself is *not political*. I would like to emphasise this. It is possible to read the main theses of Kropotkin so that the political is revealed beyond the boundaries of the human and the historical, in nature. This could open up the opportunity to talk about chimpanzee politics, the politics of ants, bees, plants and mushrooms. However, this is hardly the only direction in which Kropotkin proposes to go. As I'll show below, Kropotkin's sociability passes through a number of thresholds in its formation, only one of which is the threshold of politicization, and a reevaluation of the political potential of the natural may, at its radical pole, be associated with the *depoliticisation* of politics itself, and not with the politicisation of nature.

So, nature is constrained by laboratories and museums, which are institutions of amnestic interference with nature: such interference, at one end, is dictated by amnesia, and at the other end, it results in an amnestic disorder of nature, which itself appears in these institutions as stunned, devoid of freedom. At this point, one could make a sharp leap and assume that 'free nature' is nature-in-itself, nature freed from all conscious interference, from all presence of consciousness. Such a leap is methodologically unjustified. In one of his theoretical works on geography, Kropotkin protests against physiography without man: 'I cannot conceive Physiography from which Man has been excluded' (Kropotkin 1893, 355), that is, the natural landscape cannot be viewed through the exclusion of the (conscious or unconscious) lives that inhabit it. However, research optics must be decentralised by excluding the point of view of a species that has privileged access to the landscape. Beyond the laboratories and museums, free nature is nature without a 'control centre', but not without life or thinking. Kropotkin is not interested in a 'world-without-us', but a world-without-oppression, another name for which might be the old-fashioned word 'harmony'. Here's how it is described:

> Harmony [. . .] appears as a temporary adjustment, established among all forces acting upon a given spot – a provisory adaptation; and that adjustment will only last under one condition: that of being continually modified; of representing every moment the resultant of all conflicting actions. Let but one of those forces be hampered in its action for some time and harmony disappears. Force will accumulate its effect; it must come to light, it must exercise its action, and if other forces hinder its manifestation it will not be annihilated by that, but will end by upsetting the present adjustment, by destroying harmony, in order to find a new form of equilibrium and to work to form a new adaptation. Such is the eruption of a volcano, whose imprisoned force ends by breaking the petrified lavas which hindered them to pour forth the gases, the molten lavas, and the incandescent ashes. Such, also, are the revolutions of mankind. (Kropotkin 1897, 6)

Harmony in its temporality and variability is an extreme form of interacting forces. Average forms exist only as temporary agreements with constraint from an external force, as an accumulation of forces for explosions and for the creation of the extreme forms (of novelty) in which the ability is manifested in action. So the average form is a form of conspiracy. Force cannot but act (on itself in accumulation or on another force in action). Forces are inseparable from forms; they are forms-of-forces or forms-of-life (such combinations often appear in Russian translations of Kropotkin's texts).

So, free nature is nature as a harmony of elements, which is a plastic unity in which none of the acting forces is essentially limited in its action. Kropotkin is well aware that this is, rather, a 'speculative ideal' towards which nature 'strives' (it, however, cannot be separated from the action of the elements). Harmony is virtual. Actually, since there are always forces that are limited in their action, freedom is the 'ontological right to rebellion' of each oppressed force; the freedom of nature is a freedom of rebellion. The problem, therefore, is not that nature cannot be separated from the givenness but that nature is never given completely free, always given constrained. Since nature is never given in freedom, since there are always forces that are limited in their action, the rebellion is given as postponed for later, as a coming rebellion. This raises a question: We know the laboratories and museums of oppression, but are laboratories and museums for rebellion possible? (Kropotkin believes in this possibility.) One way or another, mutuality is the factor that increases the ability of the elements to act, increases the ability of rebellion, while isolated individualism is the result of the separation of the element from the ability to act and is a phase of accumulation of effects, a reservoir of not yet manifested actions that are inevitable – one way or another otherwise, they will appear in the future.

Orientation 3. (Feelings) All the Way Down (Extremum of Animation)

In one of the notes to *Mutual Aid*, Kropotkin declares the thesis, repeated in many of his works: 'Society has not been created by man; it is *anterior* to man' (Kropotkin 2018, 181, emphasis added). This thesis lies at the heart of both the argument used in criticising the state form of social life, the argument against the ruling minority (the people is anterior to the lords) and the method of Kropotkin's research, focused on considering what might be called the 'Great Anteriority of Mutual Aid'. We can hardly be mistaken, on the whole, in calling the Kropotkin method the method of *anteriorisation*: pushing the principle of mutual aid down into the depths of the pre-human (into animal life, life of insects, plants and so forth.) There is no shortage of anteriority formulas in Kropotkin's texts; I shall give only a few examples – in the order of their descent down towards the 'origin'. Reflecting on sociability, he writes about it 'having evidently its origin at the earliest stages of the evolution of the animal world, perhaps even at the "colony-stages"'. He adds: 'I consequently directed my chief attention to establishing first of all, the importance of the Mutual Aid factor of evolution, leaving to ulterior research the task of discovering the origin of the Mutual Aid instinct in Nature' (Kropotkin 2018, 3).

A similar consideration: 'Mutual aid is met with even amidst the lowest animals, and we must be prepared to learn some day, from the students of microscopical pond-life, facts of unconscious mutual support, even from the life of micro-organisms' (Kropotkin 2018, 13–14). What is the meaning of this permanent shift of the border of detection of mutual aid among living beings downwards, to ever simpler forms? There are at least two such meanings. First, Kropotkin is sure that the longer this or that stable phenomenon has developed, the more stable it is. If mutual aid among people is borrowed from pre-human nature then it is a more stable form of life's organisation than, for example, the very young state form. However, if we take the ulterior research's (speculative) point of view, that is, expand anteriorisation to 'the origin of the Mutual Aid instinct in Nature', bring it to the extreme (i.e. to infinity),[2] it turns out that it is inseparable from life as such, bringing the intensity of extreme forms into the origin itself. So second, Kropotkin seeks to identify a growing, progressive life with mutual aid at least asserting it as

[2] See Deleuze on how 'the extreme can be defined by the infinite' (Deleuze 1997, 42).

one of the indispensable essential sides of life. Mutuality as the resultant of actions is an extreme form of (co)existence of lives, while 'war' is only a (negative or zero) sum of the average forms. Mutual aid and 'war' do not differ as two opposite sides of life; they differ as extreme and average forms of life. Due to the fact that extreme forms cannot be obtained by adding average forms, at the ontological level of the 'origin' there is no life outside the relationship of mutual aid: being completely excluded from such relationships, life cannot last a moment.

Anteriorisation: we find mutual aid *all the way down* the evolutionary path of life. However, is it possible to cross the threshold of the organic in anteriorisation? Where is the ontological limit of this shift? Kropotkin is extremely cautious in his use of speculative statements, and when it comes to the anteriorisation of the principle of mutual aid beyond organic life, he is rather switching over to the language of poetry. He says that the call for the avoidance of competition 'is the *tendency* of nature, not always realized in full, but always present. That is the watchword which comes to us from the bush, the forest, the river, the ocean' (Kropotkin 2018, 48), and to discover the sources (and patterns) of moral sentiment, we must 'descend to animals, plants and rocks' (Kropotkin 2005). In *Anarchism: Its Philosophy and Ideal*, he writes about 'small atoms which dash in all directions, vibrate, move, *live*, and by their vibrations, their shocks, their *life*, produce the phenomena of heat, light, magnetism or electricity' (Kropotkin 1897, 4, emphasis added), and in *Ethics*, crossing the macro- and micro-levels, he gives the entire poetic picture:

> [Philosophy] accustoms man to conceive the life of the universe as a never-ending series of transformations of energy [. . .] The recent studies in the wide borderland dividing the inorganic world from the organic, where the simplest life-processes in the lowest fungi are hardly distinguishable – if distinguishable at all from the chemical redistribution of atoms which is always going on in the more complex molecules of matter, have divested life of its mystical character. At the same time, our conception of life has been so widened that we grow accustomed now to conceive all the agglomerations of matter in the universe – solid, liquid, and gaseous (such are some nebulae of the astral world) – *as something living* and going through the same cycles of evolution and decay as do living beings. (Kropotkin 1924, 3, emphasis added)

In poetic language, Kropotkin speaks in favour of *panpsychism*, the general truth of which he rarely doubts. (In one of his articles on biology, he speaks out against the concept of 'matter endowed with a soul' (Kropotkin 1912, 517), but this is not a criticism of panpsychism, but a rejection, first, of the dualism of soul and body and form and life, and second, the assertion of death in its transformative positivity.) Today, the question of panpsychism is at the forefront of ontological issues, but most ontologists who have chosen panpsychism admit the embarrassing character of this choice – if not the pornographic nature[3] of the panpsychistic picture of the world and the associated *shock* (on the importance for our research to move to where the shock is, see above). Poetry and morality allow Kropotkin not to notice this and maintain decency.

Beyond poetry and moralism, however, Kropotkin's ontological maxims fit easily with the arguments of today's ontology for panpsychism. In his classic essay, Thomas Nagel bases panpsychism on four premises: 1) Material composition, 2) Non-reductionism, 3) Realism and 4) Non-emergence (Nagel 1979, 181). The first is that living things consist of the same elements as non-living things. The second is that mental properties cannot be reduced to material ones. The third is that the mental is still a property of the material, there is no soul separate from the body. Finally, the fourth is in the rejection of brute emergence as the emergence of something from nothing.

Kropotkin, obviously, would share all four premises with Nagel, with some specific clarifications. Eagerly citing Darwin's words of the ant brain as 'one of the most marvelous atoms of matter in the world', he adds: 'Is it not due to the fact that mutual aid has entirely taken the place of mutual struggle in the communities of ants?' (Kropotkin 2018, 16–17). Material composition, if it can be mental, suggests a moment of sociability. Nagel and the majority of modern panpsychists, looking for the starting point of the indivisibility of the mental and the material, analyse mainly an individual being, the brain, hemispheres, neurons and so on (Nagel 2002, 225–228), that is, what Kropotkin calls an *isolated* individual. He himself, on the contrary, begins his process of anteriorisation with collectives, indirectly asking the question: Is the isolated individual *animated*? While answering in the affirmative (of course!), he is nevertheless forced to admit that the isolated individual is animated by something like 'residual animation' borrowed from mutual aid relations and inevitably fading away outside these relations, in the event of exacerbation of isolation. Therefore, anteriorisation occurs not with the individual, but with collectives.

Kropotkin's non-reductionism is not so clearly outlined, although indisputable. It appears to him as the irreducibility of (upward) transformation, as the impossibility of describing, for example, social processes in terms of physics: 'Humanity is not a rolling ball [. . .] and if you wish for a comparison, you must rather take it in the laws of organic evolution than in those of an inorganic moving body' (Kropotkin 1897, 27). As we have seen, the transformative movement of nature is described by Kropotkin as going through a series

[3] See Steven Shaviro's excellent note on the living panpsychistic world which is 'obscene and pornographic' (Shaviro 2014, 47).

of plastic thresholds between the destruction of the old form and the creation of a new one. In various works, Kropotkin lists such thresholds at the transitions: from physics to physiology, from physiology to ('family') economics, from economics to (social) politics and finally, from politics to the state. At each threshold, a transformation takes place, which, on the one hand, places the new form against the background of the previous one – places the new form *in* the previous form as in the environment, and on the other hand directs the new form *against* the old in the order of the *struggle for life*. The new form defends itself by struggle in the face of and against the background of the previous form.

Perhaps the most interesting collision occurs in the transformative movement of nature where the state appears, asserting itself through the struggle with society. Kropotkin experiences obvious difficulties in explaining the emergence of the state. Too often, the problem is disposed by making a hasty conclusion that the state embodies something unnatural. But the state is not an alien predator that fell from the sky. And in the logic of Kropotkin himself (orientation 1), it fights against society and subjugates it for reasons no less natural than those that force birds to build nests, and peasants to use the power of domestic animals in their households and eat their meat. The state is also a form of the struggle against the forces of nature, but the nature against which it fights is *sociability itself*. The state always fights against the extremisation of forms-of-life in their encounters (Kropotkin often describes cases when any sociability is viewed by the state as an extreme, any free community is viewed as a threat). The state, speaking as speculatively as possible, is a life-of-form; the opposite of a form-of-life, it lives through the *separation* of life and form. There is no symmetry between life-of-form and form-of-life; there is *a difference in kind* between them (as well as between the average and extreme forms): we can briefly express this by saying that mutual aid is impossible in the state. Life-of-form is also a form-of-death: it is the production of death – and at the same time it is the threshold of the reconstitution of life in a new form, the threshold of the production of a new form-of-life on an anti-state basis (Kropotkin 1908, 42).

It seems that today, we are on the same threshold. Kropotkin's non-reductionism can be especially emphasised at this point: despite the fact that the state's form is played out on bodies, it – being firmly connected with consciousness – cannot be described in terms of physics or biology and cannot be reduced to the states of bodies. In a sense, it is the soul separate from the body (or, which is the same, the soul of a separate isolated body), in the words of Michel Foucault, the state is the soul as 'the prison of the body' (Foucault 1995, 30). The political metaphysics of the state is completely opposite to panpsychistic anteriorisation, it is always based on two operations: the separation of form from life (soul from body) and the return of form as a prison – back to life. As a result, we get a picture completely opposite to the realism of forms-of-life (in which form is inseparable from life), a picture in which the soul is not only separated from the body, but also (very selectively) distributed among bodies. Kropotkin, in turn, fully shares the premise of realism: there is no soul separate from the body, form and life are inseparable. The premise of non-reductionism and the premise of realism, according to Nagel, are most difficult to agree with one another. Indeed, how to think of the mental as irreducible to the material and at the same time as inseparable from it? This requires a completely new, very radical conception, based on 'the idea that there is something more fundamental than the physical' (Nagel 2002, 233). Could Kropotkin's concept of mutual aid (most speculatively read) serve as such a conception? At first glance, it seems not. In his magnum opus he is content with asserting mutual aid as *one of the two* factors of evolution. This dualistic stop is dictated by strategic considerations: *Mutual Aid* was written in order to undermine the *monopoly* of the law of mutual struggle as the only law of evolution, for such an undermining it is enough to establish mutual aid as *another* law. However, is this enough for *complete victory*? The answer to this question is closely related to the question of 'free nature' (orientation 2). The law of mutual struggle (in nature) is as real as the state is real (in human society). And just as the state cannot be abolished by a simple declaration that its nature is death (a revolution is required to eliminate it), so the law of mutual struggle, interspecific oppression or, for example, *natural disasters* cannot be removed from nature by a simple declaration that '[i]n the beginning was the Mutual Aid', (requires a kind of liberating *involution* of mutual aid).

The premise of non-emergence, which also finds an echo in Kropotkin's evolutionism, receives its most vivid expression where Kropotkin discusses the human moral feeling. The latter, Kropotkin is convinced, does not appear out of nowhere, of some supernatural source, but is the result of the development of sociable feelings, the source of which is in the very nature of nature. Following the logic of panpsychist argumentation, in which it is precisely the rejection of brute emergence that is decisive, and following the principle of anteriorisation, we can assume that Kropotkin should have pushed sociable feelings all the way down into nature. It is clear that if a moral feeling did not come to humanity from a supernatural source, if it did not emerge for inexplicable reasons from completely asocial elements of nature as war, then the same can be said about cranes, roe deer, bees, ants, microorganisms, plants and rocks – *all the way down.* Panpsychism's speculative view, according to which blind feeling should exist from the very beginning (Shaviro 2014, 97), Kropotkin would correct by insisting that there is no entirely unsociable feeling.

Of course, in poetic form this idea is difficult to accept (except as something that inspires), and, if it makes sense, the development of a theory of mutual aid among elementary particles (or rather *elemental* forces) should be a matter of the future.

CONCLUSION: EARTH BETWEEN GAIA AND MEDEA

The key question that arises after encountering Kropotkin's system of nature is the question of the relationship between different species of living beings and between organic and inorganic life. It is whether mutual aid can cross the transformative thresholds of nature. Is mutual assistance between (unconscious and conscious) species or between organic and non-organic life possible, and if so by what means? This question is a test of the plasticity of Kropotkin's concepts. Of course, Kropotkin does not ignore interspecies mutual aid. Thus, he describes the relationship between different species of ants, between ants and aphids, between seagulls and sea swallows, between cranes and other aquatic birds (as well as cranes and humans), between different species of parrots and so on. However, this topic does not become key for him anywhere (and where Kropotkin turns to mutual assistance among people, it completely fades into the background). Again, the reason is strategic: Kropotkin is arguing primarily with a separate thesis of Darwin concerning the defining nature of intraspecific struggle (more precisely, with the distortion and absolutisation of this thesis in Darwinism). However, his own thesis in the end itself can be easily distorted and absolutised: mutual assistance within a species can simply mean an interspecific war of all against all, in which the species simply takes the place of the individual. Kropotkin's paradoxical position on the First World War – support for the Entente countries – seems to serve as an example of how Kropotkin himself allowed such distortions and absolutisations.

Curiously, Kropotkin did not notice how the concept of mutualism was introduced into biology, describing the mutual assistance that takes place between different species of living beings. This concept was introduced by Heinrich Anton de Bary several years before the release of Kropotkin's first articles on mutual aid for *The Nineteenth Century*. (But in fairness it should be said that for a long time – until recently – mutualism 'was the stepchild of ecology, neglected, malnourished and not studied theoretically because the prevailing paradigm was "nature red in tooth and claw"' [Stadler and Dixon 2008, vii].) *Mutualism* is defined as mutually beneficial interaction of different species of organism, assuming that in such relations not only an excess of resources necessary for the participants is produced, but also the possibility of complication and development of mutualistic relations themselves as a certain excess of sociability. The most detailed descriptions of the mutualisms are those into which ants enter: with aphids, coccids, membracids and lycaenids, as well as mutualisms between ants and plants. If historically the first studies of mutualism focused on highly specialised pair relationships, then in recent decades there has been an increasing number of studies of mutualistic networks, which include tens or even hundreds of species.

It should be noted that Kropotkin's conception does not in the least exclude mutualism; on the contrary, it presupposes it as a fruitful expansion and taking mutual assistance to the extreme. Two poles can be identified in mutual aid: conservative and inventive. This is done by Kropotkin himself, speaking, on the one hand, about mutual aid as the self-preservation of the species (under conditions of maximum environmental pressure), and on the other hand, about mutual assistance as a pleasure in society, play, sports, a 'fit of gladness' (Kropotkin 2018, 37).[4] And if the conservative pole of mutual aid is constructed according to the logic of *identity*, rather rigidly enclosing the species on its survival, then the inventive pole, on the contrary, sharpens the *difference* and presupposes a weakening of identification, going beyond the boundaries of the species – when the animal does not resemble itself and develops a carefree sociability almost with the first comer. These two poles are interconnected: the increased protection achieved in the struggle for existence provides a more sustainable environment for the expression of carefree creativity and cooperation. Kropotkin placed interspecies mutual assistance at the pole of inventiveness and believed that play and creativity are signs of consciousness, which is an opportunity for the development of the highest ethics of mutual aid, covering the whole species (and further – all living things). Research into mutualism could make a correction here: interspecies inventiveness is found *all the way down* (e.g., between fungi and plants), and it does not depend on the level of development of 'consciousness'.

Let's take an even more radical step. Often Kropotkin describes the relationship of groups of animals and human societies with other species as relationships with the environment.[5] Moreover, the Lamarckian thesis that individual variability is the result of the direct action of the environment on organisms was the position that Kropotkin defended in the community of biologists, largely contrary to the trends that existed at the beginning of the twentieth century (Kropotkin 1910, 86–107). In this regard, *mutualism* could be defined by Kropotkin as an *instrumental* involvement of the environment into a community, into an *armature* of mutual aid – remember that Kropotkin often defines *mutual assistance* itself instrumentally as '*arm* in the struggle for life' (Kropotkin 2018, 33, emphasis added). And it is precisely from this

[4] In Russian translation this phrase is translated as 'explosion of joy' (взрыв радости).
[5] For example Kropotkin (2018, 15–16, 30–31 and 34).

point that one could conceptualise mutual aid that crosses the thresholds of organic and non-organic life. Kropotkin distinguishes between several types of instruments: individual ('beak and claw') and collective (anthills, burrows, nests, trails). But, perhaps, an individual living body can be considered as a very specific instrument in the armature of mutual support. It is the living bodies that make up the armature of mutual aid in the dramatic example of a migration of fallow-deer which Kropotkin witnessed on the Amur. In the human world, individual instruments are separated from bodies (although today we know that the appearance of instruments separated from the body is not a feature of the human world; *tool behaviour* also descends *all the way down*), but the instruments of human collectives (roads, bridges, means of transport, architecture) begin to play a key role in the development of sociability – until they are captured by states. Collective instruments (and collectives as armature of instruments) of living beings carry something like a 'terraforming' *charge*, to which Kropotkin attached great importance. It is here that the struggle with nature acquires its liberating meaning (see above concerning the laboratories of rebellion; here, we can call them laboratories of *animation*). When Kropotkin writes about the voices of mutual aid from the bush, the forest, the river, the ocean, he most likely literally means animals that inhabit the most different corners of the Earth, making them habitable, making them – by means of mutual aid armature, including organic bodies and nonorganic life – inhabited by life and, as it were, *instrumentally animated*. Kropotkin opposed Lamarck's thesis about the possibility of organs being invented by living organisms, but he transferred the functions of the invented organs to instruments. And often Kropotkin described armatures of mutual aid as an organic whole (Kropotkin 2018, 124).

Putting forward the hypothesis of the desiccation of Eurasia, Kropotkin predicted a sad desert future for the Earth and suggested now to start working on its prevention by reanimating the deserts, urging his readers and listeners

> to think of the measures which should be taken for combating [. . .] the coming drought. Such measures, I mean, as tree-planting on a large scale in the menaced regions, with the aid of artesian wells [. . .] or any other measures which the knowledge of the danger and further research may suggest. (Kropotkin 1904, 734)

Without going into the details of how this hypothesis ultimately came true, let us emphasise Kropotkin's terraforming conclusions: If a planet dies and steadily approaches the state of lifeless Mars, it should be *technically reanimated* with a mutualistic armature of collective instruments: life must rebel (against the planet). The struggle with nature in this context acquires *technical* and *plastic* meanings: here it is indistinguishable from mutual aid (already between the planet and life on it). This conclusion allows us to place Kropotkin in the context of modern environmental discussions, located between two extreme hypotheses – the Gaia Hypothesis and the Medea Hypothesis – between the hypothesis of the Earth as a self-organizing system (the enemy of which is often exposed to humans) and the hypothesis according to which the Earth is a terrible mother, killing its own spawn (all living things). These two poles are analogous to the optimistic and pessimistic extremes in understanding nature, which we talked about at the beginning, and, probably, Kropotkin would reject both alternatives, believing that both miss mutual aid as a real process, the result of which is *not predetermined* by anything, as a process requiring invention. Gaia is a mythologeme that elevates mutual aid to a homeostatic absolute (average form). Medea is a mythologeme in which mutual aid is absent in the final outcome (the average form too).

But ultimately, mutual aid and the struggle for life is a struggle for extreme forms-of-life – *all the way down.*

BIBLIOGRAPHY

Deleuze, Gilles. 1997. *Difference and Repetition.* London and New York: Continuum.

Foucault, Michel. 1995. *Discipline and Punish: The Birth of the Prison.* New York: Vintage Books.

Graeber, David and Andrej Grubačić. 2020. "Introduction from the Forthcoming Mutual Aid: An Illuminated Factor of Evolution." *PM Press blog.* https://www.pmpress.org/blog/2020/09/03/in-loving-memory-david-graeber/. Accessed 31 January 2021.

Kropotkin, Peter. 1897. *Anarchism: Its Philosophy and Ideal.* London: Freedom Press.

Kropotkin, Peter. 2005. "Anarchist Morality." *Libcom.* https://libcom.org/library/anarchist-morality-I-peter-kropotkin. Accessed 31 January 2021.

Kropotkin, Peter. 1924. *Ethics: Origin and Development.* Translated by Louis Friedland and Joseph Piroshnikoff. New York: The Dial Press.

Kropotkin, Peter. 2018. *Mutual Aid: A Factor of Evolution.* Middletown: Jonathan-David Jackson.

Kropotkin, Peter. 1893. "On the Teaching of Physiography." *The Geographical Journal* 2(4): 350–359.

Kropotkin, Peter. 1904. "The Desiccation of Eur-Asia." *The Geographical Journal* 23(6): 722–734.

Kropotkin, Peter. 1912. "The Inheritance of Acquired Characters: Theoretical Difficulties." *The Nineteenth Century* (March): 511–531.

Kropotkin, Peter. 1908. *The State: Its Historic Role.* London: Freedom Press.

Kropotkin, Peter. 1910. "The Theory of Evolution and Mutual Aid." *The Nineteenth Century* (January): 86–107.
Malabou, Catherine. 2005. *The Future of Hegel: Plasticity, Temporality and Dialectic*. London and New York: Routledge.
Malabou, Catherine. 2008. *What Should We Do with Our Brain?* New York: Fordham University Press.
Nagel, Thomas. 1979. "Panpsychism." In *Mortal Questions*, 181–195. Cambridge: Cambridge University Press.
Nagel, Thomas. 2002. "The Psychophysical Nexus." In *Concealment and Exposure: And Other Essays*, 194–235. New York: Oxford University Press.
Shaviro, Steven. 2014. *The Universe of Things: On Speculative Realism*. Minneapolis: University of Minnesota Press.
Stadler, Bernard, and Tony Dixon. 2008. *Mutualism: Ants and Their Insect Partners*. Cambridge: Cambridge University Press.
Willet, Cynthia. 2014. *Interspecies Ethics*. New York: Columbia University Press.

Chapter 10

Solidarity Is Not Reciprocal Altruism

Jonas Faria Costa

Classic game theory assumed that agents could only reason at the individual level. This is an assumption not only of ontological individualism but also of methodological individualism. But this assumption was unnecessary, a heritage from the previous generations of economists and the strong fear of the communist menace at the time. I will explain the roots of this assumption and its limitations, most specifically, how it faces problems when explaining cooperation. Next, I will show how this assumption slipped into evolutionary theory, through the works of John M. Smith (1982) and Richard Dawkins (2017). Yet, as Peter Kropotkin's (2009) work on mutual aid illustrates, evolutionary theory need not assume individualism. To develop this, I will present a contemporary version of game theory that allows the possibility of collective reasoning. This will allow me to explain why altruism is a form of individual reasoning and why solidarity is a form of collective reasoning. On this reading, solidarity is not reducible to the radical individualism present in neoclassical economics and Dawkins's evolutionary theory, that is, it is not reducible to reciprocal altruism. As long as we do not maintain the assumption of individualism, game theory and evolutionary theory can provide an account of solidarity.

INDIVIDUALISM AND GAME THEORY

One central dogma in capitalist ideology is the idea that individuals are egoists. That is, left unchecked, society would collapse. We need bosses to direct us. We need politicians to administrate us. We need the police to keep us from becoming monsters. The idea that the law of nature is the law of competition between individuals is old. The discussion that humans might essentially be selfish appears already in Plato's *Republic* (2012). In that dialogue, the characters discuss what justice is, and Thrasymachus says that 'what is just [. . .] is nothing more than what is in the interest of the stronger' (Plato 2012, 18, §338c). The idea is that doing wrong and not being punished is a good thing, as it brings me joy, and suffering wrongdoing and not being able to punish is a bad thing, as it brings me suffering. So, weak people gather together and make a contract to avoid suffering wrongdoings (Plato 2012, 44–45, §358e, §359a, and §359b). A strong person would be able to maximise her happiness without following any sort of justice system. This idea persisted, through the Latin proverb *homo homini lupus est* ('a man is a wolf to another man'), and in the works of philosophers such as Bernard Mandeville (1970) and Thomas Hobbes (1996). The core idea is not that people hate each other, but that each wants to maximise their own happiness, even if at the expense of other people's welfare. This is at the foundation of game theory, which will be the main topic discussed in this chapter.

There is also another aspect to this individualist idea, which is methodological individualism. In order to analyse society and human behaviour, one has first to consider man in isolation and only then in interaction with other people. It is the myth of a Robinson Crusoe.[1] This leads to a model of agency in which the agent is rational (i.e. wants to maximise its welfare) and is individualistic (i.e. welfare is calculated at the individual level of happiness and rationality is not collective).

Classic Game Theory

Economists, such as Leon Walras (1954) and Vilfredo Pareto (1972), set the ground for game theory, which only became a field of study with the work of John von Neumann and Oskar Morgenstern (2004). Instead of using the term 'happiness' or 'welfare', they used the term 'utility'. Their idea was that we could form better theories about the mechanism of prices and production if we first analyse 'the behaviour of the individuals which constitute the economic community' (von Neumann and Morgenstern 2004, 8). An individual is rational if he tries to maximise his own individual utility. Rationality and individualism are the axioms of classic game theory. Take one person in isolation, and she will have a hierarchy of preferences, for example, she prefers chocolate to vanilla. Now, put that person in interaction with another, and the outcome will be the product of their interactions – that is a game.

Here is one example of a game. Adam and Beth got caught while committing a crime. The police want them to confess. The police put them in separate

[1] For a detailed analysis of the use of Robinson Crusoe in neoclassical economics, I highly recommend Söllner (2016).

		Adam	
		Cooperate	Defect
Beth	Cooperate	(-1, -1)	(0, -10)
	Defect	(-10, 0)	(-4, -4)

Figure 10.1 Prisoner's Dilemma.

rooms, so that they cannot talk to each other, and gave each the same offer: If you defect, by confessing that the other did the crime, and the other does not defect, then you will not go to jail at all, but the other person will spend ten years in prison. If they both defect, then each will spend four years in jail. If neither defects, then each will spend only one year in jail. This forms the matrix shown in Figure 10.1.

That game is the famous Prisoner's Dilemma. A rational agent will try to maximise his utility. If Beth chooses *Defect*, then Adam will spend less time in jail if he also chooses *Defect*. If Beth chooses *Cooperate*, then Adam will spend no time in jail if he chooses *Defect*. No matter what Beth chooses, Adam is better off by choosing *Defect*. The same strategy is valid for Beth, which means that both will choose *Defect*. It is a dilemma because both would be better off if both could coordinate and choose *Cooperate*. Both would get a better payoff by not acting according to 'rationality'. If you maintain the axioms of classic game theory, there is no way to solve this problem in a one-shot game (i.e. a game only played once).

Solving the Prisoner's Dilemma: Armed to the Teeth

There is a way to solve the dilemma while maintaining the axioms of classic game theory. If there is a chance of future interactions, then it is better to *Cooperate*, because it can create a virtuous cycle where both *Cooperate*, instead of a vicious cycle where both *Defect* (see Axelrod 1984). However, this will only work if the player does not know when the last interaction will be. This is because it is always rational to play *Defect* in the last round. Since that is what is rational, the player can predict that both would play *Defect* in that last round, which means that the best thing to do in the last-but-one round would be to play *Defect*, as it would maximise your individual payoff overall, considering all the previous cycles of *Cooperation*. It is easy to see how the cascade effect would make it rational to play *Defect* in the very first interaction. Nonetheless, if the players do not know when the last interaction will be, then it becomes rational to cooperate.

The idea is that, as long as the other person is cooperating, it is rational to keep cooperating as well. If the other person stops cooperating, then the rational reply is to retaliate, by choosing *Defect* as well. So, if a player does not know when it will be the last round, then the player can infer that if he does not cooperate, then the other will retaliate. In other words, there is a fear of punishment, which makes it rational to play *Cooperate* (see Aumann 1959). This reasoning can be applied to any sort of interaction that allows retaliation. It provides a theoretical explanation of how two selfish individuals can form an association. It explains how Robinson Crusoe and Friday can cooperate or how two Robinsons can cooperate. The idea that people are selfish was popular among the authors that established game theory as a research field. John von Neumann thought that 'it is just as foolish to complain that people are selfish and treacherous as it is to complain that the magnetic field does not increase unless the electric field has a curl. Both are laws of nature' (von Neumann as quoted by Eugene Wigner, in Wigner 1967, 261). There is a thin line between this idea and the idea that society is nothing but selfish people interacting.[2]

The argument of future punishment was used to justify the arms race between the United States and the Soviet Union; build atomic bombs because retaliation guarantees protection. Thomas Schelling (1966) used this game-theoretic argumentation to explain how peace can be achieved: if two nations are heavily armed and can retaliate against each other's attack, then neither will attack. Schelling argued, for example, that the Mongols, during Genghis Khan's time, would put their hostages in front of their army lines, so that if they were attacked, the first ones to die would be the hostages (Schelling 1966, 6). Schelling also said that China and the Soviet Union were known to put hostages near target points to avoid getting bombed. Schelling argues that having a hostage is having the capacity to retaliate (Schelling 1966, 6).

The idea that producing more arms and atomic bombs is the key to maintain peace was preceded by another more dangerous idea. When the United States managed to acquire the atomic bomb technology before any other country, there was a wide-spread opinion that it should use it to destroy the Soviet menace. Von Neumann was a radical anti-communist. However, this opinion was not only held by radicals such as von Neumann. Bertrand Russell, the famous philosopher, held the same opinion (see Russell 2001, 410). Notice that they were saying the United States was a free society in the 1940s, that is before the civil rights movements in the 1960s. It makes one wonder what 'freedom' they had in mind. During those times, not presupposing that humans are essentially individualistic would be seen as a socialist

[2] Consider, for example, Margaret Thatcher's remark that 'There is no such thing as society' (in an interview for *Women's Own*, 1987).

idea, and socialist ideas were seen as dangerous. Consider, for example, Margaret Thatcher's words:

> There is no such thing as 'safe' Socialism. If it's safe, it's not Socialism. And if it's Socialism, it's not safe. The signposts of Socialism point downhill to less freedom, less prosperity, downhill to more muddle, more failure. If we follow them to their destination, they will lead this nation into bankruptcy. (Thatcher in a speech to Conservative Central Council, 1976)

Game theory, coupled with the assumption that individuals are selfish, provided a theoretical justification not only for the arms race but for the capitalist ideology as a whole. What is interesting is that the idea that a person tries to maximise her own individual payoff is just an assumption. It works as an axiom, upon which the mathematics of game theory operates.

Where This Individualism Assumption Comes From

Why did they make this assumption about individual rationality? There are a few things we need to take into consideration here. The origins of game theory can be traced back to Charles Waldegrave, mentioned by Pierre Rémond de Montmort (1713), at the beginning of the eighteenth century. Waldegrave provided a solution to a two-person card game. From that point on, there was much mathematical analysis of games, such as Ernst Zermelo's analysis of chess strategies (see Schwalbe 2001). What all of these analyses have in common is that they are about the interaction between rational decision makers with clear goals. In a game, players have clear objectives, and they want to win.

These mathematical analyses provided the tools for economists, such as Cournot (1897 [1838]), Marshall (1898) and Walras (1954 [1874]), to develop mathematical theories of economics, which gave birth to neoclassical economics. One big difference between these economic models and the mathematical analysis of games, such as a chess game, is that the players in a chess game have a clear objective. In a market, a firm wants to maximise profits. The firm sells products to consumers. But what are the goals of the consumers? Classical economists, such as David Ricardo (2002 [1817]), considered that the value of a product, or at least the ideal value of a product, depends on how much labour was put in it. One of the innovations made by neoclassical economics was to consider that value (and therefore price) depends on the relation between the marginal costs of supply and the consumer's marginal utility. For instance, if a person has 500 g of bread and only 10 g of cheese, she might be willing to exchange 100g of bread for 10g more of cheese. However, if the person has 250 g of bread and 100g of cheese, then she is willing to exchange only 50g of bread for 10g of cheese. Walras (1954 [1874]) defined *value* as anything useful to the person whether it is necessary or superfluous. In other words, value is subjective.

If value is subjective, then it depends on the individual's state of mind. If I am thirsty, I will value water, even if I am on an isolated island. In such a situation, if I have to choose between making fire or searching for water, I will choose to search for water. The same reasoning can be applied to superfluous things. What matters is that choice depends on preference, and preferences are subjective. This means that value is ontologically reducible to statements about an individual. It is the ontological primacy of the individual, which leads to methodological individualism. It is here that the story of Robinson Crusoe kicks in.

Daniel Defoe wrote *Robinson Crusoe* in 1719, but only a century later it started being used by economists. William Lloyd, one of the founding fathers of neoclassical economics, was the first to use Defoe's story to explain the notion of marginal utility (see Lloyd 1834, 20–24). If value is subjective, then a story about an isolated man can be a good way to explain the concept of utility. After Lloyd, many other economists started using Robinson Crusoe in their argumentations, such as Carl Menger (2007 [1871], 134–135). Menger is one of the main authors of the Austrian School of economics. Crusoe was so much used, especially by the Austrian School, that it became a framework of study: the Robinson Crusoe economy. The idea is that it is easier to explain and analyse marginal utility by considering a person in isolation. Morgenstern, who co-wrote *Theory of Games and Economic Behavior* with von Neumann, was heavily influenced by the Austrian School, having studied in Vienna with Friedrich von Wieser (1891).

Morgenstern and von Neumann mention Crusoe, but what they have in mind is the idea of a Robinson Crusoe economy (Morgenstern and von Neumann 2004, 10–12). Their critique is that a man in isolation has control over all variables. He might not have control over the weather, for instance, but such variables can be grasped through the use of probabilities. A person in a social interaction, however, cannot control all the variables. In an interaction, a person cannot even use probability to think about what will happen. This is because the other person is also a decision maker, guided by rational principles. Morgenstern and von Neumann concluded that the methods used by Crusoe economy are not useful to economic theory (Morgenstern and von Neumann 2004, 12). However, they do not deny methodological individualism. For classic game theory, social interaction is reducible to statements about individuals. Rationality is considered only at the individual level. Social action boils down to strategic interaction, which is each individual trying to get the best payoff they can for themselves.

Classic game theory assumed individualism because the authors who established game theory are part of a long tradition that uses methodological individualism to understand human agency. One could argue that a rational agent does not have to be selfish. He can incorporate into his own payoff the payoff of others, that is, he cares about what happens to others. However, this is still a form of individual rationality.

Altruism Does Not Solve the Hi-Lo Dilemma

It was only a matter of time until experiments were done with real people, proving that people are not like the rational agents in game theory. In experiments with people playing a Prisoner's Dilemma, half of the participants chose *Cooperate* in one-shot games (Sally 1995). People are not as selfish as classic economics theories thought we were. So, game theory had to adapt. Some stipulated bounded rationality, that is, people are not perfect calculation machines, there is a limit to how much we can think that others think that we think that others think (Simon 1957). Others proposed that people can be altruists. Altruism, in that case, would be to incorporate into your payoff the welfare of the other person. This means that the other person spending time in jail counts negatively in your utility. Notice, however, that this sort of altruism is still individualistic and it cannot solve the dilemma.[3]

Let us consider the example I gave of a Prisoner's Dilemma earlier. But this time, let us consider that Adam and Beth are married, so each one's welfare is part of the other's utility function. In that case, if one of them stays ten years in jail and the other does not go to jail, then each will get a payoff of minus ten. If both go to jail for four years, then each gets a payoff of minus eight. And if both stay only one year in jail, then each gets a payoff of minus two. The game has changed. It is no longer a Prisoner's Dilemma (Figure 10.1). It is now a Hi-Lo (Figure 10.2).

		Adam	
		Cooperate (High)	Defect (Low)
Beth	Cooperate (High)	(-2, -2)	(-10, -10)
	Defect (Low)	(-10, -10)	(-8, -8)

Figure 10.2 Hi-Lo.

[3] Some economists say that game theory is neither about prediction nor about human behaviour (see Rubinstein 1991), but just a mathematical analysis of interaction. However, as Fritz Söllner shows, 'there are countless instances in the literature about decisions being made or alternatives being chosen *because* they maximize utility' (Söllner 2016, 58).

There are three possible outcomes: both choose *Cooperate (High)*, both choose *Defect (Low)* or each chooses something different. Making the same choice is always better than making different choices. If Beth plays *Defect (Low)*, then Adam should play *Defect (Low)*. But if Beth plays *Cooperate (High)*, then Adam should play *Cooperate (High)*. Choosing *Defect (Low)* is not more rational than choosing *Cooperate (High)*. Regardless of both being altruists, they still cannot solve the dilemma.

So far, I have explained how classic game theory assumed individual rationality and some of its limitations. I will now explain how evolutionary theory passively and indirectly maintained such an assumption.

EVOLUTIONARY THEORY: HOW INDIVIDUALISM SLIPS IN

Game theory, in conjunction with biology, formed a new branch: evolutionary game theory. John Maynard Smith (1982) had the ingenious idea of applying the structure of iterated games to explain evolution. 'The criterion of rationality is replaced by that of population dynamics and stability, and the criterion of self-interest by Darwinian fitness' (Smith 1982, 2). It was a revolutionary idea, in that it substituted payoff, which was considered a subjective state by neoclassical economists, for reproduction success, which is objective. In addition, instead of thinking of agents choosing strategies, an animal already has its behaviour determined by its genes.

Smith, however, managed to maintain the individualistic dogma from classic game theory. In and of itself, game theory does not have to be individualistic, as I will show in a later section. The individualism was just an assumption, a heritage from the previous generations of economists and the strong fear of the communist menace at the time. Similarly, evolutionary game theory does not need to be individualistic. Nevertheless, individualism slips in. In Smith's case, the first time he shows how evolutionary game theory works, he uses the Hawk-Dove matrix, which has a structure similar to the Prisoner's Dilemma. It is a competition for a resource between two animals (Smith 1982, 11). If one animal has access to the resource, he will leave a higher number of offspring, but if both try to access the resource, then they will fight, and the injuries diminish the payoff associated with that outcome. This means that 'payoff' is calculated on having a larger number of offspring and getting or not injured (where an injury diminishes the 'payoff' because it eventually reduces the chances of having more offspring). 'Rationality' is changed to the strategy of the animal. For example, certain animals are 'hawks', in that they will try to access the resource and fight for it. Others are 'dove', they will refrain from engaging in a fight at the expense of having access to the resource. 'Rationality' is thus substituted by behaviour, where behaviour is understood as phenotype. A change in the genes can change the behaviour of the animal and thus its strategy. The strategies that will survive are the stable ones, that is, those that, in the long run, it tends to still exist in the population, and the population, of course, keeps existing.

Robert Axelrod did a computer experiment to test which strategies have a better outcome in a competition of Prisoner's Dilemma (Axelrod 1984). Each programme would play against each other, and it was not fixed how many iterations there would be. The champion programme, TIT FOR TAT, had the following strategy: always start playing *Cooperate* and repeat what the other programme chooses henceforth. If the other programme played Defect in the first round, then TIT FOR TAT would play *Defect* in the second round. This could create a vicious cycle unless the other programme decided to play *Cooperate*. So, every now and then, TIT FOR TAT would play *Cooperate* even if the other programme had played *Defect* in the previous round, to break the vicious cycle. TIT FOR TAT is fully compatible with what orthodox game theory predicts for iterated Prisoner's Dilemma. TIT FOR TAT tends to dominate the competition, which means that such a strategy will become frequent, because it leaves a higher number of offspring with the same behaviour, and it is stable.

Once again, we can explain the association between selfish individuals. Evolutionary game theory provides us with a strong narrative of how certain animals exhibit cooperative behaviour. This is an essential aspect of Dawkins's argumentation, in his work *The Selfish Gene* (2017). Mutualism, either within a species or between species, is explained as reciprocal altruism (see Smith 1982, 167). That is, cooperation helps both. Two TIT FOR TATs will cooperate because it is good for both. An animal helps another because, in the long run, it helps itself. Dawkins argues that the struggle for existence happens at the level of the phenotype. A gene that inclines the gene machine (which is the animal body) to have a stable strategy tends to maintain itself in the gene pool and to become present in the gene pools of the other individual animals.

Smith finishes his book by briefly talking about how animals that can speak can create a contract to guarantee certain stable strategies (Smith 1982, 173). It is the same idea as presented by Thrasymachus and Glaucon in Plato's *Republic*. It is better to be strong and never get punished, but for the weak, it is better to gather and make a contract to guarantee punishment and avoid being worse off.

I am not arguing against evolutionary theory. What I am arguing is that, when it comes to decision makers, evolutionary game theory adds nothing different from classic game theory. That is, evolutionary game theory will provide the same analysis of society as classic game theory. Decision makers can choose their strategies, and payoff becomes subjective once again, because reproduction success might not be what the decision makers prefer. On pain of sounding repetitive, there is no need to assume that decision makers can only perform individual reasoning. What is interesting is that some authors use evolutionary game theory to justify the assumption of individual rationality. This will get clearer when we analyse Richard Dawkins's arguments.

Dawkins's Insistence on the Individual and What Reciprocal Altruism Is

Dawkins argues that the analysis of behaviour should be done at the phenotype level (Dawkins 2017, 327). The gene is a replicator. It is something that tends to replicate itself. There is, then, a discussion about the vehicle of that replication. A gene alone does not replicate. It forms a pool of genes, where one cooperates with the other, much like a society of Robinson Crusoes. Together, they form that machine that we call the body. The body is the vehicle. The discussion is whether the vehicle is the body or the group of bodies. Dawkins argues that the group does not exhibit the same kind of cohesion that a single body does. Groups can get infiltrated by alien bodies, so there is not as much stability in the gene pool as there is when it comes to individual bodies. 'The group is too wishy-washy an entity' (Dawkins 2017, 329). Notice that these are pragmatic criteria not to consider the group as the vehicle. For example, how much stability is necessary to consider a group as the vehicle? On a theoretical level, we could imagine a population of humans with identical genes, who reproduce by cloning. Dawkins's standards imply that such group would not be 'too wishy-washy an entity'.

Dawkins argues the gene is not only the gene in one individual body. It is all its replicas (Dawkins 2017, 114). In other words, a gene gives a certain behaviour, and it is the behaviour, understood as strategy, that is selected in natural selection. A strategy is only selected if it is stable. Thus, a strategy is selected based not on one single individual performing it, but on its frequency and impacts in the iterations between many individuals. The struggle for existence is, for example, between the strategy 'hawk' and the strategy 'dove'. However, the vehicle is not the group but the individual because it is through the individual that the genes are able to replicate, not through the group. Dawkins argues:

> 'Single' individual organisms such as ourselves are the ultimate embodiment of many such merges. The group of organisms – the flock of birds, the pack of wolves – does not merge into a single vehicle, precisely because the genes in the flock or the pack do not share a common method of leaving the present vehicle.

> To be sure, packs may bud off daughter packs. But the genes in the parent pack don't pass to the daughter pack in a single vessel in which all have an equal share. [. . .] A gene can foster its own future welfare by favouring its own individual wolf, at the expense of other wolves. (Dawkins 2017, 330)

Dawkins argues that genes are selfish (i.e. they tend to replicate and they 'cooperate' with other genes if it helps themself), so this 'will give rise to selfishness in individual behaviour' (Dawkins 2017, 3). Although later in life Dawkins admitted that certain parts of his book *Selfish Gene* are misleading and a bit too radical, such as 'we are born selfish' (Dawkins 2017, ix), this does not change the core of his ideas or their implications. The implication is that cooperation can only be understood as reciprocal altruism. Dawkins himself is not a gene determinist. Throughout the book, Dawkins says that it is possible for the genes in the pool that forms our DNA to leave to us (as conscious beings) to do what we think is best. This leaves room for ethics, in the sense of humanity being able to think about what we should do beyond whatever is our nature. In Dawkins's logics, such behaviour will only exist if it helps the genes that lead to it to keep existing. However, Dawkins does put a limit to such a form of free will, and it is at the level of the individual since the individual is the ultimate embodiment of the genes (see Dawkins 2017, 330). All in all, Dawkins's idea is Thrasymachus's idea in new clothes.

Again, on a theoretical level, there is no need to consider that the individual body is the ultimate expression of the genes. If what matters about the genes is the behaviour they cause (i.e. the strategies), then what is in question here is not the individual body, but agency. Agency can be analysed at the individual level, but it can also be analysed at the collective level. We can talk about the behaviour of a bee and the behaviour of the hive, where the former is determined by the latter. I am arguing that certain individual behaviours (i.e. individual strategies) are derived from collective behaviour (i.e. group strategy). The ultimate expression of a gene need not be at the individual level. Notice that I am not arguing against ontological individualism here, but against methodological individualism. This has one important implication, namely, that prosocial behaviour need not be reduced to reciprocal altruism.

If game theory and evolutionary theory need not assume that radical individualism, then we should be open to considering collectivist accounts of social behaviour. It is possible to use evolution and game theory to provide an account of solidarity. In the next section, I will present one evolutionary account of social behaviour that does not assume that radical individualism, namely, Kropotkin's account of mutual aid (2009). Then, I will present a contemporary account of game theory that explains how collective reasoning works, namely, Bacharach's account of team reasoning (2006). The concept of mutual aid is compatible with collective reasoning. This allows me to explain why solidarity cannot be reduced to reciprocal altruism.

Kropotkin's Mutual Aid Is Not Reciprocal Altruism

Kropotkin argued that mutual aid is as much, if not more, a law of nature as the struggle against one another (Kropotkin 2009, 32). Some of the behaviours identified by Kropotkin could be understood as reciprocal altruism. However, Kropotkin also identifies strong forms of cooperation, which cannot be understood as reciprocal altruism. Consider the following passage:

> 'It is the conscience [. . .] of human solidarity. It is the unconscious recognition of the force that is borrowed by each man from the practice of mutual aid; of the close dependency of *every one's happiness upon the happiness of all*' (Kropotkin 2009, 24 – my emphasis).

Kropotkin inverts the classic economic understanding of happiness. Reciprocal altruism maintains the idea that each person tries to maximise their individual utility. However, what Kropotkin means is that individual utility is closely related to 'collective' utility. In other words, individual happiness can be derived from the happiness of the group. I will explain in the next section how this leads to a different way of understanding the interaction between agents.

Solidarity cannot be reduced to reciprocal altruism. A friendship cannot be reduced to an association for mutual gain. If that was the case, then a friend would be nothing more than a tool. If mutual aid is reciprocal altruism, then it is a form of strategic interaction. If friendship is just a strategic interaction that helps gene replication, then this is not friendship – it is a negotiation.

Maybe some people interpret Kropotkin's concept of mutual aid as reciprocal altruism to defend Kropotkin from the criticism that he confused his political aspirations with science.[4] After more than a 100 years since Kropotkin wrote his book, it is getting more apparent now that humans are not 'wolves to each other'. Humans exhibit a very complex form of cooperative behaviour. Michael Tomasello's (2009) experiments with toddlers corroborate the idea that humans have a primitive cognitive capability to understand the plural subject 'us' as the subject of an action.

---

[4] For example, in the preface for Freedom Press' edition of *Mutual Aid*, Daniel Rooum says that Kropotkin's idea of mutual aid is reciprocal altruism (Kropotkin 2009, 12). That is a mistake, because it maintains the individualism assumption, just like Smith and Dawkins did. This will lead to some problems, as I have already explained using the Prisoner's Dilemma and the Hi-Lo. Solidarity, as a core value in anarchism, is not compatible with the neoclassical economics framework.

Team Reasoning and What Solidarity Is

Game theory needs change. Besides the previous branches I have presented, there is one more. It is called team reasoning, formulated by Michael Bacharach (2006). In classic game theory, when an agent plays a game, the agent will think 'What should *I* do?' This kind of reasoning leads to, in a one-shot Prisoner's Dilemma, to choose *Defect*, and in a Hi-Lo, to choose *High* if the other chooses *High*, or to choose *Low* if the other chooses *Low*, that is, it is indeterminate. Team reasoning is the idea that an agent can think 'What should *we* do?' (Bacharach 2006, 141) That means both a utility transformation and a rationality transformation. When you think at the level of the group, that is, when you perceive your action as part of a group action, it means that what will lead your choices is not your preference ranking, but the group's preference ranking (the group's utility function). Also, it means that you perceive the group as acting, so you first think about what the group should do, and from that derive your personal agency, which is your role in the group's agency.

I have presented before how altruism can transform a Prisoner's Dilemma into a Hi-Lo, and that altruism cannot solve the Hi-Lo because it follows individualistic reasoning. Playing *High* is only rational if the other person plays *High*. If the other plays *Low*, then what is rational for you is to play *Low*. This is true for both an egoist person and an altruist. Team reasoning can solve the Hi-Lo. The agent will think 'What should *we* do?' We should play *High-High*. I should play my role in the group's course of action, which means that I should play *High*. Team reasoning can also solve the Prisoner's Dilemma. If the best thing for the group is *Cooperate-Cooperate*, then each agent will play *Cooperate*.

There is a discussion about how we can make sense of a group's payoff function. It goes beyond the purposes of this chapter to deal with this. There is also a discussion about when a person will perform team reasoning. For Bacharach, it is due to psychological factors (Bacharach 2006, 10). Draw a cube, with all its edges. When you look at the picture, you will either see the cube facing one direction or another, but never both at the same time. That is the nature of illusions. Bacharach thought that something similar happens to people. Either they frame the game as a case of team reasoning, or they do not. This means that to frame the situation as a 'we' is a primitive cognitive capability. By primitive, it means that it cannot be reduced to other cognitive capabilities.

The idea that 'we' is primitive goes against the individualist dogma. From a purely game-theoretical perspective, nothing prevents us from applying 'we' as an axiom. The idea of considering the agent as an individualist reasoner was just an assumption. When biologists use game theory, they should always keep in mind that game theory is built upon presumed axioms. The same way that, from a purely game-theoretical perspective, we can presume the 'we-agency', from a purely evolutionary theory, we can also make use of a 'we-reasoning'.

If we form a notion of 'us' and from that derive what we should do, then we are being driven by our feeling of solidarity. Notice how this is different from reciprocal altruism. In reciprocal altruism, 'us' is just a shorter way to say 'me and you', understood in individualistic terms. I can maximise *my* happiness by helping you because you will help me. Solidarity, however, is different. It is the idea that there is an irreducible 'us'. There is *our* happiness, upon which my happiness is based, and yours as well. We help one another because that is what is better for the group. This way of thinking leads to team reasoning, which is different from altruism. If we reduce mutual aid to a concept of reciprocal altruism, we will be accepting the individualist dogmas of neoclassical economics.

In other words, if we accept the possibility of collective reasoning, then there is room to talk about group utility, which can be irreducible to individual utility. If decision-making is done using collective reasoning, then the rationality of your agency derives from the rationality of the group agency. This means that the rationality of one member's agency depends on the other member's agency. This is a high level of interdependence, and it is different from reciprocity. It is not anymore helping the other because this might be good for you in the future. It is about helping others because that is the best for the group. The idea here is that a worker helps another worker because they are both members of the working class. When one worker does not join a strike, for example, he harm the group as a whole, including himself.

CONCLUSION: BEYOND INDIVIDUALISM

Returning to Plato, the way Socrates answers Thrasymachus and Glaucon's question about what happiness and justice are, is to start the analysis at the level of the city (Plato 2012, 57, §368e). So, we can derive individual happiness from the happiness of the collective (Plato 2012, 122–123, §420c–e, §421a–b). In game theory, happiness translates into utility. If we consider that humans are essentially social animals, that we need each other, then we can start our analysis of what is good by analysing what a good city is. From the welfare of the city, Socrates derives the welfare of the citizens. The individual understood as a citizen, that is, making sense of what is a human by considering what the city is.

Kropotkin would very much disagree with Plato's idea of a strong state, but a collectivist account need not support authoritarianism. Team reasoning is an account of how people can form a unity in their agency without hierarchy.

A group does not need one person thinking for the whole group. Each person in the group can reason at a collective level. Also, this is a form of methodological collectivism. The discussion about what establishes the group payoff need not impose the majority over the minority. Such a discussion would go beyond the scope of this chapter.

This chapter aimed to show that evolutionary theory maintained the individualist assumption from classic game theory, and the problem is that some authors, like Dawkins, aim to explain human behaviour using classic game theory without putting into question the individualist assumption. This leads to an individualistic notion of prosocial agency, that is, as reciprocal altruism. I argued that it is possible to assume that people can reason at the collective level. This leads to a collectivist notion of prosocial agency, that is, as solidarity. We can understand solidarity as mutual aid, but mutual aid should not be reduced to reciprocal altruism, as that would be to admit the neoclassical framework of human agency. Or, as the expression goes: solidarity, not charity.

BIBLIOGRAPHY

Aumann, Robert J. 1959. "Acceptable Points in General Cooperative n-person Games." *Contributions to the Theory of Games* 4: 287–324.

Axelrod, Robert. 1984. *The Evolution of Cooperation*. New York: Basic Books.

Bacharach, Michael. 2006. *Beyond Individual Choice: Team and Frames in Game Theory*. Princeton, NJ: Princeton University Press.

Cournot, Antoine A., Irving Fisher, and Nathaniel T. Bacon. 1897 [1838]. *Researches into the Mathematical Principles of the Theory of Wealth*. New York: Macmillan.

Dawkins, Richard. 2017 [1976]. *The Selfish Gene*. 40th anniversary edition. Oxford: Oxford University Press.

Hobbes, Thomas. 1996 [1651]. *Leviathan*. Translated by Richard Tuck. Revised student edition. Cambridge: Cambridge University Press.

Kropotkin, Peter. 2009 [1902]. *Mutual Aid: A Factor of Evolution*. London: Freedom Press.

Lloyd, William F. 1834. *A Lecture on the Notion of Value*. London: Roake and Varty.

Mandeville, Bernard. 1970 [1714]. *The Fable of the Bees*. Translated by Phillip Harth. London: Penguin.

Marshall, Alfred. 1898. *Principles of Economics,* Vol. I. 4th ed. London: Macmillan and co.

Menger, Carl. 2007 [1871]. *Principles of Economics*. Auburn: Ludwig von Mises Institute.

Montmort, Pierre R. 1713. *Essay d'analyse sur les jeux de hazard*. Seconde édition. Paris: Chez J. Quillau.

Pareto, Vilfredo. 1972. *Manual of Political Economy*. Translated by Ann S, Schweir, and Alfred Nye. London: Macmillian.

Plato. 2012. *Republic*. Translated by Christopher J. Rowe. London: Penguin.

Ricardo, David. 2002 [1817]. *The Principles of Political Economy and Taxation.* 3rd ed. London: Empiricus Books.

Rubinstein, Ariel. 1991. "Comments on the Interpretation of Game Theory." *Econometrica*, 59(4): 909–924.

Russell, Bertrand. 2001. *The Selected Letters of Bertrand Russell: The Public Years, 1914–1970.* Edited by Nicholas Griffin. New York: Routledge.

Sally, David. 1995. "Conversation and Cooperation in Social Dilemmas: A Meta-Analysis of Experiments from 1958 to 1992." *Rationality and Society* 7(1): 58–92.

Schelling, Thomas C. 1966. *Arms and Influence.* New Haven: Yale University Press.

Schwalbe, Walker. 2001. "Zermelo and the Early History of Game Theory." *Games and Economic Behavior* 34(1): 123–137.

Simon, Hebert A. 1957. *Models of Man: Social and Rational.* New York: John Wiley.

Smith, Maynard J. 1982. *Evolution and the Theory of Games.* Cambridge: Cambridge University Press.

Söllner, Fritz. 2016. "The Use (and Abuse) of Robinson Crusoe in Neoclassical Economics." *History of Political Economy* 48(1): 35–64.

Thatcher, Margaret. 1976. Margaret Thatcher's *Speech to Conservative Central Council, "The Historic Choice".* https://www.margaretthatcher.org/document/102990.

Thatcher, Margaret. 1987. Interview with Margaret Thatcher for *Women's Own.* https://www.margaretthatcher.org/document/106689.

Tomasello, Michael. 2009. *Why We Cooperate.* Cambridge, MA: MIT Press.

von Neumann, John, and Morgenstern, Oskar. 2004 [1944]. *Theory of Games and Economic Behavior.* 60th Anniversary Commemorative Edition. Princeton, NJ: Princeton University Press.

von Wieser, Friedrich. 1891. "The Austrian School and the Theory of Value." *The Economics Journal of the British Economic Association* 1: 108–121.

Walras, Leon. 1954 [1874]. *Elements of Pure Economics.* Translated by William Jaffé. London: George Allen and Unwin LTD.

Wigner, Eugene P. 1967. *Symmetries and Reflections: Scientific Essays of Eugene P. Wigner.* London: Indiana University Press.

Chapter 11

Selfish Genes, Evil Nature

The Christian Echoes in Neo-Atheism

Ole Martin Sandberg

In the opening chapter of *The Selfish Gene*, Richard Dawkins writes: 'Be warned that if you wish, as I do, to build a society in which individuals cooperate generously and unselfishly towards a common good, you can expect little help from biological nature' (Dawkins 2006, 3).[1] If we want to find sources of morality and social relations, we should not look to nature as it teaches us nothing but selfishness and ruthless competition. A human society based on the gene's laws 'would be a very nasty society in which to live' (*Ibid.*, 3). His book is thus not meant to glorify this fundamentally selfish nature or to say that it determines our destiny because he goes on to say that even though we are 'born selfish' we can still 'try to *teach* generosity and altruism' (*Ibid.*, 3).[2] He posits a radical distinction between our biological nature, humans as animals or 'gene machines', and our social culture which is unique for humans and sets us apart from the rest of nature: 'Among animals, man is uniquely dominated by culture, by influences learned and handed down' (*Ibid.*, 3). This uniquely human invention, culture, gives us the ability to transcend and even break away from our nature: 'we have the power to turn against our creators. We, alone on earth, can rebel against the tyranny of the selfish replicators' (*Ibid.*, 201).

While Dawkins is a firm proponent of the theory of evolution, these ideas strongly indicate that he believes humans are capable of breaking the chain of evolution and become something radically new: A species that is no longer bound by nature and has separated itself from its biological ancestors. There is no indication of the plasticity usually assumed in evolutionary accounts:

---

[1] I will be referring to the 2006 edition of *The Selfish Gene* because part of my interest here is in the additions that appeared after the original publication.
[2] Emphasis in original. All italics in quotations throughout this text are original.

the gradual morphing of one thing into another where the latter retains parts of the former but puts them to a different use. The Dawkinsian history of evolution is a long uninterrupted chain of ruthlessly competitive animals that suddenly breaks when the rational and cultured human emerges. Likewise, each human organism ontologically consists of chains of selfish units (strings of DNA and genes), which can be controlled by rational beings rebelling against their inner nature.

This view is hardly consistent with Charles Darwin's version of evolution, which is based on continuity between species. Furthermore, even though Dawkins is today mostly known for his firebrand atheism, the view has echoes of Christian cosmology and morality. This is not exactly a new debate – Dawkins's views are almost indistinguishable from those of the nineteenth-century English biologist Thomas Henry Huxley who divided the world into two separate realms: that of nature and that of human society and ethics. This view was critiqued by the Russian naturalist Peter Kropotkin, who insisted that human morality must be given a naturalistic explanation located in our nature. This chapter explores that debate and discusses how it applies to Dawkins's selfish gene-theory. Finally, it draws upon Friedrich Nietzsche whose atheism has little in common with the 'new atheism' movement Dawkins has championed. Nietzsche was also influenced by Darwin but came to quite different conclusions. He feared evolution would not benefit the strong-spirited but rather promote the 'slave morality' of the masses. I argue that although they disagreed politically, Kropotkin explicitly rejects the 'life-denying' morality and concept of equality that favours 'mediocrity' that Nietzsche opposed. Throughout the chapter I discuss whether the different positions lead to biological essentialism and determinism, concluding with the argument that human behaviour is not just impacted by our biology but also by the stories we tell ourselves about our nature.

WHAT IS 'SELFISHNESS'?

The central thesis of *The Selfish Gene* is that the relevant unit of evolution is the gene, not the organism. The gene is what continues over generations, if successful, or perishes if not. Individual organisms do not survive or reproduce themselves; they merely pass on some of their genes. This gene-centred view has helped biologists explain seemingly altruistic acts among animals: An animal might jeopardise its survival in certain cases but if it helps the survival of kin carrying the same genes then it would be advantageous from the gene-perspective. The individual organism is merely a vehicle for reproducing genes. Dawkins's point is that a gene that results in a specific trait would not have survived evolution if that trait were harmful to the reproduction of the gene that causes it. In this sense, 'selfish' simply means that which survives.

This is a useful thesis, but it can be forced to do more work than it is capable of. The thesis does not in itself support the claim that the individual organism is selfish because of its 'selfish' genes. To conflate those two levels of analysis would be a 'fallacy of composition'. It merely means that genes that cause their own extinction will not be passed on to future generations. This does not say much about which traits they can give rise to, as different traits can be beneficial in different circumstances. Even if they give rise to behavioural traits that benefit the survival of the individual organism, that says nothing about the motives of that organism. Selfishness in the evolutionary sense, whether at the gene or organism level, does not necessarily imply psychological or behavioural selfishness at the organism level. And yet, that is what Dawkins concludes when he writes that because of our genes 'we are born selfish' (Dawkins 2006, 3).

In the introduction to the thirtieth-anniversary edition of *The Selfish Gene* Dawkins admits this mistake and asks the readers to 'mentally delete that rogue sentence and others like it' (Dawkins 2006, ix). It is clear that he regrets the use of the word 'selfish' in the title of a book he primarily wanted to be a defence of the gene-centric theory of evolution. He even claims that '[t]he Cooperative Gene would have been an equally appropriate title for this book, and the book itself would not have changed at all' (*Ibid.*, ix). This is a rather odd claim. It is clear from the initial pages that the book is not merely a scientific treaty defending the gene-centric approach to evolution. It has a strong normative message. This message would not make any sense if we replaced the word 'selfish' with 'cooperative' so that the opening chapter said that a human society based on the gene's law of universal *cooperation* would be a very nasty society in which to live and that if you wish to build a society in which individuals cooperate towards a common good, you can expect little help from biological nature because we are born *cooperative*. Such warnings make little sense. It is more than a few 'rogue sentences'. The emphasis on natural selfishness is the explicit theme of the book. Like in this passage where he slips directly from the level of genes to the behaviour of individual organisms: 'I shall argue that a predominant quality to be expected in a successful gene is ruthless selfishness. This gene selfishness will usually give rise to selfishness in individual behavior' (Dawkins 2006, 2). And this one that conflates 'selfishness' in the evolutionary sense with selfishness in the behavioural sense:

> If you look at the way natural selection works, it seems to follow that anything that has evolved by natural selection should be selfish. Therefore we must expect that when we go and look at the behaviour of baboons, humans, and all other living creatures, we shall find it to be selfish. (*Ibid.*, 4)

The quote continues: 'If we find that our expectation is wrong, if we observe that human behaviour is truly altruistic, then we shall be faced with something puzzling, something that needs explaining' (*Ibid.*, 4). But that would not be a puzzle at all if the book had emphasised cooperativeness instead of selfishness. Dawkins is not merely defending a scientific thesis with a technical use of 'selfishness'. He uses the word in its standard, normative, sense and the book contains a strong moral message: 'Our genes may instruct us to be selfish, but we are not necessarily compelled to obey them all our lives' (*Ibid.*, 3).

BREAKING OUT OF NATURE

Dawkins sees nature and the creatures in it as amoral and selfish but also believes humans can suppress our natural inclinations. Where does this capacity come from, since not from nature? To explain that, Dawkins throws out the gene as the sole basis of evolution (Dawkins 2006, 191) and introduces a new factor: 'memes'. Memes are the idealist corollary to the materialist genes: they are the basic units of culture and ideas that replicate themselves and are passed on from organism to organism. He still maintains genetic evolution as the foundational principle for the majority of human existence, but it is not sufficient for an understanding of the evolution of 'modern man' (*Ibid.*, 191). For eons, life has been governed by natural evolution but 'a new seizure of power is now just beginning' (*Ibid.*, 22).

The idea that humans are unique and the result of a radical break with our evolutionary ancestors – with evolution itself – does not sit comfortably with the general tenets of evolutionary theory. Darwin emphasised gradual and quantitative changes and pointed to our relationship and similarities with our simian ancestors. He did not advocate our disavowal of the family line or see us as essentially and radically different. But Dawkins is certainly not the first to see humans as the exception to the logic of evolution.

A contemporary of Darwin, Alfred Russel Wallace, also conceived the theory of evolution through natural selection but he could not see how this process would have led to the moral and intellectual capacities of humans. Like Dawkins, Wallace thought there must be a parallel factor, a unique human essence that could shield the human mind from the malicious processes of biological evolution. The belief that natural selection was insufficient led Wallace on a path to extra-natural ideas and spiritual practices (see Kottler 1974, 163) which Dawkins would scorn. Another uncomfortable ally can be found in the Catholic Church, which in 1996 partially accepted the theory of evolution but declared that humans were an exception: 'With man, then, we find ourselves in the presence of an ontological difference, an ontological leap, one could say' (John Paul II 1997). The pope was aware that this is an inconsistency: 'Does not the posing of such ontological discontinuity run counter to that physical continuity which seems to be the main thread of research into evolution?' (*Ibid.*) The same question might well be posed to Dawkins.

The most appropriate comparison to Dawkins, though, is another contemporary of Darwin. Although he is never mentioned in the book, *The Selfish Gene* seems like a modern version of the thoughts of Thomas Henry Huxley who wrote: 'From the point of view of the moralist the animal world is on about the same level as a gladiator's show' in which only 'the strongest, the swiftest, and the cunningest live to fight another day' (Huxley 1895, 199–200). Huxley describes life in the state of nature, in which 'primitive men' must have found themselves, as 'a continual free fight, and beyond the limited and temporary relations of the family, the Hobbesian war of each against all was the normal state of existence' (*Ibid.*, 204). Like Thomas Hobbes, Huxley believed this natural state could and should be stopped by the invention of society and the state: 'The history of civilization – that is, of society – on the other hand, is the record of the attempts which the human race has made to escape from this position' (*Ibid.*, 204). While nature does not contain anything moral, society does, and it is only in society – or rather, the state – that humans become truly humans, that is, realise the unique quality that distinguishes them from other animals. Only in society can 'the primitive savage' be transformed into 'ethical man' who escapes from 'the animal kingdom' to establish a 'kingdom of man' (*Ibid.*, 205). The behaviours and motivations of 'man as a mere member of the animal kingdom' and 'ethical man – the member of society or citizen' are in direct contradiction. The animalistic man does whatever 'takes his fancy', while 'the ideal of the ethical man is to limit his freedom of action' (*Ibid.*, 205).

Huxley divides the world into two realms. The struggle for existence in which evolution occurs he calls 'the cosmic process', while human civilisation is a result of what he calls 'the ethical process'. One is a product of nature, the other of culture; one determines our baser and selfish instincts while the other guides our higher virtues, and the two are in constant conflict: 'the ethical progress of society depends, not on imitating the cosmic process, still less in running away from it, but in combating it' (Huxley 1895, 83). This is to be done by individual and social self-restraint and suppression of our instincts. Alone, the individual cannot do this, so it must be backed by laws and moral precepts 'directed to the end of curbing the cosmic process and reminding the individual of his duty to the community' (*Ibid.*, 82). Huxley sees human civilisation as a long and gradual escape from nature, although it is not a struggle in which we can ever achieve full victory. The reason is that the ethical process is partially self-defeating. Huxley draws upon the Malthusian theory of exponential population growth which could be held in check in primitive societies by war, murder and infanticide, but as morality evolves we lose these checks (*Ibid.*, 208). This leads to overpopulation and a potential return to the struggle for existence. Huxley disagrees with the political prescripts of Malthus's and the later 'social Darwinists' that welfare reforms would merely cause the poor to breed more children than they could feed, and that it would be better to let 'nature' take its course. It is in the desperation of the poor that the struggle for existence – the fight over resources – plays out, and this is what society is there to prevent. If it does not, 'animal man, finding that the ethical man has landed him in such a slough, resumes his ancient sovereignty, and preaches anarchy' (*Ibid.*, 215).

Dawkins too is concerned about Malthusian population growth. Although he hardly ever mentions Malthus, the Malthusian principle of exponential growth has been at the core of Dawkins's writings from the start and he frequently paraphrases him.[3] Dawkins explicitly declares: 'Mankind is having too many children' (Dawkins 2006, 110), and he deploys the Malthusian argument that increases in food-production 'may well make the problem worse, by speeding up the rate of the population expansion' (*Ibid.*, 111). Dawkins finds it morally imperative that we take measures to restrain our biological instinct to reproduce. Such measures are possible because humans 'have the conscious foresight to see ahead to the disastrous consequences of over-population' (*Ibid.*, 111). But as he immediately acknowledges, it is the assumption of the book that we are 'guided by selfish genes, who most certainly cannot be expected to see into the future, nor to have the welfare of the whole species at heart'. So where does this capacity come from? It must be located outside of nature, and to succeed it must suppress our bodily nature.

This is Huxley's cosmological dualism revisited, but it is also a dualism that has much longer roots and is ingrained in the culture of both Huxley and Dawkins. I am talking, of course, of the predominant Christian worldview where the world is divided into the earthly and the heavenly realms and humans into flesh and spirit. When nature and our bodies are considered wicked, corrupt and sinful, morality and salvation can only be found in the transcendental realm of pure spirit. Since we are not pure spirit, we must constantly struggle to restrain our bodily desires. Self-restraint and asceticism are not unique to Christianity – we also find them in Buddhism for example – and

[3] The first time Dawkins makes an actual reference to Malthus is, as far as I can tell, in a footnote in *The Greatest Show on Earth* (Dawkins 2009, 399) but he frequently paraphrases him without attribution. Compare the following quotes: 'Population, when unchecked, increases in a geometrical ratio. Subsistence increases only in an arithmetical ratio' (Malthus 1798, 14). 'Hence the population will tend to grow exponentially until checked by competition for resources or raw materials' (Dawkins 1997, 285). Malthus describes the positive checks on population growth as 'war, pestilence, and famine' (Malthus 1798, 101) while Dawkins writes that 'famine, plague, and war' will set the limits (Dawkins 2006, 111). Malthus writes about delayed marriage as the first preventive check on population growth (Malthus 1798, 63), a proposal Dawkins repeats (Dawkins 2006, 111).

dualism can be traced back at least to Plato. But the repression of the carnal and corporeal was a distinctive element in the foundation of Christianity, especially in Paul (see Romans 8:6–10), and with Augustine it became one of the centrepieces of Christian doctrine (Cherry 2018, 89). The idea that humans are unique and exceptional, that we have special capacities that set us radically apart from the rest of 'creation', is also in line with the dominant interpretations of Christianity.[4] Huxley and Dawkins both follow a long tradition of seeing humans as inherently sinful, a state we can only overcome by consciously striving towards a transcendent goal: to break out of nature and break with our nature.[5] They also locate the source of this wickedness in our tendency to reproduce, that is, in sexuality, which is also associated with the Fall of Man that caused Original Sin. To quote Max Stirner (2017, 198): 'Our atheists are pious people'. Dawkins, who has in recent decades mostly been known as a professional atheist, has gotten rid of God, which is not that hard a task in our time, but failed to get rid of Christian morality and metaphysics. Nietzsche called this a particular 'English' form of atheism that merely proves how dominating the Christian value system has been: It can continue even without God to guarantee the transcendental morals. But Nietzsche insists that 'when you give up Christian faith, you pull the rug out from under your right to Christian morality as well' (Nietzsche 2005, 194).

KROPOTKIN'S ANTI-DUALISM

There has been a range of critiques of Dawkins's book since its publication.[6] But since the theory is so similar to Huxley's it is worth drawing attention to the critique Huxley received in his time, particularly that of the Russian naturalist and anarchist Peter Kropotkin, who also worked in the footsteps of Darwin. Of particular interest is his critique of the dualistic worldview. This dualism is necessary for both Huxley and Dawkins as they start by describing the natural and biological processes as fundamentally opposed to any morality, and then insist that we nevertheless have conceptions of 'the good' and capacity for moral progress. Addressing Huxley, Kropotkin wrote that the

---

4 There are of course always exceptions, as Christianity is not monolithic. Two notable figures within the Catholic tradition who both had some distinctly different views on nature and animals are Francis of Assisi and Hildegard von Bingen.

5 Compare with Frans de Waal's comment on Dawkins: 'The image of humanity's innate depravity and its struggle to transcend that depravity is quintessentially Calvinist, going back to the doctrine of original sin' (de Waal 2009, 17).

6 Some critical works in biology are Sober and Wilson, *Unto Others* (1998); de Waal, *Good Natured* (2009); and West-Eberhard, *Developmental Plasticity and Evolution* (2003). For philosophical critiques see especially Midgley, *Evolution as a Religion* (2002) chap. 15.

'evolutionist philosopher has to solve a deep contradiction which he himself has introduced into his philosophy' (Kropotkin 1924, 12).

The Huxleyian-Dawkinsian theory is that for millennia there was 'no evil and no good, nothing but blind pitiless indifference' (Dawkins 1996, 133) which developed in a process in which only the most ruthless traits could be successful and reproduced. According to Dawkins, 'blindness to suffering is an inherent consequence of natural selection' (Dawkins 2004, 9). But out of this emerged something that is the complete opposite – it came with the unique human mind which created society and laws and ethics as well as caring about suffering. Yet it did not emerge because those things were beneficial to our survival and reproduction; that would make it a natural result of evolution. Somehow it emerged *despite* the laws of nature which it works to counteract. Huxley was aware of the contradiction but willing to bite the bullet: 'I can only reply, that if the conclusion that the two are antagonistic is logically absurd, I am sorry for logic' (Huxley 1895, 12). Dawkins, on the other hand, fails to see that there is any problem. He brushes it off by saying 'What is dualist about that? Obviously nothing' (Dawkins 2006, 302). But that is not obvious. The question is where the ability for self-restraint comes from if it contradicts our biological nature? He says it is located in our brain but is our brain not also a result of evolution? If evolution gives us nothing but selfish desires whence did we get the ability to do anything else? By placing the origin of morality outside the process of natural selection, it cannot be given a naturalistic explanation.[7] It is transcendental. Kropotkin writes:

> But where are the roots, where is the origin of the ethical process? It could not originate from observation of Nature, because, according to Huxley's assertion, Nature teaches us the opposite; it could not be inherited from pre-human times, because among the swarms of animals, before the appearance of man, there was no ethical process even in an embryonic form. Its origin, consequently, lies *outside of Nature*. Hence, the moral law of restraining personal impulses and passions originated like the Mosaic Law – not from already existing customs, not from habits that had already become ingrained in human nature, but it could appear only as a divine revelation, that illuminated the mind of the law-giver. It has a superhuman, nay, more than that, a supernatural origin. (Kropotkin 1924, 285)

[7] Today the primatologist Frans de Waal repeats Kropotkin's critique when he says: 'By thus locating morality outside of nature, these scientists have absolved themselves from trying to fit it into their evolutionary perspective' (de Waal 2009, 16). Stephen Jay Gould makes a similar point in *Ever Since Darwin* (Gould 1992, 261).

Kropotkin rejects this dualism and insists on a consistently naturalistic explanation. The problem, according to Kropotkin, is not in the theory of evolution but the Malthusian interpretation of the factors that determine natural selection. Darwin used Malthus's phrase 'the struggle for existence', albeit as a metaphor, but most of the Russians who otherwise accepted Darwin's theory were sceptical of this element (see Todes 1987). They simply did not see the struggle for existence caused by overpopulation in conditions of limited resources. This might be explained by the fact that the British naturalist primarily studied life in the Caribbean Islands, which is constrained on little space, while the Russians focused on the vast open landmasses of Siberia. The conditions of life, and hence of evolution, are different in such circumstances. Kropotkin recollects his first expedition: 'we vainly looked for the keen competition between animals of the same species which the reading of Darwin's work had prepared us to expect' (Kropotkin 1902, 9).

This does not mean there is no struggle and thus no natural selection in these habitats. The struggle is not the fight over resources but a struggle against the elements and the harsh environment. In such circumstances, it is plausible that the factors of evolution and adaptation are different. Kropotkin set out to describe one such factor: Mutual aid or the tendency of animals to come together in social groups where they help each other survive. This is no departure from Darwin who stressed that his metaphorical use of the phrase 'struggle for existence' did not only refer to physical combat but also the adaptation to particular environmental conditions, and to 'dependence of one being on another' (Darwin 1859, 62). Darwin wrote that 'with those animals which were benefited by living in close association, the individuals which took the greatest pleasure in society would best escape various dangers; whilst those that cared least for their comrades and lived solitary would perish in greater numbers' (Darwin 1871, 80). This is Darwin's evolutionary explanation of the origins of social instincts 'which must have been acquired by man in a very rude state, and probably even by his early ape-like progenitors' (Darwin 1871, 86).

Darwin sought to locate the foundations for moral instincts and social behaviours in nature, and in biological drives that predate humans. Since most animals live in social groups, as did our pre-human ancestors, they too must have instincts that facilitate social behaviour. For Hobbesians such as Huxley and Dawkins, the 'state of nature' is one of ruthless competition, and only through conscious foresight and rational deliberation can society and social behaviour be developed. This has it upside down. As Kropotkin reminded Huxley, 'the appearance of societies on the earth preceded the appearance of man' (Kropotkin 1924, 152); thus cooperation must have come before 'modern man'. Darwin's theory of evolution is based on the principle of 'natura non facit saltum' – that evolution happens by slight successive variations and does not take leaps (Darwin 1859, 194). Huxley did not agree with this principle and privately debated it with Darwin from the first reading of *Origin of the Species* to the end of his life (Huxley 1894). For Huxley, nature must have taken a leap when it created humans. It is pertinent to stress that the social instincts, which are necessary for social behaviour, are merely a foundation, a starting point, for 'higher ethical feelings' (Kropotkin 1924, 16), not morality itself. For that to develop, according to Darwin, we need mental faculties, language and the sociability that takes place in culture (Darwin 1871, 72). These things Huxley and Dawkins agree with, but they see them as separate from the natural instincts, not complementary to them. For Dawkins, morality is founded in culture and language and works against nature. He is thus not a determinist because he deploys both the metaphor of the biological chain and the discursive chain: DNA might be in undisputed charge today, but with memes a new seizure of power is possible (Dawkins 2006, 22). In Darwin's model there is no need for such a radical break.

Kropotkin builds upon Darwin but adds other elements to the development of morality. As a geographer, he is interested in environmental factors, which to humans include social relations. As mutual aid, which he identifies with Darwin's 'social instincts', becomes more established in a community we can develop a sense of 'justice' – the desire to be treated as equals – and only to the degree that social relations become more equitable, and class distinctions fade away, can we finally develop what he sees as a proper morality (Kropotkin 1924, 30). He too, is thus not a biological determinist, because environmental and social factors have the largest roles. 'Mutual aid' is the biological foundation of an 'ascending series' that includes 'justice', and 'morality', with the latter being more 'unstable' (*Ibid.*, 30–31). We could call it a chain that starts with some rigid biological links but then becomes more plastic and indeterminate as social links are added to it. Thus, the sociability that is the result of the biological need for mutual aid might, in one environmental and social setting, result in a desire to help others while another person with a different input might express it as a desire to get social recognition through domination or status. Biological needs alone do not determine behaviour any more than genes determine phenotype as both rely on other factors, including social and environmental, for their expression.

Kropotkin is thus not, as some postanarchists claim, an essentialist in the sense that he thinks morality and benevolence are universal human features.[8] Todd May and Saul Newman both insist that anarchists like Kropotkin believe that 'the human essence is a good essence' (May 1994, 62) and that 'human subjectivity is essentially moral and rational' (Newman 2007, 48).

[8] Two critical assessments of the postanarchist critique can be found in Franks (2007); Antliff (2007).

Kropotkin addresses this most directly in the essay 'Are we good enough?' where he notes that 'if all men were good-hearted, kind, and just, they would never exploit one another' (Kropotkin 1998, 81). But clearly, anarchists are aware that people do exploit one another – Kropotkin spent most of his life struggling against oppression and injustice. Therefore, he says, 'when we hear men saying that the Anarchists imagine men much better than they really are, we merely wonder how intelligent people can repeat that nonsense' (Kropotkin 1998, 83). He reverses the trope and says that it is precisely because people are *not* the 'compassionate fellows which we should like to see them' that anarchists want to eliminate the institutions 'which permits them to oppress and exploit one another' (*Ibid.*, 82).

If the postanarchist accusation of benevolent essentialism was right Kropotkin would have a theoretical contradiction no smaller than that of Huxley's. May and Newman both attribute to him the view that people are 'naturally good; if the obstacles to that goodness are removed' (May 1994, 63), with those obstacles being the oppressive power of the state that 'stultifies the development of humanity's innate moral characteristics' (Newman 2007, 38). But whence did this oppressive power come from if human nature is so benevolent? It cannot come from humans if 'power exists in an oppressive and antagonistic relationship with man' as Newman claims is the anarchist position (Newman 2007, 37). This would simply be another cosmological dualism with the opposite values, not a consistent naturalism as Kropotkin intended. To be consistent, Kropotkin must place the capacity for both morality *and* amorality in human nature; and that is what he does. He explicitly acknowledges that we have capacities for 'greed, vanity and thirst for power' (Kropotkin 1924, 336) as well as for solidarity. He is not advancing a one-sided view of a monolithic human nature but sees us as consisting of a 'multitude of separate faculties, autonomous tendencies' which means we are 'always changeable' (Kropotkin 1927a, 119). Which tendencies within us become dominant depends upon environmental, that is, social, factors, and which of them we strengthen by practice and habit: 'to act unjustly means to train your brain to *think unjustly*' (Kropotkin 1924, 337).

FINDING SATISFACTION IN LIFE

Catherine Malabou (this volume, 16) poses the question of why people should act in solidarity. She rightly points out that if mutual aid and altruism defined a biological human 'essence' then there would be no need to inquire into the motivation for solidaristic behaviour; it would simply come naturally as an instinct. Clearly, that is not the case. The opposite answer, provided by Dawkins, does no better. According to Dawkins, our biological essence is one of ruthless selfishness and it requires a conscious suppression of the instincts for us to act ethically. The drawback to this model is that it is inherently unstable, which Dawkins acknowledges. An ethical theory that requires the conscious suppression of one's biological desires and instincts is difficult enough for an individual, but that individual is also faced with the problem that everyone else might not have the same self-control, or even the preference, to restrain themselves, which would make the moral individual vulnerable to being exploited by the others. This is the dilemma of Hobbes's 'state of nature'[9] and a feature of the game-theoretical 'Prisoner's Dilemma' according to which rational self-interested individuals cannot cooperate for their common good (see Costa, this volume). Dawkins argues that even though people can engage in reciprocal cooperation by using their '*conscious* foresight' (Dawkins 2006, 73) to act in their long-term interest there is a constant danger that cooperation will break down because some individual is tempted by short-term gain. In other words, there is a constant battle between reason and instincts.

But does cooperation require conscious calculation and suppression of our instincts? When regular people are exposed to the Prisoner's Dilemma they defy the assumptions of the economic models about human behaviour. In decades of experiments, people consistently show a high degree of trust and cooperation. Rather than calculating potential benefits of various strategies they tend to be affected by factors that have nothing to do with the immediate incentive structure: face-to-face contact, casual communication and so on (Sally 1995). Meanwhile, those who approach it with strategic calculation tend to do quite poorly (Frank et al. 1993). This is not that surprising. Many evolutionarily beneficial behaviours would be less efficient if they had to rely only on our rational deliberations and conscious decisions: when we burn our fingers, we instantly withdraw them from the flames without deliberation (Sober and Wilson 1998, 316). Neuroscientist António Damásio describes how people intuitively learn the patterns of a game by relying on deeper emotional reactions not available to subjects with specific brain damage who try and fail to analyse it rationally (Damásio 1995, 213). Conscious foresight and rational calculations are not always needed for us to do what is in our long-term interest. If living in cooperative social groups is beneficial for human survival then nature would have done wisely to equip us with instincts that help us take pleasure in the company of others (Darwin 1871, 72) instead of waiting for us to develop unique intellectual capacities.

Dawkins's idea that cooperative behaviour can only come about through rational and conscious suppression of bodily instincts brings to mind

[9] 'For he that performeth first, has no assurance the other will perform after [. . .] therefore he which performeth first, does but betray himself to his enemy' (Hobbes 1998, 91).

Nietzsche's critique of ascetic morality: 'To *have* to fight the instincts – that is the formula for decadence: as long as life is *ascending*, happiness is equal to instinct' (Nietzsche 2005, 166). The two prominent anti-theists could not be more in disagreement on this issue. Dawkins laments that the genes have been in 'undisputed charge' and hopes that the memes represent a new seizure of power (Dawkins 2006, 22), while Nietzsche mocks this position: 'The drives want to act like tyrants; an even stronger counter-tyrant needs to be invented' (Nietzsche 2005, 165). Nietzsche was profoundly influenced by the theory of evolution (Johnson 2010, 2) but disagreed with the conclusions. Progress could not come out of the struggle for existence, he believed, because the weak and the average would dominate the stronger and exceptional through their greater numbers, their prudence and cunningness (Nietzsche 2003, 259). In *Genealogy of Morals,* he develops a counter-narrative to the Darwinian Theory. In Nietzsche's version, the physiologically weak and pathological types, the priest-caste, created a moral system based on resentment of the power and life-force of the strong, the warrior-caste, and they made a virtue of their own weakness. This 'slave-morality' eventually seized power and became dominant. One of the methods was mutual aid, which allowed the priest-cast to appeal to the lowest levels of society and led to the establishment of communities (Nietzsche 2009, 113). To take pleasure in the company of others, which for Darwin must have been a factor in the evolution of social species, Nietzsche associates with weakness, while the 'strong people strive to separate *from* each other' (Nietzsche 2009, 113). Thus the weak band together and impose their value-system upon the strong who do not get to reproduce; the result according to Nietzsche is the 'opposite' of what Darwin theorised (Nietzsche 2003, 258).

This is a misunderstanding of Darwin, who emphatically did not say evolution favours those who are 'strong', physically or in any other sense.[10] 'Survival of the fittest' means, among other things, that those who cooperate can have an evolutionary advantage. Nietzsche's strong-willed individuals might be strong in some other sense, but if their desire to be alone leads them to perish alone, then they are not evolutionary strong (Atterton 2019, 423). Nietzsche's position also contains the contradiction Kropotkin pointed out, except inverted: If Nietzsche believed evolution would lead to the 'inevitable domination' of the 'average, even *below-average* types' and the elimination of the 'better-constituted types' (Nietzsche 2003, 258) how can he hold out the possibility that the noble, strong spirits will prevail? Here he too introduces a parallel force that can shelter individuals from the processes

---

[10] Nietzsche-scholars agree that Nietzsche by all accounts did not read Darwin and frequently 'attacks him for positions Darwin doesn't hold' (Richardson 2004, 16; see also Johnson 2010, 3; Pearson 1997, 86; Moore 2002, 22; Atterton 2019).

of evolution: the 'will to power' which is an internal force that can manifest in any living being unaffected by external circumstances (Wilson C. 2013, 362). This internal force, which Nietzsche explicitly asserts against Darwin (Richardson 2004, 12), gives him the hope that humans, or at least a select few, can transcend the evolutionary process and become something unique: With the higher spiritual and creative geniuses 'nature, which never makes a leap, has made its one leap in creating them' and allowed them to 'emerge out of animality' (Nietzsche 1997, 158–159). In *Zarathustra*, he urges us to be embarrassed by our simian forefathers (Nietzsche 2006, 6) as we await the arrival of the over-man who has finally broken free of the chain of evolution. Perhaps the distance between Nietzsche and Dawkins is not so great after all.

Misunderstandings of Darwin aside, might there still be something to the critique of egalitarian morality as life-denying resentment? Nietzsche saw this psychological trait in all movements for equality, especially among anarchists (Nietzsche 2009, 56). James Wilson argues that Nietzsche's critique is relevant '*if* belief in the moral equality of human beings were inevitably based on resentment' (Wilson J. 2007, 220). In contrast to the 'slave morality', Nietzsche posits a 'noble morality' which grows out of a 'triumphant affirmation of one's own self' (Nietzsche 2009, 25). This is precisely the type of morality Kropotkin advocates. Kropotkin died before he could finish his grand work, *Ethics*. The last, unwritten, chapter was meant to be a discussion of Nietzsche. We cannot know exactly what he would have said but find clues elsewhere. First, Kropotkin's ethics is far from life-denying. He rejects the anti-naturalistic moralism advocated by Huxley and Dawkins and insists that in order to find happiness as well as morality we need to confirm life: 'We must find moral satisfaction in *life* and not in some form of extra-vital condition' (Kropotkin 1924, 12). Ethics, he says, should be about 'the growth and the development of life' (Kropotkin 1924, 323). This sounds similar to Nietzsche's 'will to life' which emphasises 'growth and expansion' (Nietzsche 2001b, 208).[11] Nietzsche introduces this concept in a critical comment to Darwin where he insists that the 'struggle for survival is only an *exception*' (*Ibid.*) – a view he shares with Kropotkin.

Second, and surprisingly, Kropotkin shares some of Nietzsche's sentiments about equality, while they also fundamentally disagree. To Nietzsche, concepts such as equality and justice represent herd-mentality and a 'levelling down to mediocrity' (Nietzsche 2001b, 241) which will stifle the exceptional and adventurous individual. To Kropotkin, equality is fundamental, but he renounces 'the idea of mutilating the individual in the name of any ideal' (Kropotkin 1927b, 106). According to Kropotkin, equality is the foundation

[11] Kropotkin also writes 'the condition of the maintenance of life is its expansions' (1927b, 109).

for the 'complete liberty of the individual' and the 'free development of all his faculties' (*Ibid.*, 105). Nietzsche himself provides the reason: he talks approvingly of an aristocratic system where countless people 'have to be pushed down and shrunk into incomplete human beings, into slaves, into tools' so they can support and raise 'an exceptional type of being' (Nietzsche 2001a, 152). Surely Kropotkin would say that this debasement of the masses for the sake of a few individuals who cannot stand on their own feet is a reason such a system is incompatible with human flourishing. Despite this important disagreement, Kropotkin does seem to share the view that simple equality is a system of mediocrity. It is a necessary step but should not be the goal for everyone. He writes: 'If you are not conscious of strength within you, if your energies are only just sufficient to maintain a colorless, monotonous life [. . .] well then, keep to the simple principles of a just equality' (Kropotkin 1927b, 113). For others, 'something grander, more lovely, more vigorous than mere equity must perpetually find a place in life' (*Ibid.*, 107). This something more is what Kropotkin considers true morality (*Ibid.*, 108) and it is the opposite of resentment and life-denying acquiescence to weakness. It comes from the human being that is full of force and energy, it is 'nothing but a superabundance of life, which demands to be exercised, to give itself; at the same time, it is consciousness of power' (*Ibid.*, 108). This is far from the 'slave morality' Nietzsche defines as a being premised upon a denial of the other and closer to the 'triumphant affirmation of one's own self' which he considers 'noble morality' (Nietzsche 2009, 25). A crucial difference is that to Kropotkin, the solitary being is wretched 'because he cannot share his thoughts or feelings with others' (Kropotkin 1927b, 110) so the person who is overflowing with emotional and intellectual energy seeks others so he can discharge it and give to them 'without calculation' (*Ibid.*, 109).

Kropotkin does not believe a society based on cooperation and solidarity will be harmonious and friction-less. He addresses Nietzsche's claim that helping the sick and alleviating suffering leads to the 'deterioration of the European race' (Nietzsche 2001a, 56). If struggle for life is the condition for evolution, then we would indeed need a 'revaluation of all those moral "values" which tend to reduce the struggle' (Kropotkin 1924, 12). But Kropotkin has no intention of reducing struggle; he wants to direct it towards other arenas. There will always be conflicts, especially among people who have lost their mental and physical chains, because 'variety, conflict even, is life' while 'uniformity is death' (Kropotkin 1927a, 143). Sometimes there are epochs of revaluation of values where 'a man perceives that what he had considered moral is the deepest immorality' and casts the moral system overboard (Kropotkin 1927b, 112). Kropotkin welcomes this, as they are 'epochs of criticism' and signs that 'thought is working in society' (*Ibid.*, 112). 'To struggle is to live, and the fiercer the struggle the intenser the life', he writes, but adds: 'struggle so that all may live this rich, overflowing life. And be sure that in this struggle you will find a joy greater than anything else can give' (*Ibid.*, 113). That is, Kropotkin claims, the essence of morality, and perhaps here we find a partial answer to Malabou's question about why we should act in solidarity: the motivation comes from within, though not as a simple biological drive but as an intrinsic motivation – the feeling of joy that comes from acting without petty calculations of personal benefits. This motivation is more likely to manifest in a system where people are not forced to compete with each other for access to their daily needs.

CONCLUSION

Darwin's theory of evolution was a major turning-point, not just in natural science but also for humanity's self-perception. It had profound significance for thinkers in the following generations, but interpretations and implications differed wildly – from the 'social Darwinists' who took the descriptive claims of struggle for existence and natural selection to be normative claims about the legitimacy and necessity of national domination, poverty and even eugenics, to the social reformers who wanted to temper the struggle for existence through cultural and moral progression. Even Huxley, the great populariser and public defender of Darwin, disagreed with Darwin. Darwin's theory is one of gradual change, and he attempted to ground human traits in older, ancestral traits of social animals. The human capacity for moral conscience is grounded in nature, in the social instincts that make animals cooperate and survive. Darwin says: 'A man who possessed no trace of such feelings would be an unnatural monster' (Darwin 1871, 90). But for Huxley, as for Dawkins, morality is unnatural. The Huxleyan-Dawkinsian failure to find any source of ethical instincts in the natural world leads them to a dualistic metaphysics where humans are torn between two realms and are the only species with the ability to jump into the moral realm where nature no longer rules. The idea that social progress and cooperation requires the suppression of human nature and desires is a moral theory that is unlikely to succeed and can be felt as more repressive than liberating. It also has strong echoes of Christian doctrine. It is, as Nietzsche said, the 'newest and most preeminent form' of the ascetic ideal (Nietzsche 2009, 123). Nietzsche too decried the struggle for existence. Not because he thought it was immoral but precisely because he felt it was conducive to a certain type of morality. Nietzsche loathed the life-denying asceticism of Christian morality and because of his misunderstanding of Darwin, he believed evolution would, like Christianity, result in the survival and domination of mediocrity. Kropotkin builds directly upon Darwin and expands upon his metaphorical use of the phrase 'struggle for existence' which can take many forms – including members of a community cooperating in their mutual struggle against a harsh environment or perhaps against oppression. His ethics is not based on suppression of human nature or the denial of our desires but rather in creating the conditions where everyone can express 'the greatest amount of vitality' and feel 'the joy of life' (Kropotkin 1927b, 112).

So, what are we to conclude about human nature? Is our behaviour determined by our biology and, if so, is it then conducive or unfavourable to solidarity? I think this question is too simplistic. Kropotkin's friend and comrade, Errico Malatesta, was critical of Kropotkin's tendency to see unity in the universe – a mechanistic materialism where everything is governed by the same principles. This led him to see confirmation of his belief in the principles of mutual aid and decentralisation wherever he looked (Malatesta 1984, 263). Malatesta felt this outlook missed factors that are difficult to explain by mechanistic cause and effect, in particular the human will, and that it led to a false determinism: 'scienticism logically leads to fatalism, that is, to the denial of free will and of freedom' (1984, 41). Perhaps this exaggerates Kropotkin's philosophy (Kinna 2016, 185–195), but Malatesta also states that Kropotkin was quick to forget this mechanistic concept and throws himself into the struggle with the 'confidence of one who believes in the efficacy of his Will' (Malatesta 1984, 264).[12] He furthermore argues that the belief in determinism, and the inevitability of social progress, has led some to lose 'all revolutionary spirit' and withdraw into inactivity (Malatesta 1984, 276). This points to something important in the discussion of human nature and determinism: To believe in a particular theory of the world changes the way we act in the world and thus impacts the world. As I argue elsewhere (Sandberg 2020, 338), the posture of a cynical 'realist' who takes the world 'as it is' without sentiments is itself deeply affective and ideological; it does not just describe but actively shapes the world. To truly believe in a world dominated by ruthless selfishness is to adopt an attitude of distrust and suspicion that cannot foster cooperation whereby the descriptive theory becomes a self-fulfilling prophecy. I thus agree with Malabou (this volume, 25) that the distinction between the biological and the discursive is superfluous and inaccurate. Human nature is not fixed; our brains have evolved to adapt to complex situations and environments and for better or worse this plasticity also makes us susceptible to ideological and discursive claims about human nature. Which story about ourselves is correct depends on which of them we tell ourselves and enact by our praxis. Kropotkin ends his essay on morality

[12] One is reminded of Kant's statement that in order to act we must act 'under the idea of freedom' (Kant 1997, 53), that is, believe that our will can be an effective cause in the world.

(Kropotkin 1927b, 113) with a statement that defies claims of determinism and centres the human will: 'Yours is the choice'.

BIBLIOGRAPHY

Antliff, Allan. 2007. "Anarchy, Power, and Poststructuralism." *SubStance* 36 (2): 56–66.

Atterton, Peter. 2019. "Nietzsche's 'Anti-Darwinism': A Deflationary Critique." In *Nietzsche and Critical Social Theory: Affirmation, Animosity, and Ambiguity*, edited by Christine A. Payne and Michael J. Roberts, 416–433. Leiden: Brill.

Cherry, Robert. 2018. *Jewish and Christian Views on Bodily Pleasure: Their Origins and Relevance in the Twentieth-Century*. Eugene: Wipf and Stock.

Damásio, António. 1995. *Descartes' Error*. New York: Avon Books.

Darwin, Charles. 1859. *On the Origin of Species by Means of Natural Selection, or the Preservation of Favoured Races in the Struggle for Life*. London: John Murray.

Darwin, Charles. 1871. *The Descent of Man and Selection in Relation to Sex, Vol 1*. London: John Murray.

Dawkins, Richard. 1996. *River Out of Eden: A Darwinian View of Life*. Reprint edition. London: Basic Books.

Dawkins, Richard. 2004. *A Devil's Chaplain: Reflections on Hope, Lies, Science, and Love*. Reprint edition. Boston: Mariner Books.

Dawkins, Richard. 2006. *The Selfish Gene: 30th Anniversary Edition*. 3rd ed. Oxford: Oxford University Press.

Frank, Robert H., Thomas Gilovich, and Dennis T. Regan. 1993. "Does Studying Economics Inhibit Cooperation?" *Journal of Economic Perspectives* 7(2): 159–171.

Franks, Benjamin. 2007. "Postanarchism: A Critical Assessment." *Journal of Political Ideologies* 12(2): 127–145.

Gould, Stephen Jay. 1992. *Ever Since Darwin: Reflections in Natural History*. New York London: W. W. Norton & Company.

Huxley, Thomas Henry. 1894. "Letter to William Bateson," February 20, 1894. https://mathcs.clarku.edu/huxley/letters/94.html.

Huxley, Thomas Henry. 1895. *Evolution and Ethics and Other Essays*. Edited by Thomas Henry Huxley. London: Macmillan.

John Paul II. 1997. "Message to the Pontifical Academy of Sciences." *The Quarterly Review of Biology* 72(4): 381–383.

Johnson, Dirk R. 2010. *Nietzsche's Anti-Darwinism*. Cambridge: Cambridge University Press.

Kant, Immanuel. 1997. *Groundwork for the Metaphysics of Morals*. Translated by Mary Gregor. Cambridge: Cambridge University Press.

Kinna, Ruth. 2016. *Kropotkin: Reviewing an Anarchist Tradition: Reviewing the Classical Anarchist Tradition*. Edinburgh: Edinburgh University Press.

Kottler, Malcolm Jay. 1974. "Alfred Russel Wallace, the Origin of Man, and Spiritualism." *Isis* 65(2): 145–192.

Kropotkin, Peter. 1902. *Mutual Aid: A Factor in Evolution*. New York: McClure Phillips & Co.

Kropotkin, Peter. 1924. *Ethics: Origin and Development*. Translated by Louis S. Friedland and Joseph R. Piroshnikoff. New York: The Dial Press.

Kropotkin, Peter. 1927a. "Anarchism: Its Philosophy and Ideal." In *Kropotkin's Revolutionary Pamphlets: A Collection of Writings by Peter Kropotkin*, edited by Roger N Baldwin, 114–144. New York: Dover Publications.

Kropotkin, Peter. 1927b. "Anarchist Morality." In *Kropotkin's Revolutionary Pamphlets: A Collection of Writings by Peter Kropotkin*, edited by Roger N Baldwin, 79–113. New York: Dover Publications.

Kropotkin, Peter. 1998. "Are We Good Enough?" In *Act for Yourselves! Articles from Freedom 1886-1907*, edited by Nicolas Walter and Heiner Becker, 81–86. London: Freedom Press.

Malatesta, Errico. 1984. *Malatesta: Life and Ideas*. London: Freedom Press.

Malthus, Thomas Robert. 1798. *An Essay on the Principle of Population as It Affects the Future Improvement of Society*. [Reprint 1966]. London: Palgrave Macmillan.

May, Todd. 1994. *The Political Philosophy of Poststructuralist Anarchism*. 1st ed. University Park, PA: Pennsylvania State University Press.

Midgley, Mary. 2002. *Evolution as a Religion*. 2nd ed. London: Routledge.

Moore, Gregory. 2002. *Nietzsche, Biology and Metaphor*. 1st ed. Cambridge: Cambridge University Press.

Newman, Saul. 2007. *From Bakunin to Lacan: Anti-Authoritarianism and the Dislocation of Power*. Lanham: Lexington Books.

Nietzsche, Friedrich. 1997. *Untimely Meditations*. Edited by Daniel Breazeale. Translated by R. J. Hollingdale. 2nd ed. Cambridge: Cambridge University Press.

Nietzsche, Friedrich. 2001a. *Beyond Good and Evil: Prelude to a Philosophy of the Future*. Edited by Rolf-Peter Horstmann. Translated by Judith Norman. Cambridge: Cambridge University Press.

Nietzsche, Friedrich. 2001b. *The Gay Science: With a Prelude in German Rhymes and an Appendix of Songs*. Edited by Bernard Williams. Translated by Josefine Nauckhoff and Adrian Del Caro. Cambridge: Cambridge University Press.

Nietzsche, Friedrich. 2003. *Writings from the Late Notebooks*. Edited by Rüdiger Bittner. Translated by Kate Sturge. Cambridge & New York: Cambridge University Press.

Nietzsche, Friedrich. 2005. "Twilight of the Idols." In *Nietzsche: The Anti-Christ, Ecce Homo, Twilight of the Idols, and Other Writings*, edited by Aaron Ridley. Translated by Judith Norman, 153–229. Cambridge: Cambridge University Press.

Nietzsche, Friedrich. 2006. *Thus Spoke Zarathustra*. Edited by Robert Pippin. Translated by Adrian Del Caro. Cambridge: Cambridge University Press.

Nietzsche, Friedrich. 2009. *On the Genealogy of Morals: A Polemical Tract*. Translated by Ian Johnston. Virginia: Richer Resources Publications.

Pearson, Keith Ansell. 1997. *Viroid Life: Perspectives on Nietzsche and the Transhuman Condition*. 1st ed. London and New York: Routledge.

Richardson, John. 2004. *Nietzsche's New Darwinism*. Oxford: Oxford University Press.

Sally, David. 1995. "Conversation and Cooperation in Social Dilemmas: A Meta-Analysis of Experiments from 1958 to 1992." *Rationality and Society* 7(1): 58–92.

Sandberg, Ole Martin. 2020. "Climate Disruption, Political Stability, and Collective Imagination." *Radical Philosophy Review* 23(2), 331–360.

Sober, Elliott, and David Sloan Wilson. 1998. *Unto Others: The Evolution and Psychology of Unselfish Behavior*. Cambridge, MA: Harvard University Press.

Stirner, Max. 2017. *The Unique and Its Property*. Translated by Wolfi Landstreicher. Baltimore: Underworld Amusements.

Todes, Daniel P. 1987. "Darwin's Malthusian Metaphor and Russian Evolutionary Thought, 1859-1917." *Isis* 78(4): 537–551.

Waal, Frans de. 2009. *Good Natured: The Origins of Right and Wrong in Humans and Other Animals*. Cambridge, MA: Harvard University Press.

West-Eberhard, Mary Jane. 2003. *Developmental Plasticity and Evolution*. Oxford: Oxford University Press.

Wilson, Catherine. 2013. "Darwin and Nietzsche: Selection, Evolution, and Morality." *Journal of Nietzsche Studies* 44(2): 354–370.

Wilson, James. 2007. "Nietzsche and Equality." In *Nietzsche and Ethics*, edited by Gudrun von Tevenar, 211–231. Bern: Peter Lang.

Part III

'AT THE END OF THE DAY, IT'S JUST US' – THE ACTUALITY OF MUTUAL AID

Chapter 12

Plastic Encounters

COVID-19 and (De)Racialisation in Canada

Jade Crimson Rose Da Costa

Many scholars believe that the Coronavirus pandemic (COVID-19) has changed political activism (Rasch et al. 2020; Wood 2020a). Questions such as 'How has the COVID-19 pandemic created or denied opportunities for resistance" or "How has COVID-19 shaped the work of social movements?' appeared across countless digital conference agendas and calls for submissions in the spring and summer of 2020, prompting us to consider repeatedly how activism has changed in response to COVID-19. The idea behind these questions is rudimentary: the pandemic brought a halt to our everyday words, freezing the regimes of the normal that hitherto constrained and governed our behaviours, while simultaneously weaponising physical contact, a central component of social movement organising. It thus logically follows that COVID-19 would have affected how we engage in political advocacy.

While I agree with this assertion, I disagree with its underlining temporal logic: that the pandemic unilaterally affected political activists. When one asks, 'How did COVID-19 shape activism', without also asking 'how did

Acknowledgements: First, I would like to thank the editors of this volume for so thoughtfully reviewing and strengthening my chapter. Second, I want to thank my friend Kaitlin Peters for sending me the call for submissions and my friend Giovanni Carranza-Hernandez for not only reviewing the first draft of my chapter but for helping me set boundaries and practice better self-care at the onset of cofounding The People's Pantry. Most importantly, I want to thank my fellow cofounders and admin: Ellie Ade Kur, Yann Gracia, Andrea Román Alfaro, Michelle Huang (黃庭萱) and Paul Pritchard. Your collective willingness and desire to uplift the community and resist social violence and food insecurity is what made TPP possible. I am especially appreciative of Ellie, Yann and Andrea for their continued commitment to lead the direction and scope of our group, as well as the community writ large. Ellie, your insight and vulnerability has always moved me; Yann, your compassion and spirit has always uplifted me; and Andrea, your beautiful mind and soul has always grounded me. Thank you all. Lastly, I want to thank all the logistical, chef and delivery volunteers who make TPP work every single day, especially those working alongside me in the sister initiative, and who are the heart and soul of our network: without y'all, TPP would not exist. To learn more about our community, visit: www.thepeoplespantryto.com/.

activism shape COVID-19', they assume that the relationship between the two is conditional, opposed to dialectical, thereby reducing the complex interchange between collective trauma and political mobilisation to mere cause and effect. In contrast, I hold that the relationship between COVID-19 and social activism is one of dual (constructive-destructive) plasticity (Malabou 2008; 2012), whereby the collective trauma of the former interfaced with the transformative impetus of the latter to rupture, not a healthy system, but rather, the violent terrain from which both phenomena are housed: late Western modernity.

More specifically, I posit that Women, Queer, Trans, Black, Indigenous and People of Color (WQTBIPOC) activisms in Toronto, Canada, provided a basis from which local organisers could better confront, and thus shape, the pandemic. This, in turn, enabled the (albeit brief) plasticisation of whiteness, a process which was *destructive* in logic and yet *constructive* in outcome. My analysis is grounded in my experience of cofounding The People's Pantry (TPP): a WQTBPOC-led,[1] Toronto-based, free grassroots meal programme that offers home-cooked meals and groceries to food-insecure families living in or near the Greater Toronto Area (GTA).

Building on my experiences with TPP, I explore how COVID-19 created a site of social disjuncture that enabled the public to perform care beyond the epistemological violence of whiteness, thereby making space for WQTBIPOC mobilisations to gain wide-spread momentum. I provide a personal account of TPP's emergence, and in this exploration, examine how the collective trauma of COVID-19 interfaced with Toronto-based WQTBIPOC activisms to rupture prevailing notions of life, death and community. Central to my argument is that the forces which made TPP possible predated COVID-19, and that the pandemic merely provided a moment of destruction in which, ironically, the restorative ethics of WQTBIPOC activists could extend into and thus reconstruct the public realm. In arguing this, I shift focus away from the specifics of COVID-19 and towards the (un)known lived lives that foster and sustain mutual aid projects.

DEFINING *PLASTICITY*

While the notion of 'plasticity' has been taken up by various scholars, it is generally considered to be the signature concept of Catherine Malabou. As defined by Malabou (2008, 5), *plasticity* is that which concertedly receives and gives form through the annihilation of the 'very form it is able to receive

[1] When I refer to TPP, I omit the 'I' from 'WQTBIPOC' because none of our cofounders-admins are Indigenous.

or create'. Malabou uses the concept to describe the dialectical nature by which 'social reality' is (de)formed, denotating the dual process of reification and fluidification that animates our existence. The conceit behind her formulation of the term is rooted in the neurosciences, whereby she takes the neuro-dialogical processes by which the human brain ruptures from a predetermined schematic, into an adaptable organ, to frame the contrapuntal interplay between history and agency that conditions social morphology.

Malabou explores two types of plasticity: constructive plasticity and destructive plasticity. Constructive plasticity is a generative phenomenon, one akin to metamorphosis. Here, plasticity works to solve various cognitive impairments by flexibly and creatively redirecting neurological resources (Malabou 2008). In contrast, destructive plasticity comes from trauma and describes the 'formative-destructive power of the wound' (Malabou 2012, 18). In this case, there is no metamorphosis, only the permanent dislocation of one form and the subsequent emergence of a new form, one which 'is neither the sublation nor the compensatory replica of the old form, but rather, literally, a form of destruction'. Thus, we can understand Malabou's notion of plasticity as having both destructive and constructive elements, as a process that gives and receives form either through the reconfiguration *or* the obliteration of what existed before.

My approach to plasticity both extends and troubles this definition. As the queer gender non-binary daughter of a working-class, English-Hungarian settler-immigrant and a middle-class, Goan-Indian-refugee, my existence has always felt plastic. It seems as though I am made up of two energies – white and Brown; gay and straight; settler and colonialised; immigrant and non-immigrant; feminine and masculine; rich and poor – that, in the words of Malabou (2008, 76), 'ceaselessly collide within a resilient person'. Hence, Malabou's work cannot help but speak to and transform my own epistemology. Yet, for this same reason, my interpretation of the term pivots away from Malabou, borrowing from the thinking of Black feminist and queer of colour theorists who not only touch on the particularities of my worlding but, in doing so, diverge from Malabou's materialist-realistic approach (Chen 2012; Jackson 2020; Weheliye 2014).

Building on this scholarship, I engage plasticity as the reality of living under a flawed praxis of being that attempts to bind our existence to a matrix of hierarchal-binary classifications that are predicated upon the fossilisation, bestialisation and abjection of non-whiteness (Da Costa 2020a). In particular, I hold that the modern Western world was designed as a relational and racialised 'ontological totality' in which whiteness gains life through the literal or social death of non-whiteness, thereby placing BIPOC in external relationality to humanity (Weheliye 2014, 22). This view of racialisation is specific to late Western modernity: a catchall term for Western settler-colonial states, such as Canada and the United States, that are conditioned by what has been called the three pillars of white supremacy (Da Costa, 2020a): 1) slaveability/anti-Blackness – the reduction of Black people to historical relics (slaves) and thus abject; 2) genocide – the disappearing of Indigenous folk to justify our stealing of their land; and 3) Orientalism – the rendering of racialised peoples as 'less developed' and thus viable for imperial conquest.

While each pillar operates differently, they are all motivated by the same goal: to bind white settlers and their descendants to the present by either arresting BIPOC back, before or beyond time, thus denying us life within the here-and-now (Da Costa 2020a). Within this milieu, and by extension my framework, whiteness acts as an imperial force that secures its own existence through colonial and racial territorialisations that expel, kill and displace BIPOC. Accordingly, I place race at the crux of all ontological violence and consider the entirety of subjectification/domination to be conditioned by white ascendancy (Ali and Anane-Bediakoh 2020). From here, I view plasticity as the ontological chaos caused by hegemonic whiteness; as the malleable effect of existing in tension with registers of belonging that concertedly render whiteness synonymous with humanity and non-whiteness synonymous with the Other and, in doing so, have built the impossible dichotomy into all other facets of social life (Chen 2012).

With this in mind, plasticity in my analysis resonates most closely with Zakiyyah Iman Jackson's (2020, 10) understanding of the term, which she describes as the '"enduring project of the modern Western world"'. Within this sociohistorical milieu, humanity is secured through the 'abjection of Blackness' (18), the first pillar of white supremacy, in addition to the erasure of Indigeneity and the arresting of people of colour, the second and third pillars (Da Costa 2020a). As a result, Blackness is rendered into 'a plastic way of being', forever fluidified by the 'antiblack bonds of ontological effacement or irresolution' (Jackson 2020, 72). Accordingly, Jackson views plasticity, not as the process of receiving and giving form, but as the fluidification of Blackness within and through the ontologising violence of Western humanist ideologies. While Jackson's focus is on Blackness, her ontology has implications for all Western modernity: within this landscape, whiteness gains form through the concerted plasticisation (read: abjection, subhuman rendering) of Blackness especially and the non-white Other more generally.

This approach to plasticity differs from Malabou's in a few ways. For one, the concept of 'trauma' is only ever taken up indirectly and with different implications, making it difficult to apply Malabou's distinction between constructive and destructive plasticity. In Jackson's view, trauma, specifically the trauma of anti-Blackness, is implicitly built into the very essence of our being. For Black folks, it operates as a mechanism of fluidification that inhibits reification by denying the ability to hold form, while for non-Black, specifically white, folks, this same trauma enables our/their life. Similarly, white supremacy acts as a conditional trauma for all non-white peoples, even as we benefit from anti-Blackness (and or the other two pillars of white supremacy).

Within this framework, what counts as *constructive* plasticity versus *destructive* plasticity is not obvious: Blackness is neither the reconfiguration nor the annihilation of whiteness, but the abject core that conditions and secures white matter. Further, Black subjectivity is not reducible to trauma or repair as is exists in movement – in/against the ontological chaos of white hegemony. The same can be also said about non-whiteness writ large, just with the caveat that anti-Blackness, as well as genocide, result in more abjection when compared to (certain kinds of) Orientalism, such as the othering experienced by non-Black Canadians of colour (Ali and Anane-Bediakoh 2020). Nonetheless, whiteness requires the dehumanisation of all BIPOC to exist in its current (western) form. Accordingly, anti-Blackness/non-whiteness is not the formative suffering 'of the identity that endures it' (Malabou 2012, 18), but a materialised optic of white hegemony. To position it as otherwise, would be to impose a separation between Blackness/Otherness and whiteness that is not possible within the relational-racial worlding of late Western modernity.

This leads me to the main divergence between the two perspectives: while Malabou offers an exploration into how humanity can (and should) take on any form, Jackson (2020, 42) provides a discursive investigation into how the ontologising plasticisation of Blackness is governed by violent operatives of power, thus providing a 'theory of ontologised plasticity'. Jackson observes that: 'In contrast to Malabou's approach, the plastic ontology described here is neither the thing-in-itself nor an immanent ontology of the real but representational or paradigmatic: an a posteriori virtual model of a dynamic, motile mode of antiblack arrangement' (72). In other words, Jackson refurbishes Malabou's notion of plasticity from a material-historical locus of 'immanent metamorphosis' into a discursive-relational site of anti-Black racialisation, giving substantive focus to the interplay between racial violence and fluidification.

Extending Jackson's approach, I focus not on the movement of Blackness per se, but on the entire racial spectra of late Western modernity. Specifically, I illustrate how the 'tyrannies of will and imagination' that render Blackness (and non-whiteness) into a highly malleable mode of life (Jackson 2020, 72), also create possibilities to rupture whiteness. Focusing on COVID-19 and Canada in particular, I posit that because whiteness gains form through the killing and letting die of BIPOC, that the presence of wide-scale loss signalled by a global health pandemic has the capacity to destabilise it, as it troubles the boundaries between (white) life and (racialised) death. In turn, whiteness becomes a 'plastic way of being', undone by the same 'bonds of ontological effacement or irresolution' that bind it to humanity. I thus engage plasticity as a discursive-material exchange between the racialising assemblages of late Western modernity that suture whiteness to life through the otherisation of death, giving substantive focus to how COVID-19 disrupted this process in the context of my life as WQTBIPOC activist and scholar.

Importantly, I consider this exchange to be constitutive of a type of dual plasticity, whereby, akin to Jackson's approach, the distinction between destructive and constructive plasticity is unclear. If, as I claim, white ascendancy is the core of all subjectification/domination, and plasticity the measure and reality of its ontological shortcomings, then its destruction is inherently restorative. The typical language of the wound and trauma is ineffective here: whiteness is the spiritual and ideological wound *and* heart of late Western modernity, to destroy it is to break centuries of trauma that haunt and constrain our lives. Hence, when the collective trauma of COVID-19 plasticised whiteness, arguably constituting a form of destructive plasticity, the act was generative, not just through the restorative interplay between the pandemic and WQTBIPOC activisms, but for the racially wounded ourselves. In this context, destructive plasticity was conditioned by constructive plasticity and similarly therapeutic. Thus, as regards my analysis, I consider constructive and destructive plasticity to be neither wholly catastrophic nor restorative, but rather, interconnected systems of change.

The discussion that follows is both an extension of my existing sociological frameworks as well as an articulation of my personal histories with in/justice: two parts of myself that, much like the rest of me, exist in dialogical juxtaposition with one another, both as I live them and as I write them into this chapter. When I write from my personal experiences, I write with the critical inflection of an academic. I can't help it. To quote novelist Dionne Brand (2020, 20), 'this is just what an academic does'. Similarly, when I experience academia, I do so as the person I described above: as the unruly plastic plasm of power and oppression. But I experience these realities simultaneously, not concertedly, feeling frustrated at myself for claiming to 'know' anything about worlds to which I do not belong, while remaining compelled to do so with absolute authority. Thus, I exist at odds with myself: as an 'expert' who consumes the 'activist' and as an 'activist' who disavows the 'expert'. These tensions pulsate through my analysis. The activist in me welcomes them, the expert in me wrote this caveat in the hopes of excusing them.

I begin as the activist.

NEW GROUP, OLD POLITICS

The People's Pantry (TPP) started with a Facebook post. The post was made by two of our cofounders, Ellie and Yann, on 14 March 2020. Ellie wrote:

> Hello! If you're unable to leave the house for safety reasons or are just in need of food, my partner [Yann] and I have been making meals and dropping off in Toronto. We've been doing it for close friends, but want to open up to others-***prioritizing folks who are immunocompromised, living with a disability and/or my QT/BIPOC. (AK 2020)

The first time I saw this post, I was in the car with my partner as they drove us to my grandma's house to commemorate the ten-year death anniversary of my grandpa. My grandma had originally planned to hold the event on 18 January, when my grandpa had died, but there was a snowstorm that weekend so she had to postpone the event until his birthday: 14 March. This also happened to be the exact moment in which the COVID-19 pandemic hit Canada.

I remember telling my partner that I saw Ellie's post and that I wanted to do the same thing for people in or near our city of Burlington, Ontario, which is located at the southwest outskirts of the GTA. The next day, I made the following Facebook post:

> Hey everyone! Following in Eli AK 's lovely footsteps, I am offering free food prep meals to folx in Burlington, Oakville and Hamilton who are unable to leave the house for safety reasons or are simply in need of food, I am prioritizing the elderly, people living with disabilities/ who are immunocompromised, and QT/BIPOC. (Da Costa 2020b)

One of our other cofounders, Andrea, also saw Ellie and Yann's post and decided to join them in cooking food for people in Toronto, quickly bringing on Michelle and Paul, our two remaining cofounders. Soon, the six of us were individually buying, preparing, and delivering home-cooked meals and groceries to various nearby families.

After a couple of weeks, we consolidated our efforts, forming 'The People's Pantry', a Toronto-based community meal programme providing home-cooked meals and grocery care packages to people living in or near the GTA who have been disproportionately affected by COVID-19. Free of charge, no questions asked. As the only person not living in Toronto, I volunteered to manage our social media accounts, grant applications and finances. Similarly, my food work became our 'sister initiative', covering requests for Burlington, Hamilton, Oakville, Milton, Kitchener-Waterloo, Guelph and

Mississauga, all cities that exist near the southwest border of the GTA. In the span of April, our initiative grew rapidly. We now have about 500 volunteers, with four of the cofounders still acting as administrators: Ellie, Yann, Andrea and I.[2] To date, we have reached over 30,000 people in Ontario, and raised over $180,00 in funds.

In some ways, the conditions that gave rise to TPP were particular to Canada, especially Toronto. For one, Ellie and I both shared our original offers of support to a Facebook group called 'CareMongering-TO: TO Community Response to COVID-19', an online mutual aid platform that was designed to address food hoarding and grocery store overcrowding in Toronto by providing a counterculture to COVID-19-based fearmongering. Soon after the group was created, similar Facebook groups started to appear across the GTA and, eventually, all of Canada, thereby sparking the national phenomenon now known as 'CareMongering': a mutual aid movement that rapidly spread across Canada in the wake of COVID-19 (Wood 2020a).

Generally defined, *mutual aid* is the 'survival work' that ordinary people engage in to support their communities, developing bold and novel ways to redistribute resources and uplift their friends, family and neighbours in times of crisis (Spade 2020, 1). TPP operates according to this same mandate, but in the realm of food justice. Specifically, we promote community food security (CFS): 'universal access to culturally acceptable, nutritionally adequate, sustainable food through local non-emergency channels' (Johnston and Baker 2005, 313). Further, we do this while connecting the problem of hunger to racism, classism, sexism and general injustice, using mutual aid to tackle both food insecurity as well as the systems of violence that cause it.

While many countries used mutual aid to mitigate the effects of COVID-19, it was only Canada that saw the advent of 'CareMongering', a phenomenon that I trace back to Toronto and, more specifically, the city's deep activist roots. According to the Toronto activists who created CareMongering-TO, CareMongering is rooted in the histories of local WQTBIPOC activisms. In the words of one of their cofounders, Ghee Chopra, 'Caremonger is part of a lineage of care networks built by Indigenous, Black, PoC, Sick, disabled, queer, trans, and communities abandoned and oppressed by the Canadian State' (Quoted in Wood 2020a, para 11). What this quote is referencing is that WQTBIPOC activists have long operated according to a radical ethic of care, one that urges us to move beyond the limitations of an idiosyncratic self and foster a political community forged around the 'vibrancy and complexity of difference' (Nash 2011, 11).

[2] It is important to note that Andrea has now, since I originally wrote this chapter, left our group, after moving back to Peru in September 2021.

'CareMongering' is merely a new expression of this old politic; it is not novel. What is novel, however, is that the phenomenon was able to punctuate the Canadian mainstream. This happened for two main reasons. First, CareMongering began in Toronto – one of the few places in the West where organising led by WQTBIPOC 'has reached a critical enough mass to shape and, often, lead local landscapes of activism and art' (Haritaworn et al. 2018, 3). Thus, when COVID-19 happened, Toronto WQTBIPOC activists had the social power to collectively mobilise. Yet, at the same time, it was the digitalisation of social life prompted by COVID-19 that enabled us to transmute our praxis into an online group, thereby allowing it to flourish in the (now virtual) public sphere. This suggests that Toronto WQTBIPOC activists had not only the resources but the means to shape community responses to the pandemic; ergo, 'CareMongering'.

It is from here that I understand the advent of TPP. For one, we are a WQTBPOC-led group who prioritises the oppressed. All but one of our cofounders is racialised. Most of us are women and many of us are queer and/or trans. TPP got energy from us and our commitment to a common ethic of care – from our collective rejection of a singular self and mutual desire to ensure the survival of our communities. Ellie describes how: 'We came together collectively to serve our friends, our families, our peers [. . .] we're serving a lot of our own communities, we don't operate with this [. . .] k1ind of hierarchical thing, we are people showing up for our people' (Toronto/Tkaronto Mutual Aid 2020). With that being said, the main reason we were able to proliferate this energy was because of Facebook groups like CareMongering-TO: these sites offered a rare opportunity to connect with various people across and beyond the GTA, thus transforming the ethic of care that motivated our founders into a multicity mutual aid project.

What is most important about this observation is that, even though COVID-19 created the conditions for CareMongering, and by extension TPP, to emerge, neither of these things would have been possible without the longstanding efforts of WTQBIPOC activists. This claim is demonstrated by who sustained TPP after CareMongering lost momentum: other WQT/BIPOC-led groups in Toronto. Prominent groups include FoodShare Toronto, a community-based food justice enterprise, and the regional organic farms that provide their produce, specifically Black Creek Community Farm (BCCF) and Sundance Harvest. In general terms, these groups supported us by establishing mutual aid networks that delinked Torontonians from unsustainable commodity food chains *well before* COVID-19, thereby securing a 'non-profit food distribution network based on community solidarity' in the GTA from which subsequent WQT/

BIPOC-led mutual aid projects, such as TPP,[3] could flourish (Classens et al. 2014, 219).

In more literal terms, these groups have gifted us resources and supports. Collectively, FoodShare awarded us $6,500 of funding so that we could redistribute over 500 boxes of fresh produce cultivated by BCCF and Sundance Harvest to low-income and BIPOC communities through their Emergency Good Food Box programme. Individually, FoodShare has trusteed us on multiple grant applications, which has allowed us to receive provincial or state funding that we would have otherwise not been able to receive as a non-registered group. Beyond permitting us access to $80,000 in grant money, all of which has gone to directly supporting food-insecure families in Canada, our partnership with FoodShare has also enabled us to utilise government support without being chained to its racist, capitalist and colonial 'charity' practices.

Canada, like many other Western settler-colonial states, has witnessed the rise of a Non-Profit Industrial Complex (NPIC) that distorts and exploits social justice praxis. Specifically, the NPIC promotes the privatisation and corporation of social movements, subsequently turning the economic structure and survival of activist groups into their dominant feature, thereby reducing the rest of their work to a mere 'consequence or byproduct of the funding' (Clarissa and Durazo 2007, 117). Within this toxic sociopolitical climate, many mutual aid and grassroots projects must, in the words of Dean Spade (2020, 51) 'work to remain oppositional to the status quo and cultivate resistance, rather than becoming complementary to privatization'.

But this is not the case for TPP: our funding has never come at the cost of our politics, nor have we struggled to get funding. Money, quite honestly, has never controlled or regulated our work – a rarity I attribute in large part to the aid and community-centric mandate of FoodShare. Besides a standard 10 per cent trustee fee, FoodShare has given us complete agency over, and total support with, our spending. Further, each organisation that has awarded us money has allowed us to determine our budget and made it easy for us to claim funds. In fact, the first grant we received was from the United Way, and I only applied to it because someone from the organisation messaged me on Facebook and told me to. Truthfully, my experience with grassroots funding has been the same as my experience with TPP writ large: radically uplifting.

In some ways, my experience speaks to the exceptional times that we are in, while in other ways, it illustrates the power of QWTBIPOC activisms in Toronto. For one, it seems safe to assume that supporting mutual aids projects in the wake of COVID-19 is a good PR move for many corporations,

[3] Another one such group that emerged during COVID-19 is Uplift Kitchen: a Toronto-based grassroots meal programme that provides free home cooked meals to Black and Indigenous food insecure folks in Toronto and the GTA. See their website at: www.upliftkitchen.ca/ for more information.

charities and brands, suggesting that the ease by which I have secured grants is a symptom of timing, not kindness. Given what other scholar-activists in my area have observed, I am sure that if I had funding experience prior to COVID-19, it would have been far less positive (Catungal 2014). At the same time, however, TPP is led by experienced WQTBPOC Toronto-based organisers with deep roots in the city, and subsequently sustained by radical WQTBIPOC non-for-profit groups like FoodShare who actively try to disrupt the NPIC through community-based collaborations and anti-oppressive praxis (Johnston and Baker 2005). The same can also be said about BFCC, Sundance Harvest and other local WQT/BIPOC-led groups who not just resourced us but literally carved out the roadmaps for our daily practices. Hence, while COVID-19 may have created the conditions for us to emerge as we did, TPP was conceived and maintained by a longstanding network of Toronto-based WQTBIPOC activists.

OLD VIOLENCES, NEW VICTIMS

It seems that the COVID-19 pandemic played an almost cultural role in TPP's emergence, one that affected, not us per se, but those around us. Indeed, while CareMongering-TO and the digitalisation of social life help to explain *how* Toronto activists were able to publicise a radical WQTBIPOC ethic of care, neither phenomenon explain *why* this ethic was embraced by the white mainstream. To understand this, we must turn to the collective trauma of COVID-19. More specifically, the pandemic exposed the imminence of death[4] and the disinterest of the state to those across the racial, dis/ability and class spectrum, revealing the fragility of the human body while also solidifying the state's refusal to protect it (Wood 2020b). In turn, the pandemic discursively uncoupled death/loss from non-whiteness, and life/freedom from whiteness, thus creating a mass desire for a communal praxis that would have otherwise been rejected, particularly by those in and with power: monied white people.

While BIPOC, particularly Black and Indigenous people, the poor and migrant workers, remain disproportionately affected by the physical and economic harms of COVID-19 (Wood 2020b), the white and middle class still saw, and likely for the first time, the 'life of freedom and equality heralded by modern civil society' mutated by the virus (Garba 2020, para 3). Such

[4] My colleague Nadiya Ali helped me realise this claim. During a zoom conversation with Ali, and our mutual colleague Beatrice Anane-Bediakoh (2 July 2020), Ali posited that COVID-19 had forced white people to reckon with their own mortality, and that this had ruptured the white psyche in a way that allowed white people to question the racist logics upon which whiteness depends. This dialogue was essential to my understanding of my claim here.

mutations took the form of their workplaces closing, their loved ones dying prematurely, their (typically boundless) access to space rescinding and their sense of mortality escalating. Given that these are all 'freedoms' that those with full human status have long taken for granted, if not demanded, this shift had a profound effect on social life: by denying white people access to that which constitutes their liberty, and thus humanity, COVID-19 placed them in closer proximity to us not-quite-human subjects, thereby granting them a new perspective of late Western modernity. Brand (2020) describes in 'On narrative, reckoning and the calculus of living and dying':

> What the COVID-19 pandemic has done is expose even further the endoskeleton of the world. I have felt tremendous irritation at the innocence of those people (mostly, but not only, white) finally up against their historic and present culpability in a set of dreadful politics and dreadful economics – ecocidal and genocidal. (para 1)

In short, COVID-19 forced monied white people to reckon with the immanence of state violence and social death in ways that their whiteness and wealth had previously prevented.

In this milieu, where the 'human' and the 'non/inhuman' subject contend with the same terrain of violence that has always differentiated us, mutual aid becomes, as observed by social movement scholar Lesley Wood (2020a), an essential service. Wood writes: 'Transformative, anti-authoritarian social movements play an essential role in building trust…incorporating the most vulnerable, multiplying the possible ways of relating and making us less dependent on centralized power that has a historical tendency to abandon and exploit'. In other words, during a pandemic, people want transformative politics, even privileged white people. Accordingly, when CareMongering-TO provided the unique opportunity in which the radical ethic of care common to Toronto WQTBIPOC organisers could be transmuted into the public realm, people across Canada latched onto it, despite their race, gender, class, ethnicity, age and sexuality.

This is a moment of dual plasticity.

If, as I have argued, modern society is defined by the ontological chaos of hegemonic whiteness – the dialectical interplay between the reification of white life and the fluidification of the racial Other – then COVID-19 is a moment of plastic disjuncture: located at the nexus of construction and destruction, the pandemic created a rare instance in which the cosmic annihilation of whiteness became conceivable to white people at the same time as the histories of anti-white resistance gained mass momentum. On the one hand, white Canadians, like most white people in the world, were forced to occupy a plane of existence that was not clearly marked by/from racialised death, therefore highlighting the fragility of their own life and happiness. In turn, whiteness was dislocated from its necropolitical root and the possibility of a new form emerged, one unbounded by an ecocidal and genocidal endoskeleton.

Such a process is on par with the general logic of destructive plasticity: collective trauma = a new mode of destruction. Yet, at the same time, the deep linages of WQTBIPOC Toronto activisms allowed groups like TPP to emerge in response to COVID-19, presenting the public with an alternative, more effective, mode of survival at the exact moment they needed it. Hencc the COVID-19 pandemic reified WQTBIPOC's radical ethic of care at the same time it fluidified the genres of humanity that necessitate it, subsequently troubling 'the bonds of ontological effacement' (Jackson 2020, 7) that suture whiteness into Canada's national imaginary. This suggests that the ways in which the collective trauma of COVID-19 was metabolised within the country's milieu resonates more with the metamorphosing impetus of constructive plasticity.

The best evidence I have for this occurred about two months into the pandemic, when the second wave of the Black Lives Matter (BLM) movement hit Canada and hordes of white people briefly rallied against racism. At the height of the movement, many members of TPP, including myself, respectively attended a march organised by Toronto-activist group Not Another Black Life (NABL), which was held on behalf of Regis Korchinski-Paquet, an Afro-Indigenous woman in Toronto who fell from her balcony and died due to police brutality (D'sa 2020). Korchinski-Paquet's death followed the now-viral murder of George Floyd and mobilised thousands of folks in Toronto/GTA to take to the city streets in protest of police brutality and anti-Black racism.

Following the protest, I posted a photo I took at the event on TPP's Instagram. The photo featured the backside of a fellow protestor holding a 'SAY THEIR NAMES' sign with a caption in support of the movement (peoplespantryto 2020). I remember bracing myself for an onset of white rage following the post. I was confident that our white volunteers and followers would protest the image. But that did not happen. On the contrary, everyone supported the post and our stance on anti-Black racism. In fact, TPP went on to provide homed cooked meals for a subsequent action organised by NABL: a Juneteenth sit-in held outside the Toronto police headquarters calling to defund the police. We also gave meals to Afro Indigenous Rising (AIR) camp: a group of activists who reclaimed Nathan Phillips Square in Toronto after Ejaz Choudry, a Brown man, was shot and killed by police in his apartment in the neighbouring city of Mississauga. Time and time again, TPP openly supported the defund and abolish the police movement in Toronto, and time and time again, our white volunteers helped us do so.

In the weeks following that first march, posts just like mine cluttered the internet. It seemed that every racist white person I knew from high school and academia was attending a BLM rally and posting 'Black Lives Matter' on their social media. Although these posts were largely hollow acts of performative activism, liberal modalities that 'fail to take seriously "anti-Blackness" and white supremacy as organizing principles that co-construct the grounds of life and worth' (Ali and Anane-Bediakoh 2020, para 4), they gestured to something real, an almost cosmic shift: white people do not collectively say 'Black Lives Matter' – whether they mean it or not. They can't. For when they do, it forces them to consider, even if just for a moment, that their life is predicated on the destruction of BIPOC, and that realisation breaks them.

But this time, it was different: COVID-19 had already broken white people, rattling their sense of whiteness as stable and non-plastic, thereby loosening the boundaries between white life and racialised death. Why else would white people even pretend to publicly care about the lives of Floyd, Korchinski-Paquet and the many other B/IPOC killed by the state, especially when, just a few years ago, they had little to say about the similarly publicised stories of Eric Garner and Michael Brown? In fact, back then, most white folks were mad at BLM. Such a response was not surprising: valuing Black lives threatens the stability of white subjecthood. Jackson (2020, 43) observes that: 'black(ened) people are the living border dividing forms of life', marking white people from the realm of in/non-humanity. Thus, when white people contend with Black death especially and racialised death more generally, they call the borders of white life into question, which destabilises whiteness and, by extension, their very sense of being. The only reason white people would do this en masse is if the flimsiness of the border between Blackness and whiteness, death and life, the human and the Other, had not only previously revealed itself to them but had done so in way that shifted them closer to the in/non-human plane.

It is from this place of upheaval that we can understand what it meant for TPP especially and CareMongering more generally to emerge amid COVID-19. Mutual aid projects such as ours are predicated on the rejection of Western colonial-state values. While Western governments reduce and regulate public services to further concentrate resources and maintain social inequity and violence, 'Mutual Aid projects seek to radically redistribute care and well-being, as part of larger movements that work to dismantle the systems that concentrate wealth in the hands of the 1 percent' (Spade 2020, 53). Mutual aid thus creates a way of conceiving of communal belonging that counters those offered by a racist, capitalist and colonial state, which then allows people to understand social connections beyond prevailing systems of violence. For a long time, this was something only WQTBIPOC and other oppressed groups wanted, but COVID-19 changed that: COVID brought the white and wealthy closer to our plane of non/existence, making them yearn from the very ethic of care that they have been taught to distain and ignore.

I understand this cultural shift in terms of a dual plasticity, one defined by the contrapuntal interplay between collective trauma and Western humanism: forged as the anti-thesis to whiteness, and thus humanity, WQTBIPOC have long been forced to root our existence in survival, fashioning our selfhood around an ethic of care that disavows the same territorialising assemblages that subjugate us. Mutual aid is the incantation of this ethic, the practice of showing up for others based on genuine empathy. Accordingly, (Western) mutual aid is, by definition, anti-white – it is the material product of white life's abjection of the racial Other. Thus, to let mutual aid into the Western mainstream is to threaten the stability of whiteness. But when 'respectable' society is forced to struggle in the same way WQTBIPOC have always had to, as in the case with COVID-19, mutual aid becomes pro-white in its affects while remaining anti-white in its ontology. This constitutes a site of dual plasticity, one where the historical trauma of whiteness is positively fluidified: when white people, especially Canadians, embrace a praxis of care rooted in self/lessness, they inevitably bend the boundaries of white hegemony, thereby turning whiteness into what it cannot be: a plastic way of being.

CONCLUSION

To think of whiteness as plastic is ambitious, if not outright foolish. I know this even as I argue to the contrary. Perhaps the site of dual plasticity to which I theorise and attribute the fluidification of whiteness to, is simply the academic in me trying to theorise away my pain, writing a new world order into the abstract realm of academia where it will be neither tested nor rebuked by those who know better. But maybe, the activist in me saw something real, a praxis of care grounded in my (un)known lived life and is using the academic in me to translate it. Does it not seem wholly possible that COVID-19 provided an opportunity to (de)racialise life in Canada, placing whiteness in antithetical proximity to death while also creating space for WQTBIPOC activists to dominate discourses of care, providing the conditions for a dual plastic encounter? I feel like it did, and I feel as the activist. But maybe that is because I allow the academic to objectify my feelings. I mean, just because WQTBIPOC activists in Toronto affected COVID-19, and COVID-19 affected whiteness, does not mean that whiteness has been plasticised – a thought I ponder amid the fourth wave, and the escalated death count that succeeded (escaped) my analysis. Thus, unable to counter myself into a conclusion, I am left with one thought: Did these forces render whiteness plastic, or did I merely use them to plasticise whiteness?

Perhaps both are true.

BIBLIOGRAPHY

AK, Eli. 2020. "Hello! If you're unable to leave the house for safety reasons… ." Facebook, https://www.facebook.com/groups/TO.Community.Response.COVID19/permalink/2658940487674742/. Accessed 10 June, 2020.

Ali, Nadiya A., and Beatrice Anane-Bediakoh. 2020. "Anti-blackness is by design not by accident. ByBlacks." https://byblacks.com/main-menu-mobile/opinion-mobile/2586-anti-blackness-is-by-design-not-by-accident. Accessed 29 July 2020.

Brand, Dionne. 2020. "Dionne Brand: On narrative, reckoning and the calculus of living and dying." https://www.thestar.com/entertainment/books/2020/07/04/dionne-brand-on-narrative-reckoning-and-the-calculus-of-living-and-dying.html. Accessed 17 July 2020.

Catungal, John Paul. 2014. "For us, by us: Political geographies of race, sexuality and health in the works of ethno-specific AIDS service organizations in global-multicultural Toronto." PhD thesis, University of Toronto.

Chen, Mel Y. 2012. *Animacies: Biopolitics, Racial Mattering, and Queer Affect.* Durham and London: Duke University Press.

Clarissa, Ana, and Rojas Durazo. 2007. "'We Were Never Meant to Survive': Fighting Violence Against Women and the Fourth World War." In *The Revolution Will Not Be Funded: Beyond the Non-Profit Industrial Complex*, edited by INCITE! Women of Color Against Violence, 113–128. Durham and London: Duke University Press.

Classens, Michael, John-Justin McMurtry, and Jennifer Sumner. 2014. "Doing Markets Differently: The Case of FoodShare Toronto's Good Food Markets." In *Social Purpose Enterprises: Case Studies in Doing Business Differently*, edited by Jack Quarter, Sherida Ryan, and Andrea Chan, 224–245. Toronto: University of Toronto Press.

Da Costa, Jade Crimson Rose. 2020a. "Pride Parades in Queer Times: Disrupting Time, Nnorms, and Nationhood in Canada." *Journal of Canadian Studies* 54(2–3): 434–458.

Da Costa, Jade Crimson Rose. 2020b. "Hey everyone! Following in Eli AK's lovely footsteps…". Facebook, https://www.facebook.com/groups/TO.Community.Response.COVID19/permalink/2659767470925377/. Accessed 20 July 2020.

D'Sa, Premila. 2020. "Protesters March through Toronto over Death of Regis Korchinski-Paquet." *Huffpost*, May 30. https://www.huffingtonpost.ca/entry/toronto-police-regis-paquet-protest_ca_5ed2ec7ac5b679e831071ac2 Accessed 27 April 2021.

Garba, Tapji. 2020. "'The twin fetish': On political ontology and COVID-19." *COVID-19 and Cultural Studies.* https://www.uwinnipeg.ca/crics/covid-19-and-cultural-studies/the-twin-fetish-on-political-ontology-and-covid-19.html. Accessed 25 July 2020.

Haritaworn, Jin, Ghaida Moussa, Syrus Marcus Ware, and Rio Rodriguez (eds.). 2018. *Queering Urban Justice: Queer of Colour Formations in Toronto.* Toronto; Buffalo; London: University of Toronto Press.

Jackson, Zakiyyah Iman. 2020. *Becoming Human: Matter and Meaning in an Antiblack World.* New York: New York University Press.

Johnston, Jose, and Lauren Baker. 2005. "Eating Outside the Box: FoodShare's Good Food Box and the Challenge of Scale." *Agriculture and Human Values* 22: 313–332.

Malabou, Catherine. 2008. *What Should We Do With Our Brain?* New York: Fordham University Press.

Malabou, Catherine. 2012. *The New Wounded: From Neurosis to Brain Damage.* New York: Fordham University Press.

Nash, Jennifer C. 2011. "Practicing Love: Black Feminism, Love-politics, and Post-intersectionality." *Meridians* 11(2): 1–24.

Peoplespantryto. 2020. "A photo from today's @notanotherblacklife rally in Toronto…". Instagram, https://www.instagram.com/p/CA1Yb9TAlq7/. Accessed 15 August, 2020.

Rasch, Elisabet, Heike Schaumberg, and Sara C. Motta. 2020. "Rising up Against Institutional Racism in the Americas and Beyond." *Interface: A Journal for and about Social Movements* 12(1): 10–14.

Spade, Dean. 2020. *Mutual Aid: Building Solidarity During This Crisis (and the Next).* London and New York: Verso.

Smith, Andrea. 2006. "Three Pillars of White Supremacy." In *Color of Violence: The INCITE! Anthology*, edited by INCITE! Women of Color Against Violence, 66–73. Durham: Duke University Press.

Toronto/Tkaronto Mutual Aid. 2020. "Covid-19: Food Justice and Mutual Aid in the Pandemic." Facebook video, 1:04.26, www.facebook.com/110190900641866/videos/2779922052293971. Accessed 09 August 2020.

Weheliye, Alexander G. 2014. *Habeas Viscus: Racializing Assemblages, Biopolitics, and Black Feminist Theories of the Human.* Durham and London: Duke University Press.

Wood, Lesley. 2020a. "Social Movements as Essential Services." *OpenDemocracy.* opendemocracy.net/en/democraciaabierta/social-movements-essential-services/. Accessed 25 July 2020.

Wood, Lesley. 2020b. "We're Not All in This Together." *Interface: A Journal for and about Social Movements* 12(1): 34–38.

Chapter 13

Counterpublics of the Common

Feminist Solidarity Unchained

Ewa Majewska

Times of neoliberal capitalism and precarisation leave little or no space for collective organizing, and thus solidarity. In this dismantling of classical forms of dissident cooperation at the workplace, some forms of solidarity prove nevertheless efficient, or even necessary. Some of them take new shape, such as the #Metoo campaign and other forms of combatting sexism and discrimination at work. Others of these dissident solidarity practices take the form of a strike, such as the Women's Strike, both in Poland and globally. In the recent political mobilisations, particularly in #Metoo, International Women's Strike and Black Lives Matter, women's political involvement, including leadership, has been notably stronger than in the majority of earlier social mobilisations, thus it is also important to examine the meaning of this gender shift for theoretical discussions of solidarity, political agency or the subject of politics.

Solidarity is often depicted as an affect, sometimes as a social practice. Zygmunt Bauman recollects its definition based on the French *Encyclopedia* from 1765 as the readiness to assume responsibility – as in *all for one, and one for all* (Bauman 2020, 59). Enrique Dussel explains how the notion of brotherhood should be replaced by a more nuanced vision of solidarity practice (Dussel 2007). Gayatri Spivak writes about solidarity in translation, happening by means of *learning the language of others* (Spivak 1993). Catherine Malabou emphasises the altruist dimension of solidarity, as in Kropotkin (Malabou 2020), she actually calls it 'aufhebung': 'The emergence of reason appears to be a discontinuous continuity. We see how the idea of "expansion" implies both a rupture from – and a preservation of – the biological. In Hegelian terms, we might characterize the expansion of the circle [of altruism] as an *Aufhebung*' (Malabou 2020).

My core interest is solidarity as a collective social practice, transforming the public sphere and articulating the needs of the subaltern, thus I discuss various forms of counterpublics and transformations of the public sphere, before critically revisiting the 'Solidarność' movement in Poland in 1980–1981 and discussing the recent Women's Strikes and other contemporary feminist solidarity actions, in order to build a feminist, materialist notion of solidarity rooted in Hegelian thought.

ALTRUISM REVISITED

Catherine Malabou's discussion of plasticity and women's experience in philosophy and politics on the other hand makes possible a discussion of the ontology of the transitions within the feminist mobilisations, opening a materialist perspective on these often conflicted processes, and thus brings them back to their historicity and embodiment (Malabou 2011). In her recent discussion of Kropotkin's concept of 'mutual aid', Malabou returns to solidarity as an expression of plasticity (Malabou 2020). Malabou's return to Kropotkin should thus be seen as a part of a larger, feminist revision of the human and social sciences, aimed at embracing more transversal and altruist models of evolution.

In the essay *Rethinking Mutual Aid* she argues:

> It is important to notice from the outset that mutual aid, understood as a genuine concept, is not a temporarily limited set of actions determined by the emergency of a crisis. Mutual aid, in the eyes of its most influent thinkers, is an actual revolutionary dynamism, the motor of a totally renewed vision of the social. (Malabou 2020, 2)

In the same essay Malabou argues that plasticity is the central aspect of anarchism understood not just as a doctrine, but as a plethora of constantly transforming theories and practices, not fixed to any specific paradigm. The plasticity of anarchism makes it possible to think of the anarchism of plasticity as well, thus opening up ways to address the central notion of dialectics in a renewed politicised way. Thus the rethinking of mutual aid, seen here as the core of anarchism, becomes an exercise in addressing not only Peter Kropotkin's historical notion, but also the ontology of the social, with solidarity at the core of it, as shaped by usually marginalised practices of altruism and cooperation. Contrary to the most general presumptions concerning the supposedly competitive and egoist nature of the human societies and progress, various feminist and other voices demand the recognition of altruism and cooperativism as key aspects of the social, thus undermining the long line of sociology normalising the masculine socialisation as the norm and hegemonic version of human practice.

Moving between neurobiology and philosophy, Malabou already contributed to the dismantling of the solely rational, decontextualised and to some extent also dematerialised vision of the human subject, by re-installing the material, embodied, only partially conscious and voluntary agency at the core of the (Hegelian, but also more generally philosophical) human subject (Malabou 2005). In the discussions of plasticity those aspects of embodied agency are central, thus suggesting that the 'future of Hegel', and with it the future of philosophy of plasticity, is at least to some extent a feminist one. In *The Future of Hegel* Malabou writes:

> 'Plastic', as an adjective, means two things: on the one hand, to be 'susceptible to changes of form' or malleable (clay is a 'plastic' material); and on the other hand, 'having the power to bestow form, the power to mould', as in the expressions, 'plastic surgeon' and 'plastic arts'. [. . .] *Plasticité*, or 'plasticity', just like *Plaztizität* in German, describes the nature of that which is 'plastic', being at once capable of receiving and of giving form. (Malabou 2005, 8)

Moreover, she explains that plasticity means an ability to transform, but not to deform, therefore the prospect of preserving the original shape, or returning to it, is also an important part of such a process (Malabou 2005, 9). This is necessary to understand, how and to what extent Malabou's reinterpretation of Kropotkin's *mutual aid* is a materialist operation, expressing not solely the intentions or declarations of solidarity, but above all its social practice performed by the collective tissue of human organisms becoming a part of history. Solidarity seen as a part of the human future, human *destiny*, is a materialised plasticity, organised by altruism, but also by more primary drives of occupying and adapting in space, building constellations, responding to changes and sustaining the organism as well as groups of humans. It is thus a materialist concept, nevertheless embracing such entities as accidents, the unconscious or failure as necessary elements of historical process. Rooted in this materialist Hegelianism, the notion of solidarity becomes far more stable, by means of its biological and historical necessity, as well as by a sense of participation of the acts and processes of humane agency in the larger plane of nature. The solidarity Malabou invokes when returning to Kropotkin is not merely a sentiment, it is a social practice, transforming, yet not deforming, the historical process of how the human civilisation develops in its contradicting ways.

FEMINIST COUNTERPUBLICS

In Nancy Fraser's critical discussion of Jurgen Habermas's concept of the public sphere, counterpublics, while undermining the existing social divisions such as the public/private divide, also provide oppositional claims and enhance collective agency, including that of solidarity (see: Fraser 1990). Formed in the outskirts and margins of the classical, traditional public sphere, counterpublics express the need to gather and collectively debate common matters among the working classes, women, ethnic and sexual minorities. After addressing the main flaws of Habermas's notion of the public sphere and discussing various historical forms of public spheres created outside of the bourgeois, White, male circles, Fraser offers her own notion of counterpublics. She writes:

> members of subordinated social groups-women, workers, peoples of color, and gays and lesbians-have repeatedly found it advantageous to constitute alternative publics. I propose to call these subaltern counterpublics in order to signal that they are parallel discursive arenas where members of subordinated social groups invent and circulate counterdiscourses, which in turn permit them to formulate oppositional interpretations of their identities, interests, and needs. (Fraser 1990, 67)

In her critique of Habermas's exclusive model of the public sphere, Fraser emphasises the necessity of considering women as political subjects, and thus she argues for understanding contemporary feminisms as 'subaltern counterpublics'. I use the plural, because an important part of Fraser's disagreement with Habermas consists in her insistence that the uniqueness of his public sphere is anti-democratic. In Fraser's view, only a plethora of competing public spheres provides genuine debate and expression of differences, which are central to the practice of democracy. Preserving the uniqueness and oneness of the public sphere, as Habermas does, leads to the cancelling of dissenting voices, transforming the exchange of dissenting opinions into an expression of artificially imposed consent, instead of a multiplicity of voices. This is an important issue, as we often tend to believe, just as Habermas does, that if common matters should be discussed by all, this in turn should take place in one debate. Fraser demonstrates another, more transversal vision of publicness, in which various groups form their public spheres accordingly to their social positions, location, *habitus*, perhaps also gender or ethnic origins etc., and yet the public debate remains one. She discusses contemporary American feminism as such a case – technically all its members are in favour of the rights of women; however they form different, sometimes conflicting counterpublics (as in the case of pornography, about which feminists sometimes have opposing views). This pluralism not just of views, but also of counterpublics, constitutes for Fraser, and I agree with her, the guarantee of democracy, which is biased and undermined by the emphasis on one, unique public sphere that is central in Habermas's narrative. The multitude of counterpublics has also been discussed by Michael Warner, who depicted the Black and queer counterpublics, and by Warren Montag, who criticises Habermas's 'fear of the street' (Warner 2005; Hill and Montag 2000).

SOLIDARNOŚĆ – COUNTERPUBLICS OF THE COMMON

Fraser's ideas build on those of Alexander Kluge and Oskar Negt, who introduced the concept of proletarian counterpublics in 1972. Their analysis shows how the bourgeois forms of discussion and political agency dominate the understanding of political subjectivity, thus acting as ideology rather than description or normative model. Kluge and Negt rightly point to the role of commercial media in imposing the image of a White-collar, male worker as the universal form of political agency, while the factories generate their own, very different versions of public debate and political agency, often focused directly on labour and workers' rights, and thus mediated by the unions. In Poland this point sounds radically relevant, as 'Solidarność', usually depicted as a 'movement', was in fact a union, a counterpublic and mainly a proletarian one (see: Matynia 2001; Majewska 2018). Formally and structurally this most important democratic political mobilisation in Eastern Europe began as a general strike in shipyard and factories in August 1980, initiated by the workers of the Shipyard of Gdańsk, and started as a solidarity strike with Anna Walentynowicz, the crane operator, fired because of her critical opinions about the rise of food prices, which made life unbearable, as she openly said. The wave of solidarity strikes with the Gdansk Shipyard first followed in other workplaces in Gdańsk, and quickly spread to other towns and cities, finally involving 700 000 striking workers in some 700 workplaces in Poland, thus becoming the largest strike in the region, and perhaps in Europe. The strategy and method of the strike were established based on previous oppositional mobilisations – the shipyard workers learned from strikes in 1970 that an occupation strike is much more effective than street protests and from the strike in textile factories in Łódź in 1971 that demanding the presence of central state authorities and negotiating at the occupied workplace is the most effective way of obtaining what was stipulated in the demands. Thus, several researchers, including Roman Laba, Zbigniew Kowalewski and myself, argue that the early 'Solidarność' movement was proletarian (Laba 1991; Kowalewski 1985; Majewska 2018).

I call it a 'proletarian counterpublic' not solely because of the predominantly proletarian origins of its makers, but also because of the proletarian origins of the basic elements of the movement's strategies. After the successful negotiations in August 1980, 'Solidarność' became a registered, independent labour union, demanding properly socialist organisation of workplaces and care labour, democracy in media and politics, as well as better management. This entity, counting ten million registered members in March 1981, redefined the notion of solidarity for several generations, showing how it can be at once formalised, but not bureaucratic, official, but not restricted to offices, public, but not state run.

'Solidarność' expressed itself at first through the 21 Demands (Postulaty Sierpniowe), written at the Gdańsk Shipyard in the beginning of the strike in August 1980. The demands combined political freedoms with social justice, thus making the first program of 'Solidarność' a radically social-democratic one. With the further expansion of the Strike Committee and invited experts, including Tadeusz Kowalik, Poland's most prominent Luxemburgian economist, Jadwiga Staniszkis, a famous sociologist, and contacts with Karol Modzelewski – a Marxist dissident oppositionist, co-author (with Jacek Kuroń) of the famous 1965 'Open Letter to the Communist Party', whose idea it was to call the movement of 1980 'Solidarność', the discussions of the political position of 'Solidarność' embraced some more historical trends. Among them the cooperative tradition, particularly vital in Poland due to the co-op movement of the early twentieth century as well as its main theorists, Maria Orsetti and Edward Abramowski; the syndicalist tradition and anarcho-socialist thought were among the most central references (Abramowski 2013; Orsetti 2019). The thought of Abramowski, who emphasised the importance of co-ops as the first step towards the elimination of the state apparatus, which he perceived as a coercive mechanism petrifying human freedom and agency, and the possibility of establishing democratic common governance, instead of a government, was referenced on multiple occasions during the negotiations within the strike of August 1980, as well as later when 'Solidarność' worked on its programme in 1980–1981 (Abramowski 2013, 72; Magala 2012, 45). Abramowski's thought, to some extent rooted in that of Kropotkin, was central to Polish socialism in its various versions – that of the Polish Socialist Party, which took power in Poland after 1918 the more autonomous, anti-state initiatives, and the cooperativist movement. It thus influenced the Polish socialist tradition, and was respected by both the more independent members of the communist party and the more left-leaning members of the anti-state opposition. It is perhaps important to emphasise that the early 'Solidarność' did not demand the end of socialism, it demanded a fulfilment of the socialist premises that state was built upon. Anti-communism became 'Solidarność' doctrine after martial law was introduced in December 1981 and the independent union was made illegal. Until then references to socialist and socialist-anarchist thought were central in the programme documents.

The 21 Demands of the striking workplaces in August 1980 was a combination of social and political postulates. It started with the demand to legalise independent labour unions, referencing the International Covenant on Civil and Political Rights from 1977, to which the government of The People's Republic of Poland was a signatory. It demanded the liberation of political prisoners, the re-hiring of Anna Walentynowicz, the end of censorship and the participation of workers in the governance of the workplaces. It also contained demands concerning childcare, an earlier retirement age and affordable food prices. As a hybrid of topics and aspects of social and political life, the demands were often neglected by liberal political thinkers as insufficiently political, while from a Marxist-feminist perspective they did what genuine politics does – cut through the public/private divide with the aim of sublating, not neglecting, the conflicts (see: Arruzza, Bhattacharia and Fraser 2017; Rancière 2004; Staniszkis 2010; Majewska 2018).

Kluge and Negt's proletarian counterpublics are rooted in experience of labour. This is an important fact, sharply contradicting the classical liberal-conservative vision of public debate as solely available to those who do not need to care for their basic needs. This fundamental principle of evacuating politics of the realm of manual labour has been contested ever since Aristotle, recently by Jacques Rancière, who in the *Nights of Labor* and other books and essays discusses the political agency of workers, and Wiktor Marzec, who follows the proletarian political agency in the time of 1905 revolution in Poland (Rancière 1989; Marzec 2020). The examples of public debates and counterpublics these authors discuss show their roots in the experiences of working together, emphasised by Karl Marx in the chapters of *Capital* dedicated to cooperation. Antonio Negri and Michael Hardt build their notion of the common partially on these notes, emphasising the power of getting together and becoming organised within the capitalist factory and the potential to resist exploitation, which begins in these unclear conditions (Hardt and Negri 2009). The critical potential of such collective sharply contradicts the claims made by Habermas about the working classes as those, who – deprived of proper education and cultural capital – supposedly cannot oppose the media propaganda, infusing them with capitalist ideology. According to Hardt and Negri, and Kluge and Negt, although they express it in a different theoretical context, precisely through the power of collective organised factory labour, the experience of work and the impossibility to fulfil the capitalist regimes of exploitative labour, the mechanisms of critique and resistance are shaped and expressed by the 'multitude' as Hardt and Negri have it, or by the 'proletarian counterpublics', as depicted by Kluge and Negt. The 'Solidarność' movement in 1980 is a great example of such a sudden explosion of critique and resistance to exploitative and authoritarian conditions, orchestrated by the workers. Paradoxically, in the state-communist Poland the main newspaper, 'Trybuna Ludu' (the *Tribune of the People*) had a Marxist subtitle – 'Proletarians of the World, unite'. How strange must it have been for the Communist Party leaders, when they saw this communist postulate suddenly realised?

SOLIDARITY AGAINST THE STATE OF EXCEPTION

The notion of solidarity, particularly in its feminist appropriations, stands in a clear contradiction to the ultra-conservative politics of 'the state of exception' as it was theorised by Carl Schmitt, practiced by the Third Reich, and still is used as an inspiration by some of today's conservative governments, including that of Jarosław Kaczyński's ruling Law and Justice party in Poland. In his essay 'From Fraternity to Solidarity' Enrique Dussel discusses Jacques Derrida's concept of friendship, as opposed to Schmitt's politics based on the notion of enemy, and argues that: 'The question remains posed, in its foundation, in the fact that fraternity in the political community is impaled upon a contradiction that fractures it: the line passes between friend and enemy. It is not the complete enemy, the *hostis*; it is only the *inimicus* in the public sense (the Greek *stásis*) of fraternity, within the *Whole of the community*. But this fragmented fraternity, in addition to being defectively phallo-logo-centric, has nothing to do with sisterhood (sisterhood with the sister) but rather patriarchal *fratrocracia*' (Dussel 2007, 78). And then he adds:

> It is evident that Schmitt, as also Nietzsche, Weber, Derrida, and Modernity in general, understand political power as domination, and the political field is structured by a *Will to Power*, which orders this field on the basis of forces organized by the sole criterion of friends versus enemies. It will be necessary to overcome this radically. (Dussel 2007, 79)

Dussel, somehow differently from many other theorists, situates solidarity in the ability of the 'Other' to question the entire machine of the Law, be it in the context of the state of exception or a more moderate version. However, what interests me is that the step towards such a vision of solidarity is mediated by the sudden recognition of the impossibility of sisterhood in solidarity founded on the principles and practice of brotherhood. Although Dussel does not explore it further, I believe it is an important step to investigate why and how the alterity of the feminine and women in the philosophical tradition makes it perhaps impossible not only to theorise women in the context of solidarity, but also to actually imagine a definition of solidarity capable of embracing the core of its practice – the cooperation of strangers, that is, those not united by clear bonds of friendship?

FEMINIST NOTIONS OF SOLIDARITY

A feminist take on solidarity was offered by Gayatri Spivak, who discusses it as a practice of translation, consisting in the process of learning the language of the other (Spivak 1993). In the essay *The Politics of Translation* Spivak criticises the all too easy assumption that it is possible to think that 'she is just like me' when addressing the author of a foreign text. She then explains: 'Rather than imagining that women automatically have something identifiable in common, why not say, humbly and practically, my first obligation in understanding solidarity is to learn her mother tongue. You will see immediately what the differences are. You will also feel the solidarity every day as you make the attempt to learn the language in which the other woman learned to recognize reality at her mother's lap' (Spivak 1993, 191). This theory of solidarity also roots its politics in experience and in labour, as translation is work too. At its core – it is a form of work, which Walter Benjamin beautifully embeds in the Hegelian-Marxist context of alienation, claiming that translation, just as any other agency in the linguistic realm, allows encountering foreignness (Benjamin 1996). Interestingly, both fields – translation and factory labour – seem to consist in such confrontation with alienation, and produce the means to overcome it.

Solidarity can thus be seen as a form of labour, consisting in learning the language of other, without claiming sameness and ignoring differences, while directly challenging alienation. I think such definition overcomes the homogenising understandings of solidarity, rooted in brotherhood or even friendship. In the essay 'Solidarity: a word in search of a body', Zygmunt Bauman reconstructed the origins of the concept, emphasising that in times of sharp individualisation, when the model of (solo) hunter replaced the earlier attitudes of gardener, solidarity cannot be practiced as 'all for one, one for all', as it was understood in its early days (Bauman 2020, 59). The alienating rules of neoliberal management, rooted in the neo-conservative revolution since 1979, exclude altruism, necessary for any kind of responsibility taking and collective agency, thus making solidarity obsolete. However, Bauman observed efforts to overcome this condition by Occupy Wall Street. In his view solidarity needs embodiment, which also means concretisation, persistence and consequence. Overcoming estrangement, in labour and in language, solidarity builds upon a heterogeneous, non-essentialising vision of togetherness.

As Malabou argues in *Changing Difference,* women's experience in and of philosophy is one of exclusion and violence (Malabou 2011). She suggests that it is the exclusion of femininity, not necessarily of women, that constitutes the core of said exclusion. Women – if able to dismantle, rework, leave or deconstruct their femininity, are welcomed. But femininity is not. This is not necessarily an essentialising argument. It is a matter-of-fact report from philosophy departments all over the globe, that women and other persons embodying femininity are only welcomed there under the condition that they put their femininity aside. This has interesting repercussions, such as for example the long tradition of understanding Antigone as representing femininity, which requires the exclusion and foreclosure of Ismene – a bizarre fact discussed by Luce Irigaray and Bonnie Honig, among others (Irigaray 2010; Honig 2013). While Irigaray focuses on the differences between Antigone and Ismene, Honig performs a much more far reaching operation of embracing the necessity of cooperation between the two sisters in order for 'Antigone's claim' to succeed. In Honig's words, what unites the sisters, is 'a sororal, antipatriarchal pact' (Honig 2013, 182). They are bonded by their different abilities and skills, Antigone using not solely her public persona, but also – as Honig meticulously reconstructs – also her ability to cordially address her kin, and Ismene – with her kindness, care and affective communication. This is how patriarchy can be defeated. Now – as we have far less philosophical analysis of Ismene than that of Antigone, it is perhaps useful to ask what distinguishes her from other, more heroic personages of the tragedy? She is definitely caring and kind, but she also persists rather, than resists. The heroic aspects of her clearly resistant position versus Creon are replaced by passivity and supposed acceptance for the conditions he imposes. She is resilient and willful rather, than openly contesting. Her speech is also one of care rather than that of combat. Would that mean that she is any less in contempt of Creon's will? I would argue for a negative answer, however some elements her behaviour might suggest otherwise. Ismene definitely does not fulfil the classical, openly heroic political practice of resistance. Is she thus merely accepting Creon's will? If she did, Antigone would never succeed – this is Honig's argument. Does it make Ismene a less political being than Antigone? Perhaps, but as can be observed in Honig's close reading of Sophocles's piece, without her quiet complicity in Antigone's act, there would be no claim against Creon to speak of.

The vulnerability, passivity and relationality of Ismene are typical for the cultural notion of femininity. They thus constitute impossible characteristics of the political realm, symptoms of particularity in the public debate and public sphere. As we remember from John Rawls's *Theory of Justice* (1971), the moral act, and thus also politically responsible decision-making, has to apply the rule of the 'veil of ignorance', which covers any affect, relation and involvement, thus making space for the supposedly rational decision. Such a vision of political agency, rooted in Aristotle, but also in Kohlberg's analysis of the stages of the ethical development, has been undermined by feminist researchers, such as Carol Gilligan, who contested the regime of separation, exclusion of affect and relations from the realms of moral judgement or rationality, or Carole Pateman, who contests the vision of democracy as 'fraternal social pact' (see: Gilligan 1982; Pateman 1989; Rawls 1993). These 'corrections' of the moral and political subject lead to the conclusion that perhaps rationality does not require exclusion of any ties with others, and decisions can also be taken considering affects. These two – relationality and affect, had always been affiliated with femininity. Thus, such remodelling of the subject necessarily leads to a new portrait of political agency, which suddenly can also embrace figures such as Ismene. This however requires another step – the de-heroisation of the notion of what is political. And here the region of Eastern Europe has its own theoretical and historical examples that prove useful also today, particularly in the discussions of contemporary feminist solidarity.

SOLIDARITY OF THE WEAK

Embracing certain aspects of what was classically coded as 'feminine', including caring attitudes, emotionality, weakness and passivity, as well as recognising them as elements of political agency, constitutes an important shift in the understanding of politics. Traditionally, the political subject was understood as one that can be made accountable or one who could participate in the public debate. Antigone is an atypical subject of politics, but the introduction of Ismene in this context shifts the priorities, allowing care and affect into the realm of political agency. This results in a transition from a notion of politics only available to the subjects formed and socialised as privileged men towards a politics of the common, where those of other gender, class and ethnicity can be seen as political as well. Such a transition does not happen on its own, and the previous parts of this text, discussing feminist theory and protests, as well as the proletarian and feminist counterpublics, depict the ways in which such broadening of the notion of politics historically forms itself. The transformations of the notion of solidarity also contribute to its transition from an elitist version of brotherhood towards a more heterogeneous, hybrid and anarchistic version.

'The Power of Powerless', a seminal essay written by the Czech dissident theatre writer and later also the first democratic president of Czechoslovakia after 1989, Václav Havel, argues for the recognition of the political agency of the 'ordinary people', such as shop keepers or housewives (Havel does not mention housewives, I add them in line with my argument). Witnessing the stabilised clash of the Cold War empires after efforts to change local politics, in 1956 in Hungary, 1970 in Poland and 1968 in Czechoslovakia, many

Eastern Europeans felt overwhelmed by the sense of impossibility of political resistance. After so many failures, a collective act of resistance seemed impossible. Yet – it happened, over and over again, with 'Solidarność' in Poland and with oppositional agency in other countries of the so-called Soviet Bloc. Havel depicts small, everyday acts of resistance, such as not hanging the flag on state holiday (Havel 2010). These wilful acts remind of another analysis of the politics of those deprived of means to act heroically – the peasants from East Asia, described in *Weapons of the Weak* by James Scott (Scott 1986). In his accounts of peasant protests, Scott focuses on overcoming the theoretical impossibility of discussing peaceful, monotonous marches of thousands of peasants, mainly illiterate inhabitants of rural regions of Far East Asia. In his research of these mobilisations, Scott discovered what he calls the 'weapons of the weak', the unheroic, everyday forms of resistance – marching, sit-ins, chanting. These forms of political agency only seldom make careers in political theory, which – as I demonstrated above –still to a large extent depends on the exclusive, heroic and rational vision of the political, inherited after the exclusive ancient model.

FEMINIST SOLIDARITY IN ACTION: THE WOMEN'S STRIKE

The recent feminist mobilisations have mainly been analysed as new social movements and events leading to transition in legal frameworks and practices of justice (MacKinnon 2019; Verso Report, 2017); transformations of the public sphere (Majewska 2018); and new models of resistance (Lisiak 2019). New modes and strategies have also been discussed as novel in their exposure and explorations of vulnerability and weakness (Majewska 2018; Rogowska-Stangret 2017). However, the philosophical context of these new feminist formations as new forms of solidarity has found much less analysis. A crucial work in this aspect is *Feminism for the 99%* by Nancy Fraser, Cinzia Arruzza and Tithi Bhattacharya, which emphasises the prospects of the new (feminist) international, social reproduction and the strike as a global tendency (Arruzza, Bhattacharya and Fraser 2017). Another perspective, mainly focusing on the institutional mechanisms of preventing and acting against discrimination and sexual harassment, has been developed by Sara Ahmed (Ahmed 2017). In her analysis, 'diversity work' acts as a phenomenology of sexual harassment combined with wilful resistance to the powers of neglect and forgetting of gender- and race-based harm within academia. While 'diversity work' is often criticised as a mere corporate strategy to prevent and respond to discrimination based on gender and ethnicity, and thus as an insufficient measure to ensure equality, in Ahmed's work it becomes a tool to diagnose and criticise the insufficiencies of institutional anti-discrimination mechanisms at universities in the United Kingdom, Australia, United States and New Zealand.

The recent feminist protests in Poland, which started in 2016, began with thousands of women joining online groups protesting the radical conservative proposals to completely ban abortion. The evolution of these local and central mobilisations to the mass demonstrations and Women's Strike on Black Monday, 3 October 2016, was made possible by a series of intermediary steps (Majewska 2018). Before thousands of women stepped out to the streets of big and small cities, their online activity made the composition of the movement more inclusive and allowed those who had never participated in political activism to join it. A very important moment of this mobilisation took place on 23 September 2016, when Gocha Adamczyk from the left-wing party Razem invited women to post their selfie pictures in black and white with the hashtag #blackprotest, as protesting women chose black as their colour. The response was massive – some 200,000 images were uploaded by women and girls from various locations in Poland and globally. This was an unprecedented action, conducted by very ordinary and unheroic tools of social media and mobile phones. The #blackprotest became the biggest action on the Polish internet, unprecedented in size, but also in effectiveness. The Women's Strike on 3 October 2016 counted 150,000 demonstrating in Warsaw and numerous smaller cities and towns. These protests were effective – the abortion ban was not voted on, and until now this was the only case when the people defeated Kaczyński's ultra conservative government. These women's protests in Poland were fuelled by these 'ordinary' actions, often led by women, who would depict themselves as 'ordinary', to oppose the image of the 'professional' feminist activist. On 22 October 2020 the Polish Constitutional Court decided that abortion should be made illegal in cases of severe foetus malfunction, and that decision was put into action on 27 January 2021. The new wave of protests, which began immediately after the October decision, are continuing at the time of writing, police brutality is growing and various Polish and international abortion solidarity networks have been created to help women terminate pregnancies. The protests on 30 October 2020 counted already 400,000 people, with 100,000 in Warsaw alone, and others marching in 450 other places in Poland. The Women's Strike has initiated councils, which work on political demands collectively and in collective, democratic ways. Thus while thousands still protest in the streets of Poland, some hundreds are involved in building the programme of the movement and shaping its more deliberative dimensions, and others engage in solidarity networks supporting women's and trans people's needs for abortions. This combination of a sharp critique of the conservative Polish government, grassroots democratic work on political demands, the political street protests and abortion solidarity networks, makes the Women's Strike into a subaltern counterpublic, where the notion of solidarity stretches between the most general political demands and oppositional discourse, via specific demands and practices of grassroots democracy, transversal support for access to medicaments and assistance and the anti-repressive teams helping those arrested in street struggles. These actions and theoretical works compose a counterpublic of the oppressed, focused around reproduction, choice and equality, but spreading towards very general notions of how the society should be governed.

The notion of 'ordinary', especially if added to 'women' or 'people' can be misleading and misguided. However, to claim that it is impossible to define or cannot be useful in the analysis of social movements, also seems controversial, as it avoids confrontation with paradigms of social and cultural research that consciously or implicitly reduce their scope of analysis solely to the professional activists, elite groups etc. Then the notion of 'ordinary' can signal some exclusion of marginalisation, otherwise impossible to grasp. In order to discuss a mass-scale phenomenon, such as the Women's Strike, #Metoo and other campaigns and actions, it can be helpful to diagnose the narrative and theoretical gaps, such as those explaining the sudden scale of the use of #Metoo in 2017. Created by the African American feminist activist Tarana Burke, the #Metoo campaign had been running since 2006. However, it was only in 2017 that it became a massive statement and solidarity movement after the actress Alyssa Milano announced her experience of sexual harassment at work using that hashtag and urged other women with similar experiences to share them using it. The wave of such statements, where women declare they were victims of harassment, was followed by another – that of men expressing their solidarity. But the central aspect of the #Metoo action as a feminist solidarity action lies in the sudden force of the women's expression of harassment and the sense of togetherness and strength created by such announcement. The action has been discussed in several books and articles, but I believe it is worth enumerating the key aspects of such social media mediated campaign. Perhaps the most important aspect is the implicit announcement and confirmation of the mass scale of women's sexual abuse in the context of work. Most of us have heard the statistics of sexual harassment at work; however, it is very different to see the #Metoo hashtag on the social media pages of millions of women on the same day. The anonymised numbers we read about suddenly became actual people, sometimes those we know. Recognising oneself as an element of this avalanche of declarations gives a sense of belonging to a group, whose importance cannot be neglected. In her books and articles on sexual harassment, Sara Ahmed writes about the painful sense of isolation and futility of the anti-harassment claims and cases in academic institutions (Ahmed 2017).

Such feelings are weakened by the #Metoo and similar actions, creating a sense of empowerment in those who experience harassment. Those, who experienced harassment, were announcing it openly or in a more generalised way on social media in Fall 2017. For many of us this was a moment of revelation – seeing the majority of women and some non-binary and trans people sharing their experiences of violence was creating a sense of community, and for many of us announced that we are not alone, that the problem of harassment is a massive problem, and many of those who suffer from it are ready to speak up. Thus a sense of being a part of a larger movement was created, which sometimes, not always unfortunately, was followed by support directly offered by others either on social media or in other forms. Some men understood they were a part of the dominant group only after they saw these declarations of women living and working with then. Institutions and workplaces learned that it is not safe for them anymore to neglect and ignore harassment, as women and other oppressed groups are ready to speak publicly about the harm they suffer from.

The #Metoo campaign led to massive research and media coverage of various sectors of work, helping to undermine the presumptions of the supposed impossibility of preventing and counteracting the harassment. The courts started to take such claims seriously and institutions began to employ more or better tools in preventive and reactive measures. All these however can be just short-term effects if not stabilised and institutionalised. As Tithi Bhattacharya rightly claims in her article about #Metoo, the need to combine anti-discrimination and anti-harassment agency with labour unionising is striking, given the impossibility of actually combatting harassment merely through declarations and campaigns (Bhattacharya 2017). The observations of the academic sector and how impossible it is to address the harassment cases led Catharine MacKinnon to bring 300 cases from different universities in the United States to the White House and ask for help there (MacKinnon 2019). This kind of pessimism can also be observed in other sectors, which leads to the conclusion that perhaps Bhattacharya's suggestion of combining anti-harassment activism with labour unionism is not a bad idea. The #Metoo and similar campaigns are solidarity actions that also fuel such political agency, because the tendency to 'support' is there replaced by a more horizontal notion of 'solidarity'. bell hooks discusses this difference in *Feminist Theory. From Margin to Center,* and I believe it is an important one: Support can even strengthen the discrepancy between those who suffer violence and discrimination and those who do not, thus further petrifying the victims in their weakness and inferiority, while solidarity, as a horizontal type of action, makes it clearer that survivors of violence or harassment can also help others, and thus should not be solely perceived through the lens of their painful experience (see: hooks 1984).

MUTUAL AID: A WEAPON OF THE WEAK?

Campaigns such as #czarnyprotest or #Metoo provide massive support for important cases and discriminated groups. They fuel media and political interest, while at the same time allowing those who experience violence or discrimination not only to feel supported by thousands of others, but also to recognise them and act together. This is another, rarely discussed aspect of these campaigns – their role in the self-organisation of those suffering violence or discrimination. It usually begins by discussions and individual declarations of support or solidarity, which allows a comparison with the concepts of mutual aid and altruism discussed by Kropotkin, and later also by Malabou. The plasticity we observe among victims of harassment combines that of a subject of a survivor, sometimes broken and reconstituted as one more empowered or capable as well as that of collective action in itself disposing of certain plasticity. Malabou rightly emphasises that the plasticity she discovers in mutual aid is anarchistic. She also claims: 'Once again, mutual aid is not just care, or solidarity. It relies on a biological theory, pertaining to evolutionism' and further: 'An altruistic behavior may be defined as "a behavior that benefits others at some cost to oneself". It is clear that mutual aid may be regarded as the highest form of altruistic behaviors' (Malabou 2020, 3). Based in the predispositions of humans as species, acts of altruism have not, as Malabou claims, received their well-deserved theoretical analysis. However – the work on care and affective labour, developed by various strands of feminist theory, has contributed to the understanding of altruism, particularly in the contexts of maternity, care and reproduction. The fact that said works focus on the feminine involvement in such labour or even the on cultural constraints that limit women's ability to engage in such tasks only proves that perhaps the lack of in-depth analysis of altruism should be seen as gender biased, and thus that the task of revisiting the topic of altruism might be best accomplished from the feminist perspective. As I argue above, it took several decades to liberate philosophical understanding of rationality and moral judgement from their supposedly necessary detachment from relations and affect. It might take even longer for political philosophy to embrace altruism. However as social sciences begin to embrace altruism and interdependence as the humane tendencies necessary for the survival of the species, the general paradigm changes, and competitiveness ceases to be the sole characteristic responsible for human progress (see: Tomasello et al. 2012).

CONCLUSION: BETWEEN SOLIDARITY AND CARE

Altruism might be difficult for European political theory also because of its radical non-heroism. The actions of the altruist human, be it a tired mother, a nurse caring for a patient or other care-taking tasks, usually consist in repetitive, mundane, sometimes also unpleasant activities. I argued elsewhere that they might actually be found in Hegel's *Phenomenology of the Spirit*, in the chapter on unhappy consciousness. What is predominantly read as fragments on religion, can also perhaps be seen, as Judith Butler argues, as the spirit's confrontation with embodiment, however – somehow contrarily to Butler, I would not read it from an individualist perspective, but I would rather argue, that it could be read as a chapter where sustaining, caring and reproductive actions are performed and encountered by the spirit (see: Butler 1987; Majewska 2022). The unhappiness could then obviously be explained not merely by the fact of the presence of the body, which can also be found in other chapters of the *Phenomenology*, but by the dominance of repetitive caring and reproductive labour and the general context of activity devoted to sustainability, which are the most mundane and yes, solely dedicated to the biological survival of the organism. This confrontation with Hegel's *Phenomenology* and perhaps also the audacity of 'discovering' a housewife or a tired mother there, constitutes a theoretical performance that allows a strategic shift as to what counts as the subject and how to interpret dialectics in materialist ways. I believe such operations are necessary not just in order to bring new elements to existing political philosophy, but to discover how capacious some older theoretical models might already be. In the discussions concerning altruism it is thus necessary not only to reinterpret it again, but also to situate it in the philosophical contexts, where it already belongs. I believe altruism is *par excellence* the central moment of Hegel's 'unhappy consciousness', and this location allows to see its relations with the heroic versions of the struggle for recognition, as well as with culture as its necessary 'other'.

I would like to argue that the necessary mediation of contemporary altruism, mutual aid and solidarity actions in the highly commercialised environments of social media and the internet more generally, might be a necessary condition of their effectiveness, not solely their failure by means of commodification. In the recent feminist solidarity actions, as well as in the grassroots anti-Covid-19 activism, online, commercialised services play a role that should obviously be contested and criticised. Yet it is hard to imagine performing such campaigns solely by means of non-commercial, grassroots, activist media. The dependence of such campaigns on highly undemocratic corporations that use data to influence political choices and generate controversies like the Cambridge Analytica Affair requires criticism and should not allow any blunt optimism concerning massive online campaigns. However, I would also disagree with claims such as those pronounced by Jodi Dean, whose article 'Why the Net is not a Public Sphere' misleadingly confuse the entire public sphere with a part of it, and thus suggests that the internet could replace the public sphere as such (see: Dean 2003). While rightly criticising various aspects of commodification and profit orientation of the majority of providers of online services, Dean also makes it hard to understand how the internet did in fact become an important part of the public sphere, how and why it is used and abused, as well as what role it could play for genuinely progressive mobilisations, despite all the controversies. #Metoo and other massive feminist campaigns heavily depend on the accessibility of social media, on their popularity, the masses of their analysts and users. I would thus like to argue that the internet, as well as all other elements of late capitalism's culture are embedded in contradictions, complicating the theory and practice of solidarity, however in order to understand its role and functions, we cannot simply neglect or ignore them. The corrupt, commodified media and social media constitute one of the central aspects of contemporary social life, and as I argued above – they are used and resisted in various ways.

Solidarity has never been made solely by acts of blunt resistance. Sometimes such acts belong to a larger process of transition, but in most such cases they are accompanied by various alternative processes, reshaping and transforming the existing politics and/or introducing forms of the new. The altruist dimension of solidarity, making some people take action and responsibility with and for others, is a multi-layered process, proceeding transversally, in words and in silence, in various spaces of the society and often without prior warning or visibility. Counterpublics, composed of actions and debates, reshuffle the existing norms, introduce new forms of solidarity by means of collective actions and debates, demands, negotiations, critique and oppositional discourses. Solidarity is thus a plasticity of the social, in which the interventions into the public sphere are important parts of a much larger transformative process.

BIBLIOGRAPHY

Abramowski, Edward. 2013. "Znaczenie spółdzielczości dla demokracji." In *Wspólna sprawa*, edited by Remigiusz Okraska, 69–75. Warszawa: MPiPS.

Ahmed, Sara. 2017. *Living a Feminist Life*. Durham: Duke University Press.

Arruzza, Cinzia, Tithi Bhattacharya, and Nancy Fraser. 2017. *Feminism for the 99%: A Manifesto*. London: Verso.

Bauman, Zygmunt. 2020. "Solidarność: słowo w poszukiwaniu ciała." In *Solidarność, demokracja, Europa,* edited by Basil Kerski and Jacek Kołtan, 59–70. Gdańsk: ECS.

Benjamin, Walter. 1996. "The Task of Translator." In Walter Benjamin, *Selected Writings, vol. 1.*, 253–263. Cambridge, MA: Harvard University Press.

Bhattacharya, Tithi. 2017. “Socializing Security, Unionizing Work. #Metoo as Our Moment to Explore Possibility.” In *Where Freedom Starts. Sex, Power, Violence, #Metoo. A Verso Report*, 135–150. London: Verso.

Butler, Judith. 1987. *Subjects of Desire: Hegelian Reflections in Twentieth-Century France.* New York: Columbia University Press.

Dean, Jodi. 2003. “Why the Net is not a Public Sphere.” *Constellations* 10(1): 95–112.

Dussel, Enrique. 2007. “From Fraternity to Solidarity: Toward a Politics of Liberation.” *Journal of Social Philosophy* 38(1): 73–92.

Fraser, Nancy. 1990. “Rethinking the Public Sphere. A Contribution to the Critique of Actually Existing Democracy.” *Social Text* 25/26: 56–80.

Gilligan, Carol. 1982. *In a Different Voice: Psychological Theory and Women’s Development.* Cambridge, MA: Harvard University Press.

Hardt, Michael, and Antonio Negri. 2009. *The Commonwealth.* Massachusetts: MIT University Press.

Havel, Václav. 2010. *The Power of the Powerless (Routledge Revivals): Citizens Against the State in Eastern and Central Europe*. Edited by John Keane. London and New York: Routledge.

Hill, Mike and Warren Montag (eds.). 2000. *Masses, Classes and the Public Sphere.* London: Verso.

Honig, Bonnie. 2013. *Antigone, Interrupted.* Cambridge: Cambridge University Press.

hooks, bell. 1984. *Feminist Theory: From Margin to Center.* Boston: South End Press.

Irigaray, Luce. 2010. “The Eternal Irony of the Community.” In *Feminist Interpretations of G. W. F. Hegel*, edited by Patricia Jagentowicz Mills, 45–57. University Park: Pennsylvania State University Press.

Kluge, Alexander, and Oskar Negt. (2016 [1972]). *Public Sphere and Experience. Analysis of the Bourgeois and Proletarian Public Sphere*. London and New York: Verso.

Kowalewski, Zbigniew. 1985. *Rendez-nous nos usines!: Solidarnosc dans le combat pour l’autogestion ouvriere.* Montreuil: Presse Communication.

Laba, Roman. 1991. *The Roots of Solidarity. A Political Sociology of Poland’s Working Class Democratization.* Princeton: Princeton University Press.

Lisiak, Agata. 2019. “Poza girl power: dziewczyński opór, kontrpubliczności i prawo do miasta.” *Praktyka Teoretyczna* 32(2): 48–63.

MacKinnon, Catharine (in conversation with Durba Mitra). 2019. “Ask a Feminist: Sexual Harassment in the Age of #MeToo.” *Signs: Journal of Women in Culture and Society* 44 (4): 1027–1043.

Magala, Sławomir. 2012. *Walka klas w bezklasowej Polsce*. Gdańsk: ECS. [the first edition of this book was published in English as: Starski, Stanislaw. 1982. *Class Struggle in Classless Poland.* Boston: South End Press.]

Majewska, Ewa. 2018. *Kontrpubliczności ludowe i feministyczne. Wczesna “Solidarność” i Czarne Protesty.* Warszawa: Instytut Wydawniczy Książka i Prasa.

Majewska, Ewa. (2022). "Slave, Antigone and the Housewife. Hegel's Dialectics of the Weak." *Praktyka Teoretyczna* 43(1).

Malabou, Catherine. 2005. *The Future of Hegel: Plasticity, Temporality and Dialectic*. New York and London: Routledge.

Malabou, Catherine. 2011. *Changing Difference: The Feminine and the Question of Philosophy*. Translated by Carolyn Shread. Cambridge: Polity Press.

Malabou, Catherine. 2020. "Rethinking Mutual Aid. Kropotkin and Singer in debate." https://fallsemester.org/2020-1/2020/4/8/catherine-malabou-rethinking-mutual-aid-kropotkin-and-singer-in-debate Accessed 20 October 2020.

Marzec, Wiktor. 2020. *Rising Subjects: The 1905 Revolution and the Origins of Modern Polish Politics.* Pittsburgh: University of Pittsburgh Press.

Matynia, Elzbieta. 2001. "The Lost Treasures of Solidarity." *Social Research* 68(4): 917–936.

Orsetti, Maria. 2019. *Kooperatyzm anarchizm feminizm: Wybór pism.* Warszawa: Oficyna Naukowa.

Pateman, Carole. 1989. *The Disorder of Women: Democracy, Feminism and Political Theory.* Stanford*:* Stanford University Press.

Rancière, Jacques. 2004. *Disagreement.* Translated by Julie Rose. Minneapolis-London: University of Minnesota Press.

Rancière, Jacques. 1989. *Nights of Labor: The Workers Dream in Nineteenth Century France*. Translated by John Drury. Philadelphia: Temple University Press.

Rawls, John. 1993. "The Law of Peoples." *Critical Inquiry* 20(1): 36–68.

Rawls, John. 1971. *Theory of Justice.* Cambridge, MA: Harvard University Press.

Rogowska-Stangret, Monika. 2017. "Sharing Vulnerabilities: Searching for 'Unruly Edges' in Times of the Neoliberal Academy." In *Teaching Gender: Feminist Pedagogy and Responsibility in Times of Political Crisis*, edited by Beatriz Revelles-Benavente and Ana M. González Ramos, 11–24. London: Routledge.

Scott, James. 1986. *Weapons of the Weak: Everyday Forms of Peasant Resistance.* New Haven and London: Yale University Press.

Spivak, Gayatri. 1993. *Outside/in the Teaching Machine.* New York and London: Routledge.

Staniszkis, Jadwiga. 2010. *Samoograniczająca się rewolucja.* Gdańsk: ECS.

Tomasello, Michael, Alicia Melis, Claudio Tennie, Emily Wyman, and Esther Herrmann. 2012. "Two Key Steps in the Evolution of Human Cooperation: The Interdependence Hypothesis." *Current Anthropology* 53(6): 673–692.

A Verso Report. 2017. *Where Freedom Starts: Sex, Power, Violence, #Metoo.* London: Verso.

Warner, Michael. 2005. *Public Spheres and Counterpublics.* New York: Zone Books.

Chapter 14

Prefigurative Biology

Mutual Aid, Social Reproduction and Plasticity

Dan Swain

In activist imaginations, mutual aid is seen not merely as a response to immediate needs, but at the same time as establishing the basis for an alternative society. A recent introduction to the concept by activist and author Dean Spade – framed as a handbook for the activist groups that emerged during the COVID-19 crisis – insists that mutual aid involves 'both building the world we want and becoming the kind of people who could live in such a world together' (Spade 2020, 17). Understood in this sense, mutual aid is prefigurative – it is a way of instantiating elements of a desired future society in order to bring both it and the kind of subjectivity it contains into being. At the same time, though, mutual aid is understood as an ever-present possibility or tendency within us, something deeply human, or perhaps even natural. Spade talks about a 'deeply human desire to connect with others, to be of service in ways that reduce suffering, and to be seen and loved by those who truly know us and whom we love', and insists that this desire is something we can commit to, to 'make choices to act out of mutuality and care on purpose' (Spade 2020, 104). Thus, on this reading at least, engaging in mutual aid does not only allow us to learn new practices, it also involves recuperating or restoring something deeply human that has been lost or eroded in our present condition. As David Graeber puts it in his posthumously published introduction to Kropotkin's *Mutual Aid*, 'To create a new world, we can only start by rediscovering what is and has always been right before our eyes' (Graeber and Grubačić 2020).

I am grateful to my co-editors, especially Catherine Malabou and Petr Urban, and to Davina Cooper for their helpful comments on an earlier draft of this chapter. The chapter is an outcome of the project 'Towards a New Ontology of Social Cohesion', grant number GA19–20031S of the Czech Science Foundation (GAČR), realised at the Institute of Philosophy of the Czech Academy of Sciences.

It is this desire to see prefigurative promise in the very kind of animals we are that I am concerned with in this chapter. Its attraction is clear, but so are its risks. For those who imagine the world could be very different from how it is, practising mutual aid links that imagination to an understanding of who we are, to who we have been and to our present needs. And yet, the confidence that this provides can easily slip into consolation, or worse. Invocations of our natural inheritance in politics are understandably seen as suspect, prone to essentialism or biological determinism. However, when confronted with the need to maintain and reproduce life in the face of climate catastrophe, pandemics and other natural disasters, radical politics finds itself unavoidably drawn into reflection on our biological processes and capacities, our relation to non-human nature, and our natural history. In what follows, I discuss some of these challenges, first through an account of contemporary debates in the concept prefigurative politics. There, I identify two elements of particular importance to such projects – a conscious commitment to the implementation of future practices in the present and a simultaneous understanding of these practices as experimental. Already somewhat in tension, both elements are further complicated by claims of naturalness and the ideas of essentialism and determinism that can accompany them.

I then turn to consider this question alongside contemporary accounts in Marxist Feminism of socially reproductive labour. As with classical accounts of mutual aid, such labour is seen as an ever-present human necessity, but one that can be exercised in more or less emancipatory forms – sometimes in accordance with the needs of capital and states, and sometimes *against* them and *for* ourselves. Far from asserting the naturalness of such labour, they seek to emphasise the contingency and historical specificity of its (especially, but not only) gendered and commodified forms. At the same time, however, looking to the emancipatory potentials in reproductive labour invites reflection on the prefigurative potential of our practices of *life-making* in ways that can hardly avoid the terrain of biology, if not nature. I discuss a striking example of this in Sophie Lewis's account of gestational labour, which suggests a serious engagement with the biology of reproduction reveals a utopian horizon that challenges essentialist understandings of natural motherhood and birth, and invites us to learn to live differently. Pursuing this shift from nature to biology further, I suggest this might be developed through dialogue with Catherine Malabou's work. Malabou's concept of plasticity allows us to account for the importance of commitment and experimentation within practices of solidarity and mutual aid, while her non-deterministic reading of biology through epigenetics understands biology itself as a site of resistance in which natural and historical determination meet. Such a dialogue might help us understand how we can (at least sometimes) see prefigurative potentials within the production and reproduction of life itself.

PREFIGURATION, COMMITMENT AND EXPERIMENTATION

Although the term prefigurative politics is used in a variety of sometimes conflicting and contradictory ways, its central commitment is that present action can and should (and often does) *prefigure* a desired future alternative society, through some relationship of similarity, accord or anticipation (van de Sande 2019). It is seen as both a tendency within contemporary social movement practice and an explicit strategy for radicals within those practices, and is thus most commonly associated with anarchism and certain traditions of autonomist Marxism, although it also has deep roots in pacifist communities, feminist movements of the 1980s and 1990s and certain non-conforming religious traditions (Cornell 2016). In a valuable attempt to rationally reconstruct this diverse tendency, Paul Raekstad and Sofa Saio Gradin (2020, 10) define prefiguration as the '*deliberate experimental implementation of desired future social relations and practices in the here-and-now*' (italics in original). This definition captures the two senses in which prefigurative politics is utopian: It anticipates a future that is radically different from a 'here and now' – as Raekstad and Gradin (2020, 37) put it, 'before the ominpresence of free, equal, and democratic relations' – but also insists that it is possible to instantiate elements of that future in the present. Often this is framed as a response to traditions of politics that stress a stark separation between means and ends, instead insisting on either a necessary accord between them, or collapsing the distinction completely (Maeckelbergh 2011). Similarly, such traditions are often posed in response to a politics of deferral, in which questions of alternative social relations and structures are deferred to a distant post-revolutionary future. In contrast, prefigurative politics insists that, while the future will be very different, it is possible (and ultimately necessary) to reach forward and instantiate elements in the present. Prefigurative politics is thus often intimately connected to ideas of direct action, that seek to 'do it ourselves' rather than wait for authorities (Franks 2006).

While inspiring and guiding the action of many, these ideas contain many practical and theoretical tensions. Many of these, I suggest, revolve around the two elements that Raekstad and Gradin (consciously) emphasise in their definition: prefigurative action must be both *deliberate* and *experimental*. It is necessary, on the one hand, to consciously commit to the implementation of future practices in the present, while simultaneously understanding these practices as experimental, and our visions of the future as 'temporary, tentative, and subject to revision' (Raekstad and Gradin 2020, 37). This intentional character is necessary to clearly identify prefigurative politics as a strategic project (we might say, as *politics*). This is contrasted with a kind of unconscious or unexpected prefiguration: 'Early merchant capitalists did not, for example, expect or plan that their social relations would become the locus of a new social formation called capitalism' (Raekstad and Gradin 2020, 36). There is thus a moment of commitment or decision in which activists identify a given set of practices as worth implementing and exercising. This commitment, as Spade (2020, 16–44) stresses and I will discuss more below, also seems necessary to avoid practices simply being co-opted, or slipping into models of charity or saviourism that reproduce hierarchies. However, this commitment is tempered by a desire for experimentation and an openness to many possible futures. It is not possible or desirable to simply identify a desired future and 'read back' from the future to the present.

This insistence on the need for experimentation reflects several concerns that are central to the political projects of which prefigurative politics is usually a part: First, an awareness of the limits that the present poses on the capacity to imagine alternative futures. For Raekstad and Gradin (2020, 40–60) this is derived from a broadly Marxist account of the relationship between theory and practice that combines a recognition that we cannot know what the future will be like before living it with an openness that we might live in ways radically different from what we can even imagine (See also Raekstad 2018; Swain 2019a, Chapter 3; Salvage Editorial Collective 2019). Elsewhere, I have argued that an 'ends-guided' prefiguration that assumes a relatively well-defined goal to which we simply match our activity risks losing whatever is thought to be distinctive of this approach and risks collapsing into a choice between ethical commitment or social change (Swain 2019b). Pursuing a similar criticism, Uri Gordon warns of a tendency, perhaps inherent in the temporal language of prefiguration itself, to adopt a 'recursive' temporal framing, in which the future radiates back into the present, and the present gains its significance solely in terms of that future. This, though, runs contrary to what Gordon identifies as one of the motive forces of such politics: the idea that the future ought to be seen as generated out of the present and thus contains multiple possibilities that depend on present action:

> This generative temporal framing is situated in 'normal' forward-looking time, without recursion. Revolutionaries' visions for the future are themselves present-tense mental experiences and discursive exchanges. More importantly, the interpretation of the present is self-contained – dependent on ethical values rather than a promised or imagined prototype. Maturation is not guaranteed (the child 'is to be', not 'will be'). (Gordon 2018, 530)

This point of view 'implies that the ends expressed in practice undergo constant re-evaluation. Such an open-ended politics leaves any notion of future "accomplishment" at least partly indeterminate, and thus too unstable to coherently serve as a source of recursive prefiguration' (Gordon 2018, 531). Gordon also points towards the practical risks this approach creates, namely a kind of consolation for activists, in which the accord between present activity and the future mitigates against critical engagement with challenges of the present, whether climate crisis, disaster capitalism or the risk of fascism.

If prefiguration is to make sense at all, then, it has to be able to locate its actions and its alternatives in the present tense, and to understand its future goals as both emergent from those practices and subject to revision in the course of movement. In some respects, mutual aid seems to be an ideal candidate for such practices, since it is focused primarily on the meeting of present needs. It thus has a certain grounding in the present that gives it significance beyond simply modelling alternative relations. And yet, the moment we also assert that mutual aid is somehow a more *natural* or *human* practice, we seem to complicate this picture. At one point, Spade characterises the learning involved in mutual aid as not just learning something new, but as a *re*learning of something that has been lost: 'it can be hard to imagine that we could survive another way. But for most of human history, we did, and mutual aid projects let us relearn that it's possible and emancipatory' (Spade 2020, 39). Kropotkin, of course, identified mutual aid as a factor of evolution, describing how a diverse range of social and political institutions (trade unions, socialist political societies, communal groups, even ornithologist clubs) should be understood as 'manifestations of the same ever-living tendency of man towards mutual aid and support' (Kropotkin 2009, 154). The American anarchist Paul Goodman, in his 1945 May Day pamphlet, proposes a maxim that consciously combines the 'as if' action of prefigurative politics with a conception of naturalness: 'Free action is to live in present society as though it were a natural society', (Goodman 2010, 26). For Goodman:

> The free spirit is rather millenarian than utopian. A man does not look forward to a future state of things which he tries to bring about by suspect means; but he draws now, so far as he can, on the natural force in him that is no different in kind from what it will be in a free society, except that there it will have more scope and be persistently reinforced by mutual aid and fraternal conflict. (Goodman 2010, 26)

This metaphor of drawing on a force within us echoes a metaphor of Kropotkin's, in which mutual aid is a current, or flow, which 'did not die out in the masses [but] continued to flow even after that defeat'. This flow is ever present, and 'seeks its way to find out a new expression which would not be the State, nor the mediæval city, nor the village community of the barbarians, nor the savage clan, but would proceed from all of them, and yet be superior to them in its wider and more deeply humane conceptions' (Kropotkin 2009, 222).

It is easy to see both why such ideas are attractive and why they have become suspect. On the one hand, grounding our practices in our nature provides support for their superiority over other practices, and gives confidence to the idea that they can truly usher in something different. The claim that our desired future draws on and fulfils a natural and ever-present tendency buttresses confidence in the link between present and future action. On the other, claims of nature seem especially prone to the kind of consolation that Gordon warns about. If radical politics is simply about acting naturally, or living up to our nature, then we risk evading difficult practical questions. Moreover, as Goodman's remarks clearly indicate, the claim of nature complicates the temporal structure implied by prefiguration. The 'alternative' under discussion is no longer located merely in the future, but at the same time identified within us. Kropotkin's metaphor of a flow perhaps demonstrates the ambivalences of this. We can draw on a flow, and we are in some sense within the flow, and perhaps even the flow is within us. And yet, the flow operates behind our backs, and expresses itself through us and our actions. The risk is that in asserting mutual aid as natural we replace the determinacy of the future that Gordon warns about with a different kind of determinacy, whether of a supposed more natural past (or even a prehistory), or something outside of history altogether, a flow that operates behind our backs and of which our action is the mere expression. In either case, the space for experimentation seems compromised – either because we already know what our nature is and we must simply return to it, or because we are simply acting out a process over which we have little to no control. This is perhaps particularly notable in Goodman's insistence that the difference between present and future action is merely of *scope* and not of *kind*: In what sense, then, is it possible (as Spade does) to speak of our actions creating new subjects and subjectivity, of a learning that is also a transformation, if the difference is merely the quantitative expansion of existing capacities?

This also suggests a worry about the place of commitment. If mutual aid flows behind our backs and finds its way through our actions, if we are always already mutual, why must we also commit to it? Why does it require effort to learn to practise this tendency? And even when we do commit to it, in what way is it meaningfully *our* project when we do so? In what sense is the future that is built on mutual aid *our* future? These questions evoke familiar criticisms of Kropotkin, for example those of Errico Malatesta, who asks: 'In such a concept, what meaning can the words "will, freedom, responsibility" have? And of what use would education, propaganda, revolt be? One can no more transform the predestined course of human affairs than one can change the course of the stars. What then?' (quoted in Miller 1983, 338; See also Crowder, 1991) As I will return to below (and is discussed in chapters 8, 9 and 11 of this volume), there are good reasons to contest the reading of Kropotkin as a naïve exponent of biological determinism, but the question deserves an answer. Can mutual aid bridge our natural inheritance and our desired future while still allowing us to confront the challenges of the present?

MUTUAL AID, SOCIAL REPRODUCTION AND EMANCIPATORY LIFE-MAKING

One response to this worry would be to emphasise not mutual aid's naturalness, but rather its persistence and immanence – that it happens, and that it exists in forms we can commit to and develop (see Brinn and Butterfield in this volume). In her reading of Kropotkin, Ruth Kinna (2016, 107) resists his aggregation to a tradition of naïve scientific utopianism by repurposing Malatesta's critical appraisal of him as a 'poet of science'. She notes how Kropotkin, in his memoirs recalled how his brother Alexander 'had wrongly abandoned poetry for the sake of natural science' (*Ibid.*, 92). Kropotkin, in contrast, pursued a different path, in which he recast the role of geography as 'an instrument to reveal the contingencies of history, freeing it from the analysis of what existed and hooking it up with a conception of what may be' (*Ibid.*, 92). On this reading, geographical science was concerned with identifying flux and uncertainty, tracing and identifying 'collisions between ideas and practices resulted in changes that reverberated in social, political, economic and physical spheres' (*Ibid.*, 101). In Kinna's reading, Kropotkin's revolutionary hope was sustained not by deterministic certainty, but by a commitment to uncertainty, in which 'not even the most dramatic setbacks could eclipse totally the possibility of recovery' (*Ibid.*, 192). Thus, 'rather than squeeze out space for the will, as Malatesta argued, this politics was fired by a lack of certainty as much as it was by hope [. . .]. Rather than root anarchy in a conception of human nature, he grounded it in resistance' (*Ibid.*, 197). On this reading, Kropotkin's perspective remains resolutely present tense, beginning with the historical forms that were right in front of his eyes Kinna (*Ibid.*, 100) notes in particular the significance of the Paris Commune as a historically contingent event that generated new historical possibilities for communal action. Perhaps we can understand the mutual aid groups that emerge in reaction in disasters and pandemics in a similar vein – let us not worry about how they emerged but commit to them now that they are here and draw hope from their persistence.

Pursuing this further, we might see affinities with contemporary thinkers, particularly within traditions of Marxist Feminism, who emphasise the significance of socially reproductive labour. Jason Moore and Raj Patel describe how capitalism depends upon 'cheap care': 'the work of caring for, nurturing, and raising human communities. Such work is overwhelmingly unpaid because it makes the whole system of wage work possible' (Patel and Moore 2017, 124) This kind of labour has become central to renewed interest in Marxist Feminism in recent years. Its dual character – as producing both labour-power and life – is seen as creating the potential for resistance and for alternatives. As Susan Ferguson (2020, 123) puts it:

> Such labour certainly contributes to creating a commodity, labour power. But it does so by producing things to be consumed – things that support life (not capital) in the first instance. Its products are meals, clean clothes, community gardens, safe streets, hurricane relief shelters, and mended bones. They are also more ephemeral 'things', such as love, attention, discipline, and knowledge that comprise the emotional and social grounding of life. They are useful things – things produced not for sale, but to sustain life.

For Ferguson and her co-thinkers, capitalism depends on but systematically devalues this kind of work, which drives people to both attempt to develop and organise alternative forms of life-making, and to enter into combative struggles with both the state and capital over the forms that life-making takes. It is through this process that people can come to re-evaluate and reorganise these forms in a more emancipatory and self-determining direction: 'Lives can be organized against capital. Life and life-making are fundamentally about the practical human activity through which people meet their current needs and imagine new possibilities – be they pursuing food and shelter or love, play, and rest' (Ferguson 2020, 119). In his recent study of disaster relief, Peer Illner explicitly characterises mutual aid in terms of 'civil-society-led social reproduction', distinguishing it from either for-profit- or state-led social reproduction while still embedding it within 'the wider totality of reproductive labour' (Illner 2020, 122).

In this schema, practices of solidarity and mutuality are not (or not only) surviving relics of a previous era, but practices that are immanent to and reproduced by the dominance of capital while also operating in tension with it. Indeed, such approaches often emphasise the importance of denaturalising reproductive practices, especially caring and raising children, showing how they have been manifested differently historically, and how their specific historical forms have been misrepresented as natural (as naturally women's work, for example). In this case, recognition of the fact that mutuality is manifested differently in history is not about revealing a nature to which we must live up, but revealing the historical specificity of our present and how we might live differently. And yet, while resisting the idea of any one particular form of 'life-making' being more *natural* than another, social reproduction theory does insist that it is possible for communities and individuals to reflect on and repurpose their life-making activities in an emancipatory direction, understanding them as potential sites of resistance and transformation, as well as survival. Indeed, this seems essential if such practices are to avoid simply plugging gaps within an otherwise failing and crisis-ridden system. If mutual aid is a form of social reproduction, it can just as easily complement state strategies of reproduction, and even absolve the state of responsibilities towards communities ravaged by disaster (something Illner (2020, 106–110 and 118–128) observes in the Department of Homeland Security's glowing endorsement of Occupy Sandy, and warns of in the context of COVID-19. Illner (2020, 109) rightly insists that if mutual aid groups are to avoid becoming mere 'opportunities' for the state, they must not simply perform social reproduction, but *politicise* it – just as in the discussion of prefigurative politics, a certain kind of commitment remains central.

Some forms of that politicisation are straightforward – demands for better childcare, education, healthcare, as well as for the democratic capacity to decide what form they take and the free time to make them worthwhile. But focusing on questions of 'life and life-making', and how they can be organised alternatively, also seems inevitably to invite reflections on more intimate questions of our body and biology. Reflections of this sort can be found in Sophie Lewis's studies of gestational labour in both its paid and unpaid forms. Her provocative title *Full Surrogacy Now* indicates her desire to see emancipatory implications even in the deeply exploitative form take by the global market for commercial surrogacy. While opposed to the form taken by such work under capitalism, she nonetheless insists that the recognising it precisely as *work* involves an important theoretical insight. Doing so extends and reconfigures the Marxist notion of labour, and thus 'opens up the realization that pregnancy workers can bargain, commit sabotage, and go on strike' (Lewis 2019, 75), but also reveals how even the so-called normal or natural pregnancies involve not merely the work of a single mother, but also an extended network of 'surrogates' who enable this process. Lewis thus seeks to reveal the truth behind the cliché that it takes a village to make a child, and to read the actual, messy realities of pregnancy and child-rearing against a mythology that opposes an apparently uncomplicated natural pregnancy against 'artificial' forms. The defenders of 'natural' pregnancy find themselves 'in denial about the existence of gestational nonparenting and nongestational parenting', and thus 'refuse to see the naturalization already operative in everyday biogenetics' (Lewis 2019, 51).

However, such common sense biogenetics does not only fail to understand the way that children are always co-produced, it also fails to grasp how reproduction is never just reproduction. Here Lewis draws on insight she takes from Donna Haraway, who insists that contemporary understandings of genetics reveal that 'literal reproduction is a contradiction in terms' (Lewis 2019, 19). Rather than parents reproducing a child that is a continuation or copy of them, serious engagement with epigenetics reveals 'the co-production of gestators by fetuses at the genetic and epigenetic level'. This suggests that 'it is not simply a baby that is birthed during a birth, but rather two unequal beings who are both survivors of their own matrixial sym-poeisis' (Lewis 2018, 302). The purpose of this emphasis is threefold: First, to acknowledge that surrogates are not mere bearers of fetuses, but that they contribute to the development of the child both through their labour and through processes of chimeric transformation; second, to emphasise that those who are pregnant are also transformed by the process; and third, to emphasise that the child is in a very real sense something new – not simply a genetic replication of their parents, but something *sui generis*, that 'belongs to no one except themselves'. These combine in one of her key arguments ('something which the best parents on earth already know') – that the idea that 'bearing an infant "for someone else" is always a fantasy, a shaky construction, in that infants don't belong to anyone, ever' (Lewis 2019, 19).

Central to Lewis's approach is a desire to read biology against nature, or at least against romanticised 'natural motherhood'. She notes that many of those she criticises are often accused of biologism, but insists that 'ironically biologism – that is, better acquaintance with the bare biology of human gestation – is more than capable of putting an end to that fantasy' (Lewis 2019, 136). Taking biology seriously reveals:

> There is only degenerative and regenerative co-production. Labour (such as gestational labour) and nature (including genome, epigenome, microbiome, and so on) can only alchemize the world together by transforming one another. We are all, at root, responsible, and especially for the stew that is epigenetics. We are the makers of one another. And we could learn collectively to act like it. (Lewis 2019, 19–20)

It is this collective learning that Lewis calls Full Surrogacy. Thus, far from being an essentialist constraint on our emancipation, an adequate accounting with our biology would reveal our interdependence and mutual responsibility for one another, and thus reveal new possibilities for living together. For her, the consequences of this are radical – a feminist communism, in which ideas of family and parenthood are rethought alongside ideas of work and property: 'Let's bring about the conditions of possibility for open-source, fully collaborative gestation. Let's prefigure a way of manufacturing each other non-competitively. Let's hold one another hospitably, explode notions of hereditary parentage and multiply real, loving solidarities. Let us build a care commune based on comradeship, a world sustained by kith and kind more than by kin' (Lewis 2019, 26). Seeking to extend this beyond literal gestation, she also gives prominence to the practices of trans communities, who share knowledge and material resources in order to survive and fashion lives for themselves, and for whom the truth of the slogan 'biology is not destiny' is a matter of life and death (see Gleeson 2017; Gleeson and Hoad 2019).

For Lewis, then, taking seriously the biology of reproduction reveals a utopian horizon, one which she suggests is already at work in many communities that seek to organise their own reproduction. This is not without conflict – she is at pains to note the agonistic and conflictual aspects of pregnancy, and that life-making also contains morbidity and possibilities of death, especially where control over reproduction is concerned. Nonetheless, she suggests that we can reckon with and learn to *live up* to the potential that reproduction – as both a biological process and a human practice – reveals to us. In this way, Lewis provides an example of how the desire of social reproduction to denaturalise and politicise 'life-making' capacities might proceed from, rather than resist, serious engagement with our biology.

PLASTICITY, BIOLOGY AND RESISTANCE

Lewis's invitation to learn from our biology (and her focus on epigenetics) puts her on the same terrain as Catherine Malabou. While Lewis is concerned with gestation, Malabou's major focus has been the brain. Central to this is the concept of plasticity: The capacity to give, receive and annihilate form. *What Should We Do with Our Brain?* begins with the provocation that 'our brain is plastic and we do not know it. We continue to believe in the "rigidity" of an entirely genetically determined brain, about which it is impossible to ask: *What should we do with this?*' (Malabou 2008, 4). Thus, neuroscience reveals that our brain is capable of being moulded and shaped, and of shaping and moulding itself, yet we continue to labour under the illusion that we are determined beings. Malabou invites us to shatter that illusion, and to locate the brain (and perhaps by extension ourselves) at the limit between freedom and determinism. Hinting at the transformative, perhaps even utopian, possibilities that this reveals, Malabou (2008, 82) invites her readers to 'construct and entertain a relation with their brain as the image of a world to come'.

Crucially, Malabou distinguishes this plasticity from the flexibility demanded by contemporary neoliberalism. This kind of flexibility is a caricature of plasticity, in which people appear infinitely responsive to the demands and whims of the market, but are ultimately denied the capacity to make themselves: 'Flexibility is plasticity minus its genius' (Malabou 2008, 12). In a world dominated by flexibility, to use our brains properly involves a kind of resistance:

> Fashioning an identity in such a world has no meaning except as constructing of countermodel to this caricature, as opposed simply to replicating it. Not to replicate the caricature of the world: this is what we should do with our brain. To refuse to be flexible individuals who combine a permanent control of the self with a capacity to self-modify at the whim of fluxes, transfers, and exchanges, for fear of explosion. (Malabou 2008, 78)

This, then, is the sense in which our brain can provide us an image of the world to come. Recognising our plasticity gives us a basis for resistance to flexibility and reveals the possibilities for self-determination. This self-determination, though, is not the self-determination of an infinitely malleable subject (even if it is open to explosive transformations), but one that at the same time links us back to who we are. Plasticity is 'the relation that an individual entertains with what, on the one hand, attaches him originally to himself, to his proper form, and with what, on the other hand, allows him to launch himself into the void of all identity, to abandon all rigid and fixed determination' (Malabou 2008, 80).

Like Lewis, then, Malabou asks us to learn from our biology and to see within it the possibility of alternative forms that both resist domination and anticipate an alternative future. Malabou's own engagement with epigenetics extends this resistance beyond the brain into biology itself:

> If nature and culture are intimately linked through epigenetics, it means that nature and history meet within the biological, that there is a biological encounter between them. In that sense, biology ceases to be a pure deterministic field, with no symbolic autonomy, a simple raw material for political use. On the contrary, epigenetics is a biological notion that resists the political reduction of biology to a pure and simple vehicle of power. (Malabou 2015b, 53)

Here Malabou points towards an understanding of the biological as 'a complex and contradictory instance, opposed to itself and pointing to, on the one hand, the ideological vehicle of modern sovereignty, and on the other hand, that which applies its brakes' (Malabou 2015a, 292). Thus it is possible for a resistance to domination, exploitation and instrumentalisation to emerge 'from possibilities inscribed in the structure of the living organism'. On this basis, she suggests, it is possible to affirm 'the existence of a political counteroffensive inscribed in the biological' (Malabou 2015a, 292). Most recently, she has suggested that '[t]he diverse manifestations of mutual aid that we see currently emerging are precisely the expressions of such a potential [. . .] a resistance which is all at once empirical and political' (Malabou this volume, 27).

Malabou's philosophy is a materialism, but it is not, to borrow an old Marxist term, a mechanical materialism. Rather, biological life contains within it both multiple possibilities and also the symbolic concepts through which it can be appropriated: 'if we can affirm that plasticity inhabits the biological, that it opens, within organic life, a supplement of indeterminacy, a void, a floating entity, it is then possible to claim that material life is not dependent in its dynamic upon a transcendental symbolic economy; that on the contrary, biological life creates or produces its own symbolisation' (Malabou, 2015b, 43). As Natalie Helberg (2020, 597) observes, crucial to this structure is the idea that plasticity, while a natural fact of our biology, must be cognised in order to be activated: 'plasticity without a discourse that names it and makes it live for us ends up not being plasticity at all' (but mere flexibility). Thus, while symbolisation emerges from biology, it also plays an unavoidable role in naming and identifying that biology, and implicitly, this can be done in more or less coherent ways. Helberg (2020, 593) suggests: 'What Malabou terms plasticity is a basic biological capacity to transform. Still, it is a capacity that must be exercised. This is why it is so responsive to the discourse on the brain: a discourse that makes it difficult to grasp plasticity in all of its dimensions, to grasp the brain's fluidity, will not encourage us to act in ways that are consistent with the brain's potential'.

It is easy to see how engagement with Malabou's understanding of plasticity might complement and enrich the different approaches I have discussed above. Plasticity offers a way of thinking about the biological at the border between contingency and necessity, insisting on both the link to our specific, determinate form and at the same time our capacity to modify and sometimes radically explode that form. We can think our determination as biological beings, with a genetic inheritance and a historical past, without being fully captured by that determination. However, to avoid being captured by that determination involves a kind of symbolic intervention, a decision to represent our capacities as anticipating a future. Yet this no longer appears as a simple voluntarist decision, but now as something that emerges from our biology itself. We can perhaps see here a way of maintaining the two aspects of prefigurative politics that seemed most challenged by invocations of mutual aid as natural: commitment and experimentation. Just as it is necessary to recognise our brains as plastic in order for them to truly be so, it is necessary that we recognise mutual aid as radical in order for it to really be so. At the same time, this commitment is not to a specific form of living or thinking, but to exercising our capacity for reshaping and transforming ourselves and our relations with others.

Moreover, Malabou's emphasis on the possibilities of resistance inscribed in biology itself can be fruitfully brought into dialogue with social reproduction theory's emphasis on the political significance of life-making within and against capitalist exploitation. Stressing the plasticity inherent in biological forms opens up possibilities for adapting and transforming those forms in perhaps unanticipated ways. Moreover, we might draw an analogy between Malabou's treatment of flexibility and the risks of co-optation that attends many forms of alternative mutual aid and social reproduction. It is always possible to undertake these practices in a way that simply reproduces 'business as usual', and merely adapts itself to the demands of capital and existing state strategies. To avoid this requires a certain kind of political intervention, which does not come from a messianic or transcendental outside, but rather comes from *us*. It is thus possible thus to think about how our biology can transform and be transformed without this transformation appearing as a purely voluntarist decision, and this in turn might also inform debates about the relation between humans and non-human nature. For example, the *Salvage Editorial Collective* (2019, 54) has recently argued that responding to a climate catastrophe requires a 'Prometheanism', in which Prometheus 'must be, not bound by, perhaps, but *sublated* with a rigorous humility'. Plasticity, which insists on both the possibility and the limits of remaking ourselves, seems a good place to start developing this.

There will be objections to this, no doubt. Most obviously, it will rightly be insisted that both mutual aid and social reproduction are about much more than biology, and to conflate the two is to reduce its theoretical scope and risk reproducing the naturalisation of reproductive activity that many have done so much to resist. I can only agree that such a reduction would be disastrous, and serious engagement with social reproduction must concern itself with the myriad ways in which labour-power is reproduced and maintained, from education to borders to policing. But avoiding such a reduction should not be confused with avoiding biology altogether – if we are to talk about life, life-making and how it is to be organised differently, we cannot simply vacate the terrain of biology and allow it to be filled by various shades of the political right. Both Malabou and Lewis show us that we need not do so.

However, there are certainly gaps to be filled here. One concerns the relationship between resistance and learning. While resistance might be always immanent, to talk of learning suggests longer processes of transformation and change. It is partly for this reason that Ferguson emphasises the importance of combative struggles *over* social reproduction. She agrees with the authors of the *Feminism for the 99%* manifesto's characterisation of struggle as 'an opportunity and a school' that can 'transform those who participate in it, challenging our prior self-understandings and reshaping our view of the world' and allow us to 'reinterpret our interests, reframe our hopes, and expand our sense of the possible' (quoted in Ferguson 2020, 136). In this view, conflictual struggles make it possible to politicise and relate to our own reproduction in ways that are not immediately available, generating new subjects and new consciousness. How, then, might this dynamic be understood, and how can it be combined with the potentials for resistance that Malabou sees as inscribed in our biology itself, which she describes as both applying a break and launching a counteroffensive? What is the relationship between drawing on an existing capacity to resist and transforming both ourselves and the world, or, in another idiom, between resistance and revolution?

This also raises the question of goals. While most of the thinkers I have discussed so far are reticent to identify specific goals, they are nonetheless committed to broad visions of the future: For Raekstad and Gradin, a world based on the 'omnipresence of free, equal and democratic social relations', for Ferguson and her co-thinkers a form of socialism, for Lewis a gestational communism. There is a goal, as well as a movement, and thus there is some sense this goal could be reached. Does the kind of resistance that Malabou invokes have a goal, and should it? Is plasticity itself a goal, and if so, does plasticity become just another name for anarchy (or communism)? Finally, there is (again, a classical Marxist question) of agency. Who are the people, groups and classes who initiate and undergo these processes of transformation and learning? Who are they in conflict with, and where (if any) are the privileged sites of these processes? Who, in other words, is the *we* that is invited to learn from our biology (and who are we struggling against)? Asking such questions begins to raise thorny questions of organisations and institutions, not least of how to understand and approach the state and its various organs, and whether they might not be merely resisted but also transformed, destroyed or replaced. I ask these questions not because I think there are no answers, but because I think they are the grounds on which a fruitful dialogue should take place.

A final point where this dialogue might be fruitful concerns the place of history. I began with the worry that to talk of mutual aid as a factor of human evolution, or a natural feature of humanity, was precisely to dehistoricise it, to place it in a natural flow running behind our backs. Yet Malabou offers us a way of reading it is inescapably both biological and historical. Glossing Kropotkin, she suggests '"Anonymous masses" organize resistance to political hegemonies not because they are driven by a stubborn, unconscious natural trend, but because they *remember the past without having necessarily memorised it*' (Malabou this volume, 27, emphasis original). These remarks call to mind Malabou's repurposing of the famous lines from Marx's *18th Brumaire* in *What Should We do With Our Brains?* Marx's original remarks (in Ben Fowkes's translation) were: 'Men make their own history, but not of their own free will; not under circumstances they themselves have chosen, but under the given and inherited circumstances with which they are directly confronted' (Marx 2010, 146). Reflecting on this phrase Alasdair MacIntyre once suggested that 'The political aim of Marxists is to liquidate that "but". The theoretical aim is to understand it' (MacIntyre 2009, 57). MacIntyre was perhaps both right and wrong. Understanding our historical (and biological) determination is indeed part of the project of not being bound by it, or bound to repeat it; but the point is not to eliminate it, but to grasp, remember and repurpose it for ourselves.

BIBLIOGRAPHY

Cornell, Andrew. 2016. *Unruly Equality: U.S. Anarchism in the Twentieth Century.* Oakland: University of California Press.

Crowder, George. 1991. *Classical Anarchism.* Oxford: Clarendon Press.

Ferguson, Susan. 2020. *Women and Work: Feminism, Labour, and Social Reproduction.* London: Pluto Press.

Franks, Benjamin. 2006. *Rebel Alliances: The Ends and Means of British Anarchism.* Oakland: AK Press.

Gleeson, Jules Joanne. 2017. *Transition and Abolition: Notes on Marxism and Trans Politics.* July 19. Accessed 17th November, 2020. https://viewpointmag.com/2017/07/19/transition-and-abolition-notes-on-marxism-and-trans-politics/.

Gleeson, Jules Joanne, and J N Hoad. 2019. "Gender Identity Communism: A Gay Utopian Examination of Trans Healthcare in Britain." *Salvage* 7: 177–195.

Goodman, Paul. 2010. *Drawing the Line: Paul Goodman's Anarchist Writings.* Edited by Taylor Stoehr. Oakland: PM Press.

Gordon, Uri. 2018. "Prefigurative Politics between Ethical Practice and Absent Promise." *Political Studies* 66(2): 521–537.

Graeber, David, and Andrej Grubačić. 2020. *David Graeber Left Us a Parting Gift — His Thoughts on Kropotkin's "Mutual Aid".* September 4. Accessed 17th November, 2020. https://truthout.org/articles/david-graeber-left-us-a-parting-gift-his-thoughts-on-kropotkins-mutual-aid/.

Helberg, Natalie. 2020. "Insubordinate Plasticity: Judith Butler and Catherine Malabou." *Hypatia* 35(4): 587–606.

Illner, Peer. 2020. *Disasters and Social Reproduction.* London: Pluto Press.

Kinna, Ruth. 2016. *Kropotkin and the Classical Anarchist Tradition.* Edinburgh: Edinburgh University Press.

Kropotkin, Peter. 2009. *Mutual Aid: A Factor of Evolution.* New York: Cosimo Classics.

Lewis, Sophie. 2018. "Cyborg Uterine Geography: Complicating 'Care' and Social Reproduction." *Dialogues in Human Geography* 8(3): 300–316.

Lewis, Sophie. 2019. *Full Surrogacy Now: Feminism Against Family.* London: Verso.

MacIntyre, Alasdair. 2009. "Notes from the Moral Wilderness." In *Alasdair MacIntyre's Engagement with Marxism,* edited by Paul Blackledge and Neil Davidson, 45–68. Chicago: Haymarket.

Maeckelbergh, Marianne. 2011. "Doing is Believing: Prefiguration as Strategic Practice in the Alterglobalisation Movement." *Social Movement Studies* 10: 1–20.

Marx, Karl. "The Eighteenth Brumaire of Louis Napoleon." In *Surveys from Exile*, translated by Ben Fowkes, 143–249. London: Verso.

Malabou, Catherine. 2015a. "Interview with Catherine Malabou." In *Plastic Materialities: Politics, Legality and Metamorphosis in the Work of Catherine Malabou*, edited by Brenna Bhandar and Jonathan Goldberg-Hiller, 287–300. London: Duke University Press.

Malabou, Catherine. 2015b. "Will Sovereignty Ever Be Deconstructed?" In *Plastic Materialities: Politics, Legality and Metamorphosis in the Work of Catherine Malabou*, edited by Brenna Bhandar and Jonathan Goldberg-Hiller, 35–46. London: Duke University Press.

Malabou, Catherine. 2008. *What Should We Do with Our Brains?* Translated by Sebastian Rand. New York: Fordham University Press.

Miller, David. 1983. "The Neglected (II) – Kropotkin." *Government and Opposition* 18: 319–38.

Patel, Raj, and Jason Moore. 2017. *A History of Capitalism in Seven Cheap Things*. Oakland: University of California Press.

Raekstad, Paul. 2018. "Revolutionary Practice and Prefigurative Politics: A Clarification and Defence." *Constellations* 25(3): 359–372.

Raekstad, Paul, and Sofa Saio Gradin. 2020. *Prefigurative Politics: Building Tomorrow Today*. Cambridge: Polity.

Salvage Editorial Collective. 2019. "The Tragedy of the Worker: Towards the Proletarocene." *Salvage* 7: 7–62.

Spade, Dean. 2020. *Mutual Aid: Building Solidarity During This Crisis (and the Next)*. London: Verso.

Swain, Dan. 2019a. *None So Fit to Break the Chains: Marx's Ethics of Self-Emancipation*. Leiden: Brill.

Swain, Dan. 2019b. "Not Not but Not yet: Present and Future in Prefigurative Politics." *Political Studies* 67(1): 47–62.

van de Sande, Matthijs. 2019. "Prefiguration." In *Critical Terms in Futures Studies*, edited by Heike Paul, 227–233. Cham: Palgrave Macmillan.

Index

About the Contributors

Gearóid Brinn is a PhD candidate and teaches political theory at the University of Melbourne, Australia. His research focuses on radical democratic theory, anarchism and radical realism. His work has appeared in the *European Journal of Political Theory* and *Environmental Politics*.

Georgina Butterfield is an independent researcher from Melbourne, Australia. She has published and taught ecological philosophy and her research focuses on the development of non-transcendental and non-anthropocentric ecological ethics. Whilst trained as a philosopher she adopts an interdisciplinary approach drawing on wide reading in the natural sciences.

Arianne Conty is a continental philosopher and associate professor of philosophy at the American University of Sharjah, UAE. Her research focuses on the philosophy of nature, the philosophy of technology and the philosophy of religion. She has published articles in a wide range of journals, including *Environmental Values, Theory, Culture & Society*, *Journal of Speculative Philosophy, Politics* and *Religion & Ideology*.

Jonas Faria Costa is a PhD candidate in Philosophy at the University of Manchester, UK. His main research interest is on philosophy of action and social ontology. His research takes an interdisciplinary approach that encompasses social psychology, game theory and philosophy. Beyond academia, he has also collaborated with various anarchist publications and magazines.

Jade Crimson Rose Da Costa (they/them/she/her) is a gender non-binary queer woman of colour PhD candidate in sociology at York University in Toronto, Canada. Their dissertation explores how to vision a collective memory of local Black, Indigenous, and People of Colour (BIPOC) HIV/AIDS activism using a Black feminist and queer of colour approach. She founded *New Sociology: Journal of Critical Praxis*, a social justice graduate journal aimed at uplifting queer, trans, women, and BIPOC students, activists and creatives across so-called Canada and beyond. They are also a published poet, creative author and an award-winning teacher's assistant. For more information, please visit: jadecrimson.com.

Tim Elmo Feiten is a PhD candidate at the University of Cincinnati. He has published on the reception of Jakob von Uexküll in cognitive science and the relationship between ecological psychology and enactivism, as well as on the links between Max Stirner and twentieth-century French philosophy. His research deals with the history and philosophy of cognitive science and biology and their intersections with French and German philosophy.

Rasmus Sandnes Haukedal is a PhD candidate at Durham University, UK. His thesis is on the topic of the extended evolutionary synthesis within biology and its relevance to philosophy and vice versa, under the supervision of Gerald Moore.

Petr Kouba is a senior researcher at the Institute of Philosophy of the Czech Academy of Sciences. He specialises in contemporary French philosophy, phenomenology philosophy of sociality and philosophy of psychiatry. His publications include *L'exode sans Moise: L'émigration rom comme probléme politique* (Traugot Bautz, 2020), *Margins of Phenomenology* (Traugot Bautz, 2016) and *The Phenomenon of Mental Disorder: Perspectives of Heidegger's Thought in Psychopathology* (Springer, 2015).

Eugene Kuchinov is head of the Laboratory for Philosophical Studies of the Future at the Immanuel Kant Baltic Federal University. His work focuses specifically on the problems of ontological, epistemological and technological anarchy, panpsychism and animism, utopia and radical imagination. His research has been published in leading academic journals in Russia: *Logos*, *Novoe literaturnoe obozrenie* (New Literary Review), *Sinii Divan* (Blue Sofa), *Stasis*, *Neprikosnovenny zapas* (Emergency Reserve).

Ewa Majewska is a feminist philosopher and activist, living in Warsaw, Poland. She has taught at the University of Warsaw and the Jagiellonian University in Kraków, Poland, and has been a visiting scholar at UC Berkeley, ICI Berlin and IWM Vienna. She has published several books, including *Feminist Antifascism: Counterpublics of the Common* (Verso 2021) and written for various journals including: *e-flux*, *Signs*, *Third Text*, *Utopian Studies* and *Jacobin*.

Catherine Malabou is professor of philosophy at the Centre for Research in Modern European Philosophy, at Kingston University, UK, and in the departments of Comparative Literature and European Languages and Studies at UC Irvine. Her books include *Before Tomorrow: Epigenesis and Rationality* (Polity Press, 2016) *Morphing Intelligence: From IQ Measurements to Artificial Brains*, (Columbia University Press, 2018) and *Le Plaisir effacé: Clitoris et pensée* (Rivages, 2020).

Ole Martin Sandberg is a philosopher at the University of Iceland where he teaches environmental ethics and has participated in research on the philosophy of inequality, climate change, feminism, anarchist communitarianism and embodied critical thinking. He is also employed at the Icelandic Museum of Natural History conducting research on the intersection of philosophy and biology. His work has been published in *Radical Philosophy Review* and he has contributed to books on alterglobalisation and antifascism and written for various Danish left-wing media outlets.

Dan Swain is assistant professor in the Department of Humanities of the Czech University of Life Sciences and a researcher at the Institute of Philosophy of the Czech Academy of Sciences. He is the author of *None So Fit to Break the Chains: Marx's Ethics of Self-Emancipation* (Brill/Haymarket 2019/2020) and *Alienation: An Introduction to Marx's Theory* (Bookmarks, 2012). As well as Marx and Marxism, his research focuses on the concept of prefigurative politics and its role in the theory and practice of social movements.

Thomas Telios lectures in philosophy at the University of St. Gallen. His research interests include Marxism, Critical Theory, Postwar French Philosophy, Postmodern Feminism and New Materialisms. His publications include "Why Still Reification? Towards a Critical Social Ontology" (Brill, 2019) and *Das Subjekt als Gemeinwesen: Zur sozial-ontologischen Konstitution kollektiver Handlungsfähigkeit* (Nomos Verlag, 2021).

Petr Urban is a senior researcher at the Institute of Philosophy of the Czech Academy of Sciences. His research focuses on care ethics, administrative ethics and phenomenological philosophy. His work has appeared in journals such as *Frontiers in Psychology*, *Ethics and Social Welfare*, *Environmental Philosophy*, *Horizon: Studies in Phenomenology* and *Filozofia*. He is author and editor of six books including *Care Ethics, Democratic Citizenship and the State* (Palgrave Macmillan, 2020, co-edited with Lizzie Ward).

www.ingramcontent.com/pod-product-compliance
Lightning Source LLC
Chambersburg PA
CBHW021812270326
41932CB00007B/154